Amanda Minnie Douglas

A modern Adam and Eve in a Garden

Amanda Minnie Douglas

A modern Adam and Eve in a Garden

ISBN/EAN: 9783743332195

Manufactured in Europe, USA, Canada, Australia, Japa

Cover: Foto ©ninafisch / pixelio.de

Manufactured and distributed by brebook publishing software (www.brebook.com)

Amanda Minnie Douglas

A modern Adam and Eve in a Garden

THE DOUGLAS NOVELS.

A MODERN ADAM AND EVE IN A GARDEN.
THE FORTUNES OF THE FARADAYS.
FOES OF HER HOUSEHOLD.
A WOMAN'S INHERITANCE.
CLAUDIA.
FLOYD GRANDON'S HONOR.
FROM HAND TO MOUTH.
HOME NOOK.
HOPE MILLS.
IN TRUST.
LOST IN A GREAT CITY.
NELLIE KINNARD'S KINGDOM.
OUT OF THE WRECK.
SEVEN DAUGHTERS.
STEPHEN DANE.
SYDNIE ADRIANCE.
THE OLD WOMAN WHO LIVED IN A SHOE.
WHOM KATHIE MARRIED.

PRICE PER VOL., $1.50.

LEE AND SHEPARD, PUBLISHERS,
BOSTON.

A MODERN

ADAM AND EVE

IN A

GARDEN

BY

AMANDA M. DOUGLAS

BOSTON 1889
LEE AND SHEPARD Publishers
10 MILK STREET NEXT " THE OLD SOUTH MEETING-HOUSE "
NEW YORK CHARLES T. DILLINGHAM
718 AND 720 BROADWAY

CONTENTS.

		PAGE
I.	THE FLAVOR OF THE APPLE	1
II.	FINDING AN EDEN	20
III.	OUR SHARE OF THE WORLD'S WEALTH	38
IV.	TEMPTATION NO. I.	58
V.	EVE AT BARGAIN-MAKING	75
VI.	MY TRAMP	94
VII.	JOE'S FALL FROM GRACE	110
VIII.	THE HIGH STUDY OF ECONOMY	126
IX.	A PASTORAL IN HENS	147
X.	EVERY-DAY IDYLS	166
XI.	SUMMER AND SENTIMENT	189
XII.	A TOUCH OF ROMANCE	208
XIII.	ATHENS IS ROUSED	226
XIV.	WINTER BLOOMS IN EDEN	243
XV.	AND YET ANOTHER	261
XVI.	SOME IMPORTANT QUESTIONS	280
XVII.	SWEET, FATAL KNOWLEDGE	299
XVIII.	TEMPTATION NO. II.	318
XIX.	WE ENTER THE GARDEN	336
XX.	NABOBS IN A SMALL WAY	356
XXI.	COUNTING THE GAINS	375
XXII.	WEDDING BELLS	396

A MODERN ADAM AND EVE IN A GARDEN

CHAPTER I

THE FLAVOR OF THE APPLE

"News," says Eve, holding up a letter, as I came in to my nine-o'clock breakfast.

I desire it to be understood that I am not a nabob or a night-editor, but simply a telegraph operator at the great Mammoth Beach.

"News," I return, not to be outdone. "The season closes on the 20th; and, as our respective terms of service expire, we take our month's pay and our gripsack, and set out for fresh fields and pastures new."

"Well, we have expected that," answers Eve resignedly. "But mine is a great surprise — from aunt Carry."

"Has she found a new husband for you?"

"No; but she *has* found one for Kate, and you could not guess" —

"Longworth!" I answer with decision.

"Oh! how could you?" and Eve laughs. "And the funny thing is, that she writes just as if — as if he had never cared for any one else. He is on the way to a fabulous fortune, and they are to be married the last of October. Sit down, and I will spice your breakfast with all the gossip."

Eve pours the rich brown coffee deftly. There is a plate of toast, a dish of broiled oysters, some tempting oatmeal, and luscious cut peaches. The service is delicate china, the cloth snowy white. Really, a nabob might fare no better.

"You are not sorry? I wondered why aunt Carry did not try to secure him in the first place."

"Sorry!" There certainly is no regret in the tone, or the sweet young face. For Eve *is* pretty, — tall, slim, and willowy, with a proudly poised head, a small, spirited face, with dark eyes, peachy cheeks, and dimpled strawberry mouth.

"He wasn't quite rich enough, and she hoped Kate would do as well as the other two. Oh, dear! *does* a mother take any comfort in her children? Aunt Carry has thought of nothing, striven for nothing, but her girls' marriages ever since I can remember. And there is a sigh of relief all through the letter. Mr. Longworth has some share or interest in a mine in Arizona, and uncle is going out with him with a prospect of making a fortune. I only hope it may be so," interpolates Eve earnestly. "They will remain at Long Branch until the middle of October, then come up to the Fifth Avenue for a fortnight, where Kate will be married in grand style. Aunt and Helen are going to Washington to spend the winter with Clara; and she devoutly hopes Helen will pick up a husband, and her duty to her girls will be done. She thinks after the holidays she can make arrangements to send for me," Eve concludes, with a touch of hesitation.

All our lives, at least since mother's death, aunt Carry's house has been home to us. Uncle Lennard has given what he had with open hand and generous love. There has been luxury, there have also been severe pinches. But we both are in a manner homeless — Eve especially so. There is a pretty, wistful look in her eyes. And I feel conscience-smitten that at the age of twenty-seven I am not in a position to make a permanent home for one little woman.

"Of course we must go on together," I say.

"O Adam! if we only had a *sure* home of our own! Aunt Carry has been very good; but I would rather stay with you and keep house, and not feel that I was put into the world for the sole purpose of matrimony. If I could do something; and it seems as if I ought " —

"Nonsense! What do you suppose I am here for? Many a poor young chap has a wife before he reaches my term of years; and a sister cannot be more expensive. Indeed, we have lived beautifully this summer. I never enjoyed any thing so much."

"I am *so* glad."

Eve's soft eyes swim in tears.

"There, Kitty, I must eat and run. This evening we will talk it all over. Of course, you belong to me, to have and to hold" —

"To feed and to dress, unromantic thought," she responds, with a tremble in her voice.

I kiss her, and am off. The walk is rather long, but my strides soon cover it. At six I am off duty for good, and we have delightful evenings.

There are only two of us now. Two children between are dead, as well as our parents. From what I remember of my father, he must have been an odd, speculative, rather dreamy sort of man. We lived in a little country town, where he did high farming; writing a little, and reading a good deal. My mother, city bred, hated the country, except in summer, when our house was always full of visitors; and, the next town to us being quite a fashionable resort, we were rather lively.

I was just fourteen when he died suddenly, of a heart trouble. Every thing was left to mother. It was a period of great depression in country property; and she sold at a sacrifice, came to the city, and, after some up-hill work, established herself in a boarding-house. Here the sister next to me died of typhoid-fever; and my mother, worn out, followed her in less than a month.

Aunt Carry Lennard was her only sister, — a generous, warm-hearted woman, given to what she called getting the good out of life. Uncle Marvin was a broker and speculator; and they lived in the style of quite rich people. Indeed, I always supposed them wealthy, until I came to know how hollow the pretension was. I was in a business college at this time, studying telegraphy. We both went to live with uncle Lennard. His only son had gone to South America, and was in a most promising position.

At eighteen I began the world on forty dollars a month, and it looked like a fortune to me. I did not care so much for the money as the opportunity to travel. I went South the ensuing winter; I came up to the North-West in the summer; I saw some of the famous cities, had a taste of wild, adventurous life, and looked outward from the Pacific coast. Sometimes a good salary, at others a very meagre one for the work; often without a dollar, but there were plenty of "boys" in the same plight. It is a reckless, careless sort of existence, with many hardships, and, alas! many untimely deaths. When I was in desperate straits, I sent to uncle; for I knew there was a little left of my father's estate. There was much variety, there were many things that wholesome young manhood is much better off without. Is original sin our desire to have our bite at the tree of good and evil?—alas! oftener evil.

I should like now to blot out those four years. I was not as bad as hundreds of others. I saw wrecks that shocked and dismayed me; yet I was in the whirl, with not enough courage to pull myself out. Indeed, what stream was I to pull into?

Crowds of homeless chaps living in boarding-houses or rooms, and restaurant meals; herding together in a manner that should fire Christendom for their salvation. Arduous work, long hours, poor pay in many cases,—a band that has become a sort of Pariah, made and kept so by the resistless forces that grind up soul and body into profit. Heathens are sown broadcast in our own land. If some day the seething undercurrent should break out, the world will look on in dismay, where it now smiles in unbelief.

I was twenty-two when I found myself ill in a hospital in a Western city. Through the winter I had charge of a distant railroad-station, where I was ticket and express agent, operator, etc. I had to sleep in the station, for a train went through at midnight that always stopped; two others passed at four: and as, for some distance, there was but one track, great watchfulness was necessary. I could have no good continuous sleep. It was very cold, freight was often heavy; and what with overwork, some dissipation I must admit, and an accident, my career came near being ended. I was bundled off to a hospital, fortunately; but for weeks I lay half unconscious with fever.

Good nursing from kindly stranger-hands brought me back to life. Word had been sent to my uncle; and, having some business Westward, he hunted me up. Ah! what delight it was to see a familiar face, to hear a kindly voice! He wanted very much to take me back with him, but it was not considered quite prudent.

"Uncle Marvin," I said, during the last visit he was able to make, "I am sorry to bother you, but —I suppose I have a little money left?"

"I'll give you all I can spare," he answered cheerily. "My business out here has been most unfortunate. When I get home, I'll send some more as soon as I can. It has been a hard winter everywhere."

Something in his tone touched me, — the sort of bravado as if he did not want to tell the truth.

"Is my money all gone?"

"There, my boy, don't worry. There wasn't much of it; and I made aunt Carry keep the dates and the amounts, and you can look them over when you get home. You have had every penny, but you needn't mind asking me when you're hard up. Only, my boy,—do not feel hurt if I say a few words of good common sense. You are throwing yourself away too rapidly. No strength will stand such drains. I'd turn over a new leaf. You're too nice a young chap to waste your strength and energy in dissipation, and wreck yourself before you reach middle life. Surely, you have had enough of it. Get well and come back to us, for Eve's sake, for your dead mother's sake. Try to make a man of yourself, and not drift down with the evil tide, until you are a terror and a disgrace. And now good-by, my lad. Come home to us as soon as you can. You are young enough to begin all over again."

He wrung my hand with a pressure that went to my very soul. That night I did some sober thinking as I lay on my cot. A sentence I had heard somewhere ran through my mind with curious persistency,—"The way thereof is death." I had been in that way—I had seen lads younger than I go swift to destruction and death. Was it to be desired?

Another curious incident occurred the next day, which I think helped to settle my resolves. I had never been any thing of a novel-reader, but I took up a book my companion in the ward had thrown aside. It bore this title, "The Heir of Malreward."

"You won't like that," he said. "Beastly, dismal, and dull! Too preachy altogether."

I opened it somewhere in the middle, — the terrible remorse of Victor at having been betrayed into drunkenness at his father's dinner. Then I turned to the first page, and never skipped a line. I go over the book now; and though the end jars on one's desire for human victory, and the reward of virtue, it is brave, strong, and manly — a fight against the evil in the world, in one's own soul.

Uncle Marvin sent me a check for fifty dollars in the course of the next week. I was young, and had a good constitution, and presently began to recover rapidly. But I did not go home. I had a feeling of pride in trying my own mettle. I found a situation in a country town in Michigan, and through that summer saved my first money, little enough, for the salary was low. But when I returned to New York I had sufficient to repay uncle his last generous loan. I found that I was still nearly a hundred dollars his debtor, and I also realized the pinches that were sometimes quite severe under the outside show. I met with an opportunity to go South on a salary of eighty dollars a month, and at once accepted it, and through that winter finished the payment; though uncle generously handed it to Eve's account, I learned afterward. But the letter of commendation and affection he sent me repaid me a hundred times for the endeavor.

The next year I took out an endowment policy in a life-insurance company for two thousand dollars. I would have that in case of an emergency. I do not mean that I turned saint. A hearty, healthy young fellow, with a keen sense of fun, is not much given to pulling a long face. But I kept my unwritten pledge over my sad hero of Malreward, that I would be temperate, and avoid the evils that can only bring destruction in the end.

Do those who blame the hundreds going astray ever pause to think of the many temptations? — the long hours, the exhausting work, in railroading especially; the lack of home comforts and nourishing diet; meals cold and poor; deprivation of proper sleep; illness when one cannot give up, and the utter physical weariness that seems to be overcome only by stimulants; but, ah, at what a price! Those in authority above you laugh at drunkenness, as a sort of joke. When doctors cease to prescribe whiskey, brandy, and opium for countless ills, when to be sober commends you in the esteem of your employers, a long stride will be gained.

I became known among the boys by the *sobriquet* of "Old Judge," yet I have sometimes felt that my courage in fighting this fiery demon has been of some service. I have been chaffed unmercifully, tormented, threatened, and on several occasions have had to fight my way out of a half-drunken crowd by sheer force.

I began to have a respect for myself as a man must when he treats his body with the sacredness due the work of a higher power. I became much interested in the struggle going on in the great world between justice and injustice. I read up industrial phases and troubles, and so-called political economy, until it all seemed a hopeless tangle. One *must* have bread. Competition in all branches is close, but doubly so in ours, where a few months perfects one of either sex. There are some fine positions; but to the one of that kind, hard to attain, there are hundreds that barely provide food and shelter. During the summer season every thing is on the rush. With autumn comes less freighting and travelling: one is dropped off here, another there; salaries reduced in the spasm of retrenchment that always overtakes corporations.

When Eve was just past eighteen, I was in New

York in the employ of the Western Union. My
salary was fair; but board, washing, and necessary
expenses were seldom less than ten dollars a week.
I used to drop into aunt's, and occasionally take
the girls to the theatre, or escort them to some party.
The eldest, Clara, was married very well, and settled
in Washington. Louise was engaged to the son of
an oil-prince, and was married that spring. For
several years they had owned a cottage at Long
Branch: how such a piece of real luck had happened
to them, puzzles me even now. They generally in
the autumn took a suite of furnished rooms; sometimes, in a prosperous season, a whole house. The
girls were gay, jolly, and good-looking, always in
demand for balls and parties, and having no end of
invitations. They dressed handsomely, and aunt
used a livery-stable *coupé*. Uncle was brisk and
bright, with a fine, imposing presence, and supposed
to be making a great deal of money: certainly they
spent it lavishly. But they had a way of keeping
the infelicities and economies to themselves.

   Louise was married in great state, and her future
home was to be Cleveland. About this time a
young man hung around after Eve a good deal,
though at first I could not decide whether it was
she or Kate who was likely to concentrate his fancy.
But through the summer at Long Branch, it ripened

into an engagement. Aunt Carry was in her element: she had a woman's love for weddings. Kate was a year younger, and her turn would be next.

Eve was blissfully happy. I never understood why I disliked Reed Ammerman: he was gentlemanly, well-looking, and held a trusted position in one of the dry-goods palaces. He was gay, and fond of society, lavish in his expenditures, and dressed in exquisite taste. Eve was considered a fortunate girl.

We had some talks about her new life.

"I am not going to lead this shifty, showy sort of existence," she said to me one evening. "I would rather be honestly poor than have aunt's anxieties about position. It is living on the edge of a volcano that may yawn and swallow you up any time. You seem rich to-day, and to-morrow there isn't a dollar, and uncle borrowing to meet payments. I shall be glad to come to something different, and I am thankful that Mr. Ammerman has a salary."

"Do you know what it is?" I inquired.

"No; but I shall ask him as soon as we are married, and live strictly within it. I want to go to some pretty suburb, and presently buy a cottage. Aunt is sure it must be as much as three thousand from what he spends; and he is young,—just your age."

"It does seem a large sum;" and I sighed enviously, I am afraid.

"We must plan to live on two thousand, and can, when we are away from so much extravagance. The thing is, after all, that people care so little for you. You drop out, and they dance and eat without a thought of you. Why should you be spending your money for them? When I have daughters to marry, I may feel differently;" and a smile lurks about her face.

Mr. Calhoun, the superintendent of one department of this great firm, used to drop into the office on business errands; and we became quite friendly. One day he had to trust me with a secret message. They feared some crooked work was going on.

"Mr. Calhoun," I said, — and my heart seemed to bound up to my throat, — "I would like to ask you a question. Do you know what salary Mr. Ammerman gets? It may seem impertinent; but he is engaged to my sister, and I think I have a right to inquire."

"Ammerman," he repeated thoughtfully. "He is in the lace-department. About fifteen hundred a year, I think."

"Not more than that?" I asked in surprise.

"Well, perhaps eighteen hundred, though I doubt

it. Hardly enough for matrimony in such times as these," and he laughed.

"Has he any thing besides?"

A horror seized me. Mr. Ammerman spent more than eighteen hundred a year, I felt confident.

"Ah!—private means, no doubt."

A curious expression came over Mr. Calhoun's countenance, but he nodded carelessly.

I had a misgiving that I had signed my poor Eve's death-warrant. It haunted me so that I staid away from her for several days; and, dropping in rather late one evening, I found the two and aunt Carry discussing wedding-gowns and wedding-journeys. Mr. Ammerman laughed a little gayly at Eve's very moderate ideas, and I saw his extravagant plans rather annoyed her.

Alas, my poor, sweet Eve! The very next week a system of stealing was unearthed at the great store that caused consternation and grief in more than one household. One of aunt Carry's neighbors was bookkeeper of the lace-department, and it was at this house Eve had met Mr. Ammerman. The young man at the first alarm made his escape to Canada. Mr. Rathburn was not so fortunate. His wife, a charming woman, was crushed by the blow, and for days lay dangerously ill. A compromise was effected in his case by his returning to the firm all the property he had acquired. Indeed, in the excitement about the Rathburns, Eve quite escaped gossip and commiseration.

"I did love him," she confessed tremulously to me one evening when we were alone. "At least, I loved my ideal of Reed Ammerman; but I cannot love any thing so despicable as a deliberate thief. If he had been in some awful trouble, and taken a sum of money to tide him over, I could feel sorry, and have a deep sympathy for him, — but to steal month after month with no compunction, to even plan how we should live on money that he would steal in the future! It is horrible, and the very repulsion will lend me courage to overlive it. But there *is* something wrong in society approval. Everybody was glad to receive him; and, as a poor young man, few would have made him welcome."

Plucky Eve one day took her diamonds down to the head of the firm, and told her story. The ring was especially handsome: then she had solitaire earrings and a lace-pin. They went together to a jeweller's, and had them valued. The man would pay nine hundred dollars cash for them.

Mr. A—— commended Eve very highly for this piece of justice, and begged her to keep the ring; but she could not be persuaded. The next day he sent her a pair of elegant bracelets with his kindest regards.

The last of April the family went down to Long Branch. I took a position on the Grand Mammoth Beach Railroad, a famous summer resort, and found quite a pleasant home in one of the old country houses with a widow lady. Eve came up, and spent a month with me; and during this time we drew very near together. I learned to appreciate her worth, and used to wonder how she had retained her simple honesty and sweetness in the rush and whirl of incessant gayety.

"I am so tired of it all!" she sighed. "I wish I could do something useful. It looks so dreary to think of the same round year after year. How do people endure it?"

"But you will marry," I said. "You are not the kind of girl to break your heart over such a fellow as that Ammerman."

"No, my heart is not broken. But, oh, if I *had* been his wife when it came out! I think of poor Mrs. Rathburn, who is dying of consumption, they say; but I think it is the intense, intolerable shame that stings like a serpent. I wish I could give lessons in painting or music, but aunt Carry will not hear of it."

"No," I replied. "You are too sweet and pretty to fight your way through the world."

Eve sighed. "Fighting for a lover would be less

reprehensible, I suppose. It is parties and operas and teas and receptions; and how to disguise your old gowns to make them look like new; and to be pestered by debts and duns. It seems a mad chase after something — pleasure — with no real satisfaction in it. You dance and talk and flirt, and watch warily for the man with the most money."

"But why do women do it? Men would like real homes, and not all this sham and confusion," I answered.

"Would they?" and Eve gives a half-doubtful smile. "They are so much in the rush and whirl, that they are first to complain of the dulness. Uncle Marvin is uneasy when there is no company. Aunt Carry falls asleep in her chair, and Kate always dozes on the lounge. One gets so awfully worn out in society. It does seem as if there ought to be a better life for human beings."

We had many of these talks, although we were in the greatest whirl of all. Every day brought a crowd, and Sundays a jam. In fact, there were no Sundays. I had to be at my post just the same: indeed, I handled more people on our little railway that day than any other. But my house was a short distance out, and Eve found much entertainment with quaint Mrs. Williams.

When the season closed, the company sent me South to a resort they were trying to build up there; so Eve and I said a tender good-by that was to last the next seven months.

CHAPTER II

FINDING AN EDEN

EVE returned to aunt Carry's. Kate was engaged to a young man whose rich mother was very anxious he should marry. He was a wild, dissipated fellow; but Mrs. Brinkerhoff was extremely sweet to Kate, and the family was very aristocratic. Aunt Carry was really opposed to it, and my sweet Eve was shocked. Then she wrote of a Mr. Longworth, a man of five and thirty, rather loud, engaged in some sort of silver-mining; and after a little he surprised her by a proposal of marriage, which she peremptorily declined, and thereby vexed aunt Carry.

"If we could have some simple little home of our own," was the refrain of every letter.

I had so organized the matter I had taken in hand, that my assistant, a young fellow at forty dollars a month, could perform the duties; so why should a rich corporation pay eighty? Besides, the season at Great Mammoth Beach was soon to open, so I came North. Eve was overjoyed.

"Take me somewhere with you," she cried, "or

Mr. Longworth will have the life worried out of me, for aunt Carry is resolved that I shall marry him."

Meanwhile Kate's engagement came to a tragic end. Young Brinkerhoff, in a fit of delirium tremens,— insanity, the papers kindly said,— shot himself. Kate had some handsome diamonds, and did not seem much depressed by the affair. Uncle Marvin had met with several heavy losses, and they were preparing to go to Long Branch.

"But I can't go with them, for I will not marry Mr. Longworth. Nothing would induce me to begin my life in such a hap-hazard way, never knowing whether you were rich or poor, and always trying to live on the rich side. I would sooner be a nursery-governess," declared Eve.

I went down to see Mrs. Williams. She did not want to take any one to board, as she wished to do some visiting herself; but she would rent us three rooms, furnished. Eve was overjoyed with the prospect. By the middle of May we were settled, and happy as bees in clover. We had a nice large living-room down-stairs, and privilege of the parlor, and two comfortable sleeping-rooms up-stairs. There were a pretty flower-garden and grass-plot; and in the back of the yard, fenced in by themselves, were ten hens, which were an unfailing source of interest.

Our next-door neighbor was very kindly, so it was not lonesome when Mrs. Williams was away.

Certainly it was a most delightful summer. True, one of the "boys" fell in love with Eve, and quarrelled with me because he thought I aided and abetted his refusal.

"The world is too old for love-matches," said Eve. "We cannot play at Strephon and Phyllis, forever wandering in flowering meads. We must pay house-rent, and provide for butcher and baker, groceries and clothes, fires and lights, car-fares and a hundred and one things that Strephon never dreamed of, and hardly dreams of to-day; so Phyllis must consider the chances of her husband being out of work and ill occasionally."

"But you are willing to try it with me," I made answer.

"If misfortunes come, I am quite sure you will not take to drink; and there will be no children to suffer. I really wonder how very poor people dare to marry, and make their lives harder. Am I growing very mercenary? But I have seen some of it."

I had seen a great deal of it. Many a wife struggling along half-starved, some deserted after a year or two, when the young fellow found it too severe a pull; others who would have been fortunate if a brutal and indolent husband had left them to do for themselves. Twice in those early years I had been almost tempted, but the hostages to fortune came too high. No doubt, the family system is the structural unit of society. It has helped men to possess and conquer the earth. The boarding-houses provide none of the restraints or incentives of home. But the labor system of the present day makes marriages almost an impossibility. No one is educated for home life. Girls of fourteen take their places in shops, stores, and offices. To them the day is rounded by the evening's amusement, and they long for the excitement. Quiet life is too humdrum. The irregularity of employment is a fatal discouragement. The swift fingers of machinery soon piles up a store of goods, then ensues a dull season. The man looks his starving family in the face, and inwardly curses the brief affection that made him dream they would be a delight. Deserted wives are to be met with everywhere; and many husbands, when they first set out in search of work, have no intention of making the separation final. But labor is simply a commodity, and does not recognize wife or husband, parent or child. The cheapest labor is the continual cry.

And now a change was impending for us. Henceforward Eve must be my care.

We talked about it all the evening. She was pleased that aunt Carry had written so cordially, and approved Kate's marriage. There was also an invitation for her to come down to Long Branch.

Whatever happened, we would keep together. We had managed to save up a little money this summer. I was the happy possessor of about three hundred dollars; and Eve had that sum left from her portion, and a piano. She did not incline to New York, neither did she wish to go very far away from it. There were so many contractions at this season of the year.

I heard of a place in Florida, and one in Indiana.

"Why, we might go to Florida, and have an orange-grove. I believe I have inherited father's taste for the country. In the course of time, you might give up telegraphing."

I laughed at that.

Being in New York a few days later, I ran against one of the "boys."

"See here," said he, "do you remember Warren? He is out on the E. & P. road, — some sort of a little town where he is every thing rolled in one; but it's not a hard place, and late trains only twice a week. He is in an awful taking to go to Florida, and he doesn't look as if he'd live the winter out, anyway. Maybe you'd like that?"

"And I could put him in a way of going to Florida."

"Good. You had better run over and see him."

Athens, the place was called; near one considerable city, and some nine miles from another, the terminus of the road; and less than an hour's ride from New York. I resolved to go out and see what I thought of it.

Athens had once been a country of productive farms, until the mania for improvement had swept over it with a devastating hand. Streets had been laid out, some quite pretentious villas built, and rows of cottages. A lazy river flowed peaceably along at one edge, not much vexed with shipping, although several factories embellished it. The land seemed a natural succession of terraces. One beautiful, broad avenue ran along just back of the river. Here years ago the aristocracy had settled themselves, — good old Dutch people, who rejoiced in the names of Schuyler, Van Rensselaer, Van Duyne, Egbert, and so on. About a quarter of a mile back was another avenue; and the next was the county-road, a fine, Telford-paved street. Each one was about thirty feet higher than its neighbor. Above this ran the railroad; and, as you went on toward the west, the town still displayed the same gradual rise. Sometimes, indeed, a street or lane was positively steep.

Just below the station, Rutherford Avenue that was, there were some lovely houses and lawns, built at the time of the rage for country homes, and were now for sale. Indeed, the whole place seemed for sale, — great tracts of weed-grown land that had the shape of city blocks, many of them containing not more than one or two houses. Farther to the west was the town of Milford, of which Athens had once been a part. It was a lovely section of country, though speculators had wasted its substance; but this sunny October day, while it was still abloom with asters of every hue, golden-rod, the furze of the clematis, and the red berries of the bitter-sweet, I quite fell in love with it.

The station was trim and rather attractive, the high, peaked roof making it two stories. I took my walk about the place, and returned, as I saw the next train winding down through the distant trees. The waiting-room was large, clean, and in the eastern window a great mound of greenery with a few flowers. The office was at the southern end, and below it a little freight and express place and coal-bin.

Warren came out as the train slowed up. There were two passengers to get off, and a little freight to put on. I should never have recognized in the pale, sunken-eyed fellow the round, rosy country chap of three years before.

"Hillo!" I said.

"I ought to know you — but there are such swads of boys" —

"Thurston."

"Oh! Ad Thurston, — Old Judge! Well," with a wan smile, "there's no use inquiring about *your* health. How do you manage to keep in such splendid order? Out of a job? Grand Beach closed up, I suppose?"

"Yes to both questions."

"Had a jolly time there, I dare say? Excuse this horrid barking. I took a cold last March, and have never been over the cough. Say, old chap, do you know of any Southern places? I'd like to swap with some fellow."

I unfolded Thompson's scheme.

"The very thing," declared Warren. "Let's trade. Though this place isn't much, and it's a dull little hole; but the work is easy."

The salary I found was forty-five dollars a month. You were ticket-agent, freight, express, telegrapher. It was the branch road of a long main line, and took a sort of *détour* to accommodate some business towns. Up above at Springdale there was quite a hotel and summer-boarding. The first train was at 6.10. From that until ten they ran quite frequently, afterward stopping on signal about once an hour.

From four until seven quite brisk again. The last train came up at nine, except a theatre-train on Saturday night, and one on Wednesday night through the three summer months. Certainly the duties were not arduous.

"Do you suppose I could get two or three rooms for housekeeping?" I asked.

"Oh! you're married!" with the peculiar intonation in which one says, "Well, you *have* done it!"

"No; but my sister will be with me."

"There are two decentish rooms up-stairs. The old fellow who was here before me kept house with his wife. I sleep here, and take my meals just down the street."

"Let's see them," I proposed.

The roof cut off the corners, and the wide eaves shut out some of the light; but the window to the north was large. The room was the size of the one down-stairs. Indeed, it looked immense with nothing in it. There was a small chimney, and some one had used a stove. The other one was much smaller, and the stairs came up in it from the office. Warren's cot-bed was here: a little washing-stand, a chair, and a trunk completed the furniture. But the office really looked cheery. There were plants in the window, a large, old-fashioned desk, a carpet-lounge, some book-shelves, and pictures.

Warren was quite urgent. "I wouldn't find the place so bad; and at Northwood there was a theatre and considerable amusement, lots of boys; and New York was soon reached. Florida would be just the thing for him, and he knew I could stand it one winter. No doubt, I would go back to the beach in the summer."

Of course I knew I could. I returned, and laid the matter before Eve. She had no especial yearning for Florida and orange-groves. The next day we both went to view the delectable little town, and she really liked it. Then she packed up her small belongings, and went to Long Branch for a few days while I was negotiating. Aunt Carry was delighted to have her; and she staid behind to put the house in order, when they came up to New York, where about four days later she joined them. I went to Athens two days for Warren to post me, and bought his lounge, easy-chair and the cot and square of carpet up-stairs. He left me with warm expressions of gratitude, and went away with the utmost hope; but before February had ended, he had gone "over to the great majority," poor fellow.

I took possession with an odd sort of feeling, as if I had settled down into a family-man; though I knew, pretty girl as Eve was, she would marry some time. The first thing was, to get a woman to come and clean up; and in two days she made every thing shine. I donated the cot to her, and fumigated the lounge. Then, as the walls had been painted, I gave them another coat of pretty pinkish gray, and went over the woodwork. I had been quite used to furbishing up stations.

Eve ran away for one day, and came over. She declared herself delighted; but it seemed to me it must be a horrible contrast between this and an elegant hotel. She charged me strictly not to buy any furniture until she came. We had accumulated some dishes and two chairs.

"And aunt Carry has given me a great trunk full of clothes and things. They have rented their cottage for next summer at a hundred dollars a month; and, O Adam! doesn't it seem dreadful? but aunt Carry actually took up two thousand dollars on a mortgage for Kate's wedding. Uncle Marvin was not very fortunate through the summer," and Eve sighed.

"I thought the house was aunt Carry's one sacred possession," I remarked.

"So it is. Uncle Marvin wanted a quiet wedding, but Kate would not consent. He has promised to clear the house again as soon as possible. And, isn't it funny? none of them seem to remember that

Mr. Longworth ever wanted to marry me. He isn't a bit embarrassed, and is as proud of Kate as he can be. She is just the wife for him. They are all spending money as if there was no end to it."

To please Eve, I hired a dress-suit, and went to the wedding, which took place in one of the Fifth-Avenue parlors. Eve, Helen, and another young lady, were maids of honor. There was an elegant reception, and the bride looked superb. At six that evening they started for Chicago, on their way to San Francisco. Aunt Carry was really pleased that I had come.

Eve did not return until the next day. Aunt and Helen had started for Washington. I knew, by the long, tender embrace Eve gave me, that she felt she had turned the first chapter of her life. I had engaged board for her at Mrs. Corwin's, where I took my meals. The two trunks were deposited at the station.

Eve was very tired, and went straight to bed as soon as supper was over. The next day she was bright as a lark. She was sure she should like every thing and every body, and housekeeping at the station would be a sort of picnic.

"And you do not regret that you are not whirling along in a palace-car with Mr. Longworth?" I asked rather banteringly.

"O Ad! I wouldn't be his wife for all the world, though then there wouldn't be the continual struggle to seem rich! It is all show. Kate was in a whirl of delight, and thought it a great stroke to be at the hotel, because her presents were more numerous. They *were* elegant, — at least many of them; and a few of the cheaper ones she disdainfully gave to me. Mr. Longworth has passes nearly all the way through, and she was so elated. Somehow, I should want *my* husband to *pay* for our wedding journey. I just wondered how many other people in that elegant throng were pinching along in the same way, yet making a grand appearance. It is really 'swell,' — that is just the word for it. But I hope they are all happy; and we will take some comfort in *our* way. I can understand how Ulysses felt when his wanderings were at an end. He had seen much that was wonderful, but he was glad to get to his own home."

"It certainly was more inviting than ours."

"You shall not be lugubrious. And now, like Consider Miller's cow, we must 'consider,' though we are not reduced to quite such straits;" and Eve laughed merrily.

That heartened me up. But it did seem such a long step from the luxury of Fifth Avenue to two rooms in a railroad-station, and forty-five dollars a month.

The result of our consideration was, that the large room must be parlor, kitchen, and Eve's sleeping-room. We must have a cooking-stove, a carpet, a bedroom suite, a table, and some chairs. Thirty-six yards of carpet would leave a small bare space at each side, the room being nearly fifteen feet wide.

"Matting," suggested Eve, "and some pretty rugs. All the floors are matted at aunt Carry's. And we might find some second-hand goods."

"I wouldn't risk any thing but a stove. That could not give you typhoid very well."

She laughed.

We went to New York and purchased sixty yards of beautiful matting in four remnants, which cost, with freight, just eighteen dollars. We stumbled over some pretty brussels carpet in odd lengths, and two elegant pieces of velvet. As we meant housekeeping for a permanency, we might as well start with some of the articles our hearts craved.

We found the stove at Athens, in the stove and plumbing establishment. When we had our matting down, the man came and put it up; and the whole cost was eight dollars and sixty cents. I must add that it proved an excellent bargain.

We went down to Northwood. I knew the place quite well, having once for some months held a position in one of its offices. It was a thriving and prosperous manufacturing city; and we found that its stores, or rather its prices, compared favorably with our greater metropolis. We purchased a pretty ash chamber-suite, springs and mattress, and a cot, some chairs and a table.

When we reached Athens we found some posters of an auction at Clifton had been left. The owner was dead, and all the household furniture was to be sold.

"Let us go," said Eve. "Though first we must count over our money. I think we have been extravagant."

We had, owing to Eve's excellent management, accumulated during the summer a little store of about eighty dollars. We had spent sixty-seven of it already. My half-month's salary would pay board until we were settled, and give us a little besides. We had some sheets and pillow-cases that Eve had made in the summer; but no pillows, no blankets.

The succeeding day was rainy. We settled our rooms, putting down some matting in the smaller room, and setting up my cot in one corner. As we hated to shut up the north window, we stood the bedstead down a little way in the large room — Eve's that was to be. It seemed almost to cut it in two, but we could do no better. The stove-end would be the kitchen. We placed our chairs, our table, Eve's rocking-chair, and my folding arm-chair.

"And now we must invent a closet," said Eve in a sort of dismayed tone.

Thoughts of building one ran through my mind. I was quite an expert at using carpenter's tools.

"Three or four packing-boxes would make one," resumed Eve. "The summer we were in the Adirondacks we emptied our boxes and used them. We thought it no end of fun, yet we were not as comfortable as you and I will be here."

"You do take a most cheerful view of it," I said laughingly.

"If I had been born rich instead of handsome, and always lived in one house, I should not have learned the art of making myself comfortable," Eve said drolly. "You have no idea of the hardships people take for pleasure. We had a furnished cottage a month at Lake George, and there was nothing useful in it. Oh, the straits and perplexities aunt Carry and I had! Louise's lover was up there,—it was just before she was married,—and we absolutely didn't have dishes enough to go round; and as for beds—well, I used to roll up a bundle of clothes for a pillow; and I can do it here. But we look a little like living. And now I am going to unpack my trunk.

Kate gave me a set of plated knives and forks, so we will not have those to buy. And butters, and some salts; and you have two birthday china cups, and I have three, and a number of plates."

There was quite an array of dishes when she took them out. Then she had some silver of mother's, and some tablecloths and napkins. Really, we were quite rich.

"We must not spend more than ten dollars at the auction," she declared presently.

We went up the next day about noon. Most of the articles were disposed of very cheaply. We purchased two pairs of pillows, some needed kitchen utensils, a clock, a bureau, and, joy! a small closet, for eleven dollars all told.

At the end of the first week in November we were in living order, Mrs. Corwin having lent us some blankets until we could get ours. What with the large stove in the waiting-room and our range, which burned beautifully, we were cosily warm. Pictures had been arranged on some improvised brackets. I had made Eve a workstand which she covered with part of an antiquated dress, and now I was busy at a sort of bookcase to hold our intellectual treasures.

Our first supper was a success. Indeed, I had enjoyed the last week immensely, and sat down to my own table with the delight of a true householder. We did not envy the bridal couple, nor sigh for the delights of palaces. There *are* times when one feels quite content, brief seasons of a lost paradise.

CHAPTER III

OUR SHARE OF THE WORLD'S WEALTH

As if to try us the next morning, there came an offer of a situation in New York with a salary of sixty-five dollars a month.

"If it only *had* come sooner!" I cried regretfully.

"I don't know," said Eve, drawing her brows into a wise little frown. "It is true that you *can* have every thing in New York, but it costs a great deal of money. Perhaps it is better to be out of temptation's way. Out of the extra twenty dollars we would probably spend fifteen for rent, and five for car-fares. And we would have to think about company."

"Do you mean to make a hermit of yourself here?" I asked.

She laughed. "Why, I know half the people in town already. They can call on me in the office down-stairs. Some of them are very entertaining, and a little afraid of me, I think. They can't decide just where to class me. My clothes are so fine, and I have an air of"—

"Of courts," I interpolated.

"I fancy some of them suspect me to be a princess in disguise, especially that young Pryor. I feel that I shall not lack for amusement. I might not want to live here forever, but I shall enjoy it for a while. It is not half so bad as being out on a section, and I have even considered the feasibility of that. But I never told you — what Mrs. Harwood said to me on the night of the wedding, did I?" and Eve glances up hesitatingly. "You remember her, surely, — a little old lady with very white hair and very black eyes. She was quite a visitor at aunt Carry's."

"I think I do," I answered.

"She asked me if I was going to Washington; and I told her I expected to spend the winter, at least, keeping house for you. Then she said, brothers sometimes married; and when I was out of a situation, I must come to her, — that I would find one in readiness. It was very kind of her."

"O Eve! I wonder" —

"Cease to wonder, then," said she. "I do think, if Mrs. Harwood had offered me a companionship last winter when aunt Carry was throwing Mr. Longworth at me continually, I should have taken it. But now I have cast in my lot with you" —

"And if you should find it a lot of sacrifice and privations" —

"Then I can get up and go," answered Eve, with such adorable candor that I laughed. "You see, here *we* have a great advantage over matrimony. If we cannot agree, the world will merely nod triumphantly with an 'I told you so!' but we shall make no scandal. Still, I never could understand why relatives were expected to disagree, while two strangers, who have only seen each other in their best clothes and finest manners, should live like turtle-doves ever thereafter."

"I do not believe many young wives would be content to come and live over a railroad-station."

"Yes, they would be content, only they *would* be afraid of what the world would say. And I have made up my mind to regard it as a picnic."

"You are a jolly girl, Eve," I said in admiration.

"And I can be serious too. Now I want to talk seriously. Do you know, I was very much interested in Mr. Corwin's reasons for coming to live at Athens? I thought him especially entertaining the other evening."

I remembered it all after a moment or two. Mr. Corwin was a jeweller. He had a nice, sensible wife, and five children, the eldest a bright lad of thirteen. He had been speaking of the irregularity of employment for some years back, and this had decided him to get a home somewhat in the country.

An insurance company had foreclosed the mortgage on this place, and offered it — a pretty house of some eight or nine rooms, with an acre of ground — for three thousand dollars. He had paid half down four years ago, and been able to reduce the mortgage to eight hundred, besides adding some improvements, and cultivating his ground. He had now an abundance of fine fruit, not only for summer use, but for preserving as well, — berries, grapes, — and space for most of the vegetables the family needed. He was quite an enthusiast about country homes.

"I don't know," he had said on the evening of our talk, "as employment will ever be regular again. I remember when one could hardly get a two weeks' vacation: now I find that for the last three years I have averaged two and a half months out of employment. In the city, there is nothing to do but lounge around, or walk the streets. When you have a good employer, you do not want to leave him because there is a week off now and then: indeed, it might be no better in another place. So now I make my time useful. Last year I helped to paint the outside of my house. I bought the paint, and hired an excellent painter, a friend, by the day. I was astonished at the difference in the cost. I do odd jobs around, and I find that we have more real comfort at a less expense."

"But, Eve," I said, "you surely do not think of farming?"

She laughed gayly.

"And what if I did? See here, Adam! there are women going out West,—the very Far West, I mean, —who get to own vineyards and orchards and plantations and ranches. Now it seems to me there is a good deal of hard work somewhere, if a woman has very little money. If one took the little money, and did the work here, it is a question with me whether one might not have more real pleasure staying with friends, and amid civilization. I should like to help do something. I am not ambitious to be clerk or cashier in a store, or write in a stuffy office, half the time by gaslight. What I want most is a home. Can I not help make one here as well as on the Pacific coast? And I *do* realize that I like the country, but I do not want to be very far away from the city. If we could get a little place"—

"But you wouldn't want it here at Athens?"

"I am not so sure. I have studied it as I 'took my walks abroad.' It certainly *is* a lovely place naturally. Cutting it up into streets and blocks has spoiled it, but the trees and shrubs are growing up again. I wish—do you remember any thing of our old place, Adam?"

"It was very pretty. Father had a great love for beauty and gardening."

"And I've inherited the taste," she said triumphantly. "I wish the place had not been sold, and it *was* too bad to make such a sacrifice. But I suppose dear mamma thought it best, and she hated the country."

"And you want to buy a farm?" I said, rather aghast.

"Well, I should like to, presently. Listen," — and her fair face is a study, — "the wealth of the United States, if evenly divided, is supposed now to give every person nearly eight hundred dollars apiece. Now I propose that we set to work and earn ours. After we have our full share, we will not worry, but take all the comfort we can. But we ought to do our duty by the wealth of the world. And we may be able to do it in this pretty little place."

"Sixteen hundred dollars will not buy a farm."

"Well, if we can get that together, we might get some more presently. I have over three hundred dollars, so have you. It is the first step that costs."

"But, Eve, you never could content yourself to stay here for years! And the people are — why, half of them do not know whether to accord you any social recognition or not" —

"Because I have come to live in a railroad-station. Well, I can wait," and she gave a piquant nod. "I told you I meant to consider it a picnic. Don't you know, sometimes before the day is done you have met so many nice people, and made some real good friends? You will see by spring."

A train sounded in the distance. After that had been attended to, Pryor came in for a little chat. He was a bright young fellow, who kept a real-estate and insurance office, a coal-agency, and did surveying; also procured loans, and had a little of his own that he kept lending in small sums. He was about my age, a well-informed person, shrewd at bargain-making, and very entertaining.

I kept revolving Eve's plan in my mind; but it certainly was the wildest of schemes, and utterly impracticable, though I did not say so. A pretty young girl like Eve would marry, of course. I could not help remarking that here she looked a very queen. Her walk, the peculiar pliant grace of her figure, the inclination of her head, the fit of her gloves and boots, and the style of her garments, bespoke city ways and familiarities. Yet I had a misgiving, when I saw people eye her, that these very gifts and graces went against her in their estimation.

But we found so much enjoyment in the lovely

walks, for October was pure Indian summer. Eve sketched and painted a little, — she had several accomplishments. We went to church after a Sunday or two; and Eve settled herself in a pretty, old gray stone church that had stood almost a century. Next door was a vine-clad rectory, occupied by one of the church-wardens; as the rector was a young, unmarried man, of rather High-Church proclivities, and a tendency to asceticism. Mother and aunt Carry were both Episcopalians; though four of the denominations were represented at Athens.

I was somewhat amused at the reception accorded us. We were shown to a very comfortable seat, and there were curious, surreptitious glances. Perhaps Eve's stately walk rather impressed these good people as being not quite the thing for a young woman who lived in two rooms over a railroad-station. No one spoke to us. I couldn't help thinking that it would have been kindly. The Corwins were Methodists, and Mr. Pryor went to the old Reformed Church.

"I wanted so much to sing," said Eve. "There are some good voices in the choir, but they incline more to volume than to melody. And how do you like Mr. Bradford?"

"I don't like him," I made answer. "He is a regular stick."

"Rather formal and precise. I sometimes think how odd it is that so few make really good news of the gospel."

"But why did you not sing?"

"Because I knew everybody would look at me;" and she laughed a little, with just a touch of embarrassment.

We went down to Northwood one day to do a little purchasing, and found a nice library, to which I subscribed for six months, as we were both fond of reading. We had quite furbished up our two rooms, though I must admit they were not pretty to furnish.

"If it wasn't for the bedstead!" said Eve. "I believe I shall shut up the window, after all, though it is the only large one in the room, and roll the bedstead clear up. It will be more symmetrical."

"Why didn't we get a lounge or sofa?" I exclaimed with sudden regret.

"Oh, dear! if you had slept on lounges and sofas and every invention of the brain, *not* a bedstead, you would know how good it seems to be the possessor of one. And we shall have no company but those who can be entertained in your office."

When the first of November came, along with the month's salary, we felt quite elated, as we had nearly run aground. Still, Eve insisted that enough was enough.

"Not to buy a farm," and I laughed.

"We have been getting a good many odds and ends of housekeeping, and I was afraid we would not come out quite as well as this. And I haven't pinched you very much in diet, have I?"

"You had better not try that," I said warningly. "I have a bitter remembrance of such an experiment."

"When some one starved you?"

"When I starved myself."

"Experience meeting," said Eve, with a face full of dimples and laughter. "Relate."

"I kept house once."

"Oh! you did!"

"I was trying to save money. I wanted to pay uncle Marvin. I read in a paper that a man kept himself splendidly on a dollar and a half a week, besides the rent of his room. I hired a furnished room, in which there happened to be a small cooking-stove, for six dollars a month. I purchased a few articles, and started out bravely. I had to go on duty at seven in the morning, and was off at seven in the evening. I had to do my shopping on my homeward journey, and cook in the evening. Then I had to be up by six in the morning, and sometimes I ate on the fly at that. The first week it seemed fine, but it cost me over three dollars. The next week I economized rigidly, and it cost me two. I could buy the cheap meats the man had written about; and, when I had cooked them three hours, they still were tough. My bread grew dry, but then I liked toast. My room had a wretched smell of cooking; it penetrated the bedclothes and everywhere: and, if I opened windows, it was too cool. Then I had to hurry so. After a little, nothing seemed to taste so good. I would take a morning nap, and just snatch a few mouthfuls. The first month I found my expenses had averaged two fifty a week, which, with the rent and washing, made three seventy-five; and I had been far from comfortable. Still, a dollar a week was worth saving: so I went on. One night I brought home a bargain in a cheap piece of beef, and put it on to stew. It *did* have a queer smell. The next morning I was late; so I ate some bread, and drank a cup of the broth. Before I reached the office I was awfully sick. I did not go home for any dinner. At night I made a cup of coffee, and ate a little bread and cold beef. It was tough as sole-leather, and had a disagreeable taste. That night I was sick again, then I threw my bargain in beef over the fence to the cats. For several days I could retain no food whatever, and one day I dropped off my stool with an attack of vertigo. I went to a doctor, who lectured me on bad habits and dissipation. I wanted to knock him down, but I was too weak; so I told him the whole truth. He smiled kindly, and softened.

"'My lad,' he said, 'you've been trying a poor experiment. You have almost starved yourself from lack of proper food, illy prepared, and too hastily eaten meals, with not enough variety. No one ever makes any thing by taking the absolute strength out of his own body. A man who is steadily worked needs a nourishing diet. The vital question is not, How little the man can live upon, but how he can best do the work set before him. You have a severe attack of dyspepsia, and are very much reduced. Take good, wholesome board somewhere, sleep all you can, don't worry about saving money; and in a month or so, you will find yourself a new man.'

"I had kept house two months, and it had cost me in all about thirty-two dollars. Then I had to be three days off, which was six more. Doctor's bill and medicine was seven. So for the seven weeks it had cost me five dollars a week besides the discomfort, the labor and trouble, and wretched feeling; while I could have boarded for six. I never tried it again."

Eve was laughing heartily.

"I sometimes think, when I see this wonderful wisdom about very cheap living, if the writers ever *did* try it. And in cooking, you can do many economical things if you have plenty of time; and if you save your time, you must spend your money. A man or a woman employed twelve or thirteen hours a day has no time for cooking."

"Solid truth," I appended. "And to keep in good health, body and mind, you want good food."

"You have not suffered under my reign," and Eve looks me all over humorously.

"I can't see how you learned so much."

"I think I was born with a genius for housekeeping: then, to get a good deal out of a little money does sharpen one's wits."

"It rather dulled mine."

"But you did not get a good deal," laughs Eve.

November came in rainy, then it cleared up, and we had the true Indian summer.

Eve went to New York for a day, and I missed her dreadfully. She looked prettier than ever to my longing eyes when she returned; and, oh! what budgets of news!

"Two invitations to theatre parties, one to a luncheon, and an afternoon tea, a reception really to introduce two young English girls staying with Mrs. Brooke. I've had just the gayest time; and I have asked a crowd of girls over, and I know they mean to come."

"But what will you do — with company?"

"Well — I have been thinking. I shall get some pretty olive and light blue Canton flannel, and curtain off my sleeping apartment; and we must have two more chairs."

"And I haven't been idle, nor economical. Pryor was in here, and wanted to give me a season ticket for a series of entertainments at Northwood. Burdette is to lecture, Carleton to read, and several other stars. Six in all. Season-tickets one dollar and a half; and I bought two, because I knew Pryor was counting on taking you."

"You lovely Adam!" and Eve threw her arms about my neck. "Defend me from young men!"

"And Mr. Bradford called."

Eve *had* joined the singing in church. Her voice was one of those clear sopranos, which, soft rather than shrill, was of considerable compass — penetrative.

"Oh! what *did* he say?" and her face was mirthfully curious.

"He stammered something about you. Women, young women, are a little outside of his religion, which I think is of the Lara or Thebaid type. And I said a few things" —

"You were not rude?" apprehensively.

"Well" — and I reflected a little — "no, not rude, but I made him understand that one might live over a railroad-station and be a lady, well informed, and used to all the refinements and proprieties of social life. And he apologized for not calling sooner, and said there were several of the church people who were anxious to make your acquaintance."

"Let them come," said Eve with a dainty little nod; but she held her head straighter than ever.

The ordinary range of the Athenians was not very extensive, I found. The old settlers were the usual type, country people, with plenty of pedigree, and names that elsewhere carried weight; but these degenerate scions had dropped into unambitious grooves, content to eat, drink, and sleep, and let the world go by. We prate of contentment, and yet we secretly despise it as being a virtue practically more honored in the breach than the observance. Some had sold farms, and seen them cut up into building-plots, and continually regretted it: others as perseveringly bewailed their blindness in not selling when they might have done so. They all seemed to think there was a fortune in the land still. People from the adjacent cities *must* come, there would not be room enough for them; but I had learned, whether wisely or not, that cities could be crowded to repletion, because the business was there, and it was *not* in the country. Property was high enough for a prosperous city, but no one ever sold. A few traded;

now and then a mortgage was foreclosed; or some speculator, discouraged, closed out his investments cheap. "There was no public spirit," groaned everybody; but there was no private spirit either. They were waiting for a miracle to come along, and transform them into prosperity. It certainly must have been Sleepy Hollow before the railroad was built.

"People are so queer!" said Pryor one day as we were tramping over the hills, that glowed with a dusky red sunset. "If you get a chance to make a bargain, the owner claps on five hundred more, and the thing falls through. There are a number of places standing empty, that are a bill of expense, and falling into decay: others do not pay two per cent on their fancied value. The ridiculousness of asking eight or ten thousand dollars for a place, and getting two hundred dollars rent for it! Now, there is a house over yonder, that greenish one with a tower. It has all the modern improvements, and a tank that freezes up every winter, and deluges the house. Some New-York parties foreclosed a mortgage of seven thousand dollars five years ago. I could have sold it the year after for six thousand cash, but they wouldn't look at that. Two years it has not been tenanted: once they put it in good repair, and the tenant staid six months. Now it is rented for eighteen dollars a month, and the tenant

gets all out of it he can. The fences I suspect he
uses for firewood, also some of the trees. My opinion is, that the interest of six thousand dollars would
be of more account to them, for in a few years the
house will be half ruined. Now [pausing as we
came down the hill], here is a place that I think will
go cheap some day."

It was two streets above the railroad. Avenues
most of the streets running north and south were
called, and this was Oak Avenue. It stood on the
corner; and on Jay Street, a hedge of Norway spruce
almost shut it from sight; while at the back, there
was a grove of chestnut-trees. There was a picturesque house, a small barn, and dilapidated hennery,
and an acre or so of ground. On Oak Avenue,
where the house fronted, the prospect was lovely;
for the slope went down to the river, broken by the
intervening streets. The bank on the other side was
high again. You had Athens at your feet, though
nearly all of the town lay below Jay Street; and
at its southern end, there was another station,
which went by the name of the little place below,
Rutherford.

"I have been up here several times," I said.
Indeed, this was a favorite ramble with Eve as well.
"I have wondered about this house — can it be
rented?"

"Well, I am not sure. The last tenant used it dreadfully, and then went off owing three months' rent. It is for sale."

"Of course," I said in an amused tone.

"And it will be a bargain for some one. Come, Thurston, buy it yourself."

"Pray for some one to leave me a fortune. But I might rent it in the spring,—if the rent was not too high."

"The owner is bound to sell it now. It has quite a romantic history. The man who built it some twelve years ago was a Mr. Cassel. He was an engraver, and something of an artist. The Montgomery farm had just been cut up, and the station opened; and people supposed it would soon be a great place. A few years afterward his wife was killed by being thrown out of a friend's carriage. Then he shut up the house, and went away for two years, when he came back with a new wife, a gay young widow. But the place was too lonely for her, and she spent a good deal of her time in New York. Gossip said they were very unhappy; and he grew rather queer, became partially deranged, and killed himself at a hotel in New York. Every thing had been left to her. She offered the place for sale for six thousand, then five and four, and two weeks ago told me to report *any* offer to her. It is a good deal out of repair, but is well built. That north side is filled in with brick. And there were loads of lovely fruit and berries, but boys and tramps do so destroy things! I'll bring the key up sometime, and we will take a turn through it."

We entered the dilapidated gate. It was overgrown with weeds and briers. The barn was in the rear of the house: all the rest was, or had been, a garden-plot. Trees were in sad need of pruning: the grape-arbor had tumbled down at one corner, or perhaps been broken. The house was two full stories with a steep Gothic roof, which gave some rooms upstairs. Across the front, which was to the east, ran a wide porch, where honeysuckle rioted. On the southern side a two-story bay-window, and another small porch.

"I wouldn't mind undertaking some repairs, if I could rent it cheaply enough," I said.

"Mrs. Cassel is bound to sell. I think she would make an easy bargain."

"My dear fellow, forty-five dollars a month will not buy many houses, besides taking care of two persons;" and I sighed.

"I wish I could sell it," and Pryor sighed as well.

We walked out reluctantly. I wondered if, in the whole course of my life, I should save up three or four thousand dollars. What art was there, that could get a good deal out of a very little? If one could stop eating — if clothes would never wear out. We might go without books, newspapers, evening-lamps — alas! what would life be worth with mental pleasures taken out of it.

Two lugubrious fellows meandered down to the station.

CHAPTER IV

TEMPTATION NO. I

EVE went down to her theatre party, and staid all night. The next evening but one, the series of the Clayonian Club commenced with Burbank; and we found it quite delightful. Then Sadie and Bertha Brooke came over, and we had the gayest kind of a lunch. The curtain had been put up, and our dining-room looked really tasteful. The girls took it as an immense joke. Then the oddest incident occurred as they were waiting for the train to return. Mr. Bradford came in for a ticket, stared around in his near-sighted way, and Sadie, the irrepressible, gave a little shriek that was half a giggle.

"O Mr. Bradford!" she cried. "So we meet again at Athens instead of Philippi! Classic shades! Of course you know my friend, Miss Thurston?"

"I have heard her sing in church, and have met her brother."

"Oh! your church is here, isn't it? I had a vague fancy it was somewhere at Western New York."

"Train!" I exclaimed, and helped Bertha in, while Mr. Bradford took charge of Sadie.

Eve's face was one gleam of amusement.

"Wherever could he have met Sadie Brooke!" she cried. "The greatest flirt I ever knew, only there is not a bit of sentiment in any of it. I hope — no, I will not be unchristian."

"You ridiculous girl! Mr. Bradford is leagues and leagues above such pastime."

"But Sadie flirts with the soberest people. All is fish that comes to her net. It would be amusing to see him caught."

Oddly enough, a week later we had quite an influx of calls from the Athenians. I gave up my office to Eve. She had added some womanly touches, and we had flowers blooming in the window. I felt proud of my fair sister, who was a lady anywhere.

Indeed, now we seemed to have a social status. We were asked to join a young people's guild; and I took two seats in a partly rented pew at church, so that we might feel at home.

The month passed rapidly, and at its close Eve looked over the accounts.

"We have been extravagant in the way of pleasures," she declared. "Three dollars for club-tickets, two dollars for a library-ticket, and three dollars in going to and fro."

"But we shall have books five months longer, and there are three more entertainments."

"And Christmas will come next month. Well, we have not spent quite all our money."

"But we need a little pleasure."

"And the eight hundred dollars "—

"Bother that!" I interrupted.

"Getting and saving is likely to be bother enough."

But after a walk the next morning, Eve came in radiant.

"What do you think?" she began breathlessly. "I have three music-scholars, and one in painting. Forty dollars a quarter!"

"Eve!"

"Well, it is just nothing at all. Mrs. Morrison was very much taken with my playing the other evening at the Whartons's, and I said I wished I could find some music-scholars, when she offered me her two little girls. Annie plays quite well already. Then she said she had seen those pretty birthday favors at the Corwins's, and asked if I ever gave lessons in painting; and I answered that I would readily. She wants a quarter's lessons. Mrs. Clark happened in just then; and as she was dissatisfied with her daughter's teacher, and had given her up, she engaged me. Think of it! Some money all my own! And that it should come to me without any trouble! I do wish there was room for my piano."

That was at Long Branch. Aunt Carry had written Eve two quite lengthy letters, and in the second sent the invitation for the month of February. Helen was having a splendid time, and no end of admirers. But Eve decided not to go to Washington.

"You see, I can be quite gorgeously apparelled here," she said laughingly; "and my vanity prompts me to stay where I can make the most show. What would my old gowns be there?"

Eve certainly was very happy. Young people began to throng around her, and invitations were showered upon us. We had four for a Christmas dinner, and three for a party in the evening. Then there were Christmas greens and a children's treat. Mr. Bradford paid her some especial notice, and begged her to take part in the carols.

"It is so different from last winter, with teas and germans, and receptions and crushes, and racking your brains about gowns! But I enjoy the change, and it isn't half such hard work."

We did have a very pleasant time, and then Eve went to New York for a week. Sadie Brooke came over for her, and the days were crowded full of enjoyment; though she returned home looking rather fagged out.

"I do not mean to go out of an evening for the next two weeks," she declared. "We will turn over a new leaf. Why, I am ever so much more dissipated in this benighted little Athens than I was at Great Mammoth Beach."

We both laughed at that.

There was a week of wintry weather with snow and rain and sleet. Business was dull. But, oh! how cosey and snug we were in our odd little home!

I was reading aloud one evening from "My Summer in a Garden." Eve had been sewing; but presently she dropped her work, and her eyes wandered into vacancy. I paused, but she did not appear to remark it.

"Eve!" I exclaimed.

"Oh!" with a long sigh and a dreamy kind of smile as she roused from her revery. "I was not asleep."

"What were you thinking of so intently?"

"I had a vision."

"A vision!" I repeated, startled.

"Yes. I saw us both in a garden. Adam, let us stay here at Athens. It will be so lovely in the spring, and all through the summer. And if you do not earn so much, I can make a little. Let us have the garden and fruit, and flowers and poultry. Some people make money at that. And if one could have a permanent home " —

Some one came in the waiting-room, stamping the snow off his boots.

"Hillo!" cried a cheery voice. "You two people are the picture of content."

"We *are* content," answered Eve. "Could there be a more cosey interior?" and she glanced around in triumph.

I knew very well that Pryor thought it would be hard to find a prettier girl. For Eve's eyes were so softly bright, and her cheeks a dainty peach-pink.

"Yet you were wishing for something else."

"Are you quite sure it wasn't some *one* else — the lad you left behind you in New York?"

"There were so many of them!" said Eve with a graceful little shrug. "And now they are dancing with other girls, so why should I bewail them? In sober truth," — and a serious expression crossed her face, — "I was going back to what my brother terms first principles."

Pryor looked puzzled, and glanced from one to the other.

"It is not lovers or husbands, though the world insists that is a woman's greatest and most absorbing subject of contemplation. Adam and I have formed a league of amity and good-fellowship, and we want to go back to the garden."

He laughed doubtfully as if he did not quite see the point. Then he said, "Do you want a real garden, or is it some figurative" —

"German, with favors. No: what I mean is real solid earth, that will raise berries, chickens, and flowers."

"There, Thurston!" Pryor exclaimed triumphantly, "you can't do better than take the Cassel place. I had a letter from the owner to-day. She offers it for thirty-five hundred. I am almost certain three thousand will take it."

"My dear fellow," I replied, annoyed at his pertinacity, "I am in the position of the man, who, when corner-lots were selling at a dollar apiece, couldn't buy half a one."

"And she will take five hundred dollars down, with good security for the rest."

"That pretty place on the hill?" asked Eve. "I have looked at that with a longing eye, and the eye of faith also. It has possibilities."

"It is a bargain. She might throw off enough to put the place in order."

We all looked at each other like guilty conspirators, until the silence was positively ridiculous. Then Eve drew a long breath, and laughed in a ringing fashion.

"Little does Mrs. Cassel know of the deep plots against her interest," said I.

"See here," began Pryor: "suppose she had sold it five years ago for three thousand, and put the money out at six per cent. Reckon it up at simple interest — nine hundred dollars, where it's safe to say it hasn't paid her a penny. Why, it would be to her *best* interest to dispose of it as speedily as possible. My advice is, when a thing doesn't pay, and isn't likely to pay, get rid of it as soon as you can."

"I should like to go through the house," said Eve quietly.

"The first decent day we will," replied Pryor.

He talked on about places. The last train came, and I began to prepare for the night. A fine sleet had set in; but the young man pulled up his coat-collar, and lighted his lantern.

"Pryor is the most persistent fellow I ever saw," I said impatiently. "Heaven help the woman he sets out to gain if she doesn't want him!"

Eve began to fold up her work. I had a misgiving that the serpent had entered Paradise.

I dreamed that night of processions of chickens, and long rows of berry-pickers, while crates were piled mountain high.

It stormed furiously again the next day, but just at sundown the air grew wonderfully mild. I shovelled away the snow. Mr. Bradford came up on the train, and stopped in the office to chat with Eve, — a small matter that amazed me.

We read again in the evening, then we talked farm and garden.

"You have given the subject a good deal of thought, Eve," I said presently.

"Yes. Now and then I have felt like proposing to you that we should go West, and pre-empt a tract of land; but I should not like the grand and awful loneliness. I am social, and fond of my kind, even if they do flirt and tell fibs occasionally. And it puzzles me to know how you live the first year while your crops are growing, and you haven't any money. Now, if one can keep a situation, and be getting a place in order; if one can save up a little money to pay on it all the time, — there will come a year when you have your own home."

"But we couldn't buy any thing with six hundred dollars. And it might not be wisdom to put our little money where we could not get it in case of sickness or trouble. And if any thing happened to us that we could not meet payments, away would go every thing under foreclosure."

"There wouldn't even a tiny lion's whelp in the way miss your apprehensive eyes," said Eve laughingly. "I have been used to seeing ventures. Oddly enough, while I was dancing and junketing around in New York, I was studying up some of these subjects. Mrs. Stannard, Mrs. Brooke's sister, who is a rather imaginary invalid, I think, has three dozen fresh-laid eggs brought in to her every week, for which she pays fifty cents a dozen, from the first of December until the first of April. There are plenty of others — I heard of one lady giving sixty cents for white Leghorn eggs. And as for flowers — well, I never realized before how much money was spent in flowers."

"But for flowers, you must have a greenhouse; and no person on a small scale can compete with the larger gardeners, who have every appliance. And if your hens laid abundantly in winter, so would others, and down would go prices."

"At all events, I would like to try, in a home of my own where I could have matters as I desired. I wonder these stupid Athenians do not start up and do something with their land."

"There is another thing, Eve," I said gravely: "just as you were settled in this paradise of flowers and hens, there might come a tempting offer of matrimony. You are too young and quite too charming to remain a wall-flower. Even here"—

"Yes, there is Gordon Pryor devoted to *your* interests, I observe, and Dan Montgomery and two or three others; but I am afraid the flowers and hens that you mention so disdainfully would be potent rivals. Indeed, *you* might want to marry; but it seems to me, that, if we both had money in one house, we might settle it amicably."

"My dear Eve"—

She clasped her arms about my neck.

"You are not going to get rid of me so easily," she said, with something that sounded like a sob. "And I am going to help you make your eight hundred dollars, — for that will be our share at the next census, — whether you will or not."

There followed a week of rather cold but beautiful weather. Sleigh-riding was perfect, and not a day but some one came for Eve. Pryor was away four days on business, and the house had a rest.

So it was almost the last of January before we took our peep at it, cast a wistful eye where we had no possessions. It was a bright, sunny day, though roads and streets were still white with snow.

There was, as I have said, a porch in front, but it ran only half across. The southern end jutted out about six feet, and there was a large double window that opened on a balcony. Pryor unlocked the creaking door, and ushered us into a room, a sort of reception-room and hall. It was large; and quite at the end, the stairs went up with two turns, but were broad and easy. There were two windows on the north side, that overlooked Jay Street; and opposite a chimney with a grate set. A door opened on each side of this, the nearest into a pretty parlor. Here the chimney was across the corner of the room, with a quaint hard-wood mantel. On the south side this had two windows. Back of this, and opening on the hall as well, was the dining-room, with a square bay-window at the south, and just such a corner mantel as in the parlor. Indeed, one stack of chimneys did duty for the three places. Back of this room was a wash-room and a kitchen, and another chimney that answered for both. From the kitchen a back-stairs started up, and we followed these. There was only a little sort of loft over the kitchen, but in the main house four sleeping-rooms; the hall being divided in two, not so large as the others, but nicely furnished with closets. Up in the attic were three gable-ends, in one of which there was a very fair servant's room.

The paint and the walls were something dreadful. There had been some papering and some very wretched kalsomining. Several panes of glass were out, and sash-cords were broken. It had a forlorn and dilapidated air; but, as Eve observed, it had possibilities. The ceilings were moderately high, the doors and wood-work were good in spite of shabbiness.

We retraced our steps, and investigated the cellar.

It was under the main house, and had been very nice in its day of good order. There was a large closet, but the door had been carried away. The coal-bins had been partly torn down. There was an ash-shaft in the foundation of the chimney. When we went up again, we investigated. It connected with the grate; and in the dining-room was set an odd sort of thing, a kind of fireplace heater, but different from any I had ever seen, more nearly resembling a furnace in fact. There was a register through in the parlor, and three in rooms up-stairs.

"If it heats at all," said Eve, "it must be excellent."

On examination, I did not see why it should not heat; as it was extremely simple, and its manner of disposing of the ashes was commendable.

We had kept up a running fire of comment, fault-finding, depreciation, and approval. It was oddly planned, yet convenient enough, with no waste room, no great useless halls.

One small bedroom up-stairs had no mode of egress save through another, but that might not be much detriment.

Then we went out to the barn. That was not large; but it had a nice loft, and on this sunny day was positively warm. The hen-house would have to be made over altogether. It would take a good deal of time and labor, and not a little money, to get it in good order.

It was nearing train-time, and we had to return. "I'll drop in this evening," said Pryor. "Miss Thurston, it is an excellent chance."

We discussed it *pro* and *con*. I said the house was larger than our needs, and that a smaller place would cost less. I had come to have a horror of indebtedness.

"A house is not quite like any thing else," persisted Eve.

"But the interest on three thousand dollars, repairs, and taxes," I suggested.

"I could earn all that, I am sure," said she.

"But you must have clothes and journeys "—

"Aunt Carry's trunkful is not exhausted yet," with a bright smile. "I shall have another music-scholar; and when spring opens, I shall try to get a class in flower-painting."

She had set her heart on having a house and garden, I could plainly see.

"After all, suppose we do give up a good many things for the next five years — we can imagine ourselves out on the ranch; and when we have almost expired from sheer loneliness, we can go into New York."

"But I might do better than forty-five dollars a

month somewhere else. And this is a queer dead-and-alive little place."

A fourth person might have supposed us in some heated argument that evening. I am not sure but we were. And it ended by Eve having the face to make an offer of three thousand dollars for the house.

"Of course, she will not take that," said my young bargain-maker serenely. "But she may come down a little, and we can go up a little. And perhaps a month hence we may strike a bargain. And, Mr. Pryor, we shall depend upon you to study *our* best interest, and to warn and counsel if any adversary should be lurking around."

With that, Eve raises her eyes in that half entreating, wholly bewitching manner, and I can almost guess how the young fellow's heart thumps against his ribs.

"You would make a splendid real-estate agent, Miss Thurston," he says admiringly.

"Would I?" She straightens up, and the small face takes on a certain shade of haughtiness. "Well, I *hate* haggling, and cheapening and depreciating other people's belongings. If I were rich, — even moderately wealthy, — I never would have a word over any thing. If I wanted it, I would pay a fair price for it: if any one's charges were unreasonable,

I would walk away without a word. And I hate business, because there is so much discussion over bargains."

"Then you would not be so good," and he gives a little constrained laugh. "Why, I have known men who waited a year over a bargain for the sake of fifty or a hundred dollars."

"I am devoutly thankful that stores have one settled price," appends Eve. "I am ashamed of a woman who beats down."

"Eve," I said later on, "do you really think it wisdom to undertake such a wild scheme? We never *can* pay for the house, never!"

"Adam," she answers with a seraphic smile, "we will take up our common every-day lives for a few weeks, and not even dream of a return to Paradise. We may never go. But I wanted to see how it would seem just to talk about having a home of one's very own."

I dare say we both dreamed of it, but she kept her word rigidly. She would not even let Mr. Pryor discuss it; and when the word came that Mrs. Cassel could not for an instant entertain such an offer, I know I allowed myself to think of what I could do with the place, and the delight it would be. Is there some deep and secret charm in owning a bit of ground and the roof that shelters you? I even tolerated

Eve's hens when they scratched up my garden, and called myself all manner of names because I had not saved up more money.

February crept along. One day Mr. Pryor came up to the station with a very stylish black-eyed woman dressed like a princess. Some odd prescience told me it was Mrs. Cassel. I was so glad that Eve happened to be in!

There was a rather funny, wary sort of a discussion. Mrs. Cassel finally offered to split the five hundred. That was the best she could do. Eve was gentle and polite, listened with the utmost affability to a detailed account of all the place had cost, and then very sweetly suggested that it was going to cost a great deal more for repairs, — that a new owner could not be expected to pay for what was not there. No agreement was reached; and Mrs. Cassel went away rather vexed, I thought. She and Mr. Pryor walked up to look at the house.

Meanwhile we visited several other places. Indeed, half of Athens, it seemed to me, came in and offered us houses, and paid us a curious deference. I could see that we had gone up several degrees in the social scale. But in whatever direction we went, our longing feet led us thitherward. We viewed the place from every side. We were both curiously drawn to it.

CHAPTER V

EVE AT BARGAIN-MAKING

ONE morning early in March, Eve went down to the city. The "girls," as she called her bevy of young friends, kept her in warm remembrance, and thought it rare fun to come over for an hour or two. Sadie Brooke had spent one night, and confessed herself in no end of trouble with two lovers.

"I'd like to come over here and stay a month," she declared, "and in that time both of them would forget me."

I supposed Eve's day would be mostly devoted to them. She came home with a radiant face.

"You dear old Adam!" and she kissed me fondly. "Have you missed me to-day and been lonesome? For sentiment's sake, say 'Yes.'"

"For truth's sake, my dear girl."

I held her in my arms a moment. I was coming to have a strange, conscience-smitten feeling about Eve, as if there was some man in the world that I was defrauding of this sweetness and tender love.

She busied herself about our meal. There were

cold chicken, and potatoes to fry, and a dainty pudding. She was detailing odds and ends of her day's enjoyment.

"You had some luncheon?" I asked suddenly.

"Oh, yes! Do you remember Mrs. Harwood, Adam? Well, I went directly there, and staid unconscionably."

"And she asked you if we had quarrelled, or whether I had decided to take care of some other fellow's sister?"

"Exactly!" Eve laughed. "Then we talked business. And now I want to talk business with you, — about the house."

"Then, you haven't given it up?"

"We will consider the subject seriously. If you think it too much to undertake, then we will wait until we have saved a little more money. I went down to Mrs. Harwood to tell her about it, and ask some advice. I knew that she was putting money out all the time, and quite glad to find first mortgages. I confessed that our united savings and interest would amount to about seven hundred dollars, and what our income was likely to be. There was one point she asked me to consider, — what I should do in event of your death; and I told her of your insurance policy. Then she said, buy the house by all means. She will take a two-thousand-dollar mortgage on it, and give us five years to pay it, with a three years' extension if we should not be able to meet it all. The rest she will hold as a note, and we can pay it in any sums that we like. She is coming over to inspect our bargain; and, oddly enough, she knows a little about Mrs. Cassel, who is to be married in April to a rich old man, and go to Europe. And she says," laughed Eve, "that we must stand out for our offer, and that we will be sure to get it at the last. It doesn't seem real honorable to me, but I suppose it *is* business. Mrs. Harwood puts it in this light. The place never cost Mrs. Cassel any thing, and she would think nothing of spending two or three hundred dollars on her personal gratification. It is not as if she had worked and economized for it. And now she will be in affluent circumstances, while we need the money for repairs and so on, and it is *our* business to make the best bargain we can for ourselves. But three thousand dollars does seem a ridiculous sum for such a house and nearly two acres of ground."

"O Eve, you brave girl!" I began. "To think of your doing all this when I hardly dared to take the first step! But I learned through Pryor that we could take up two thousand dollars in almost any of the moneyed institutions. Didn't Mrs. Harwood say that I was a cad to let you go about it?"

"You did not send me about it, and I took care to let her know that," says Eve, bridling her proud little head. "She was only afraid you might marry, and there would be some difficulty. You see, she counts on my being an old maid."

"Eve," I reply, deeply moved, "if ever we do get the house, it must be settled upon you, because I never would have had the pluck to go at it alone."

"It will belong to both. We will both work for it, both enjoy it. I shall be all impatience until Mrs. Harwood comes, and that will be on Thursday. You must like her, Adam. She would be a very good friend to me if I needed one: she is *our* friend now."

After supper, Eve brought out her housekeeping-book, and we went over it carefully. We had been at Athens four and one-half months. Our real living expenses had averaged twenty-six dollars a month. There had been no rent to pay, and my fuel was bought at first cost. For pleasures, books, and incidentals, we had averaged seven dollars. We had spent, besides our summer savings, some twenty dollars for furniture: we had needed very little in the way of clothes, and we had now twenty-five dollars on hand. It was not much to save during that time, I confessed.

Then we counted up our assets. Eve had three hundred and sixty dollars, I had three hundred and forty odd. We could venture to pay seven hundred dollars down on the house. At the first of April, Eve would have forty dollars; and there was quite a prospect of her getting a class in painting.

Gordon Pryor came in presently, as usual. This time he had another bargain. There was a house a little farther to the north of us, to be sold under foreclosure the middle of March, for about twenty-five hundred. It was a larger and prettier house, with one acre of ground.

The next morning we went to look at it. It was a double house with a hall through the middle, and a large parlor on one side, that had a very pretentious air. There were four sleeping-chambers up-stairs, and a nice attic for storage; a furnace and a range. The fences were good, and the house in fair repair; no barn, but a very nice hennery; and some fruit. There certainly was a thousand dollars difference.

Thursday brought Mrs. Harwood. She was a bright, keen-eyed little old lady, with snowy white hair, and a kind of apple-bloom in her cheeks, a rapid talker, and she had a habit of giving sagacious little nods to emphasize her sentences. We went over the Cassel cottage exhaustively, made an estimate of what repairs would cost, though I knew I should do it for half the sum. Still, that was for Mrs. Cassel's eye. Mrs. Harwood approved of the place, and she also believed in young people laying by something.

"It is so easy," said she, "to take money out of a bank, but one cannot get it out of a house at a moment's notice."

She had a cup of tea with us, and was as much interested in Eve's small housekeeping as if she had been some connection.

We were to wait for some sign or word from Mrs. Cassel. Oddly enough, she came to hand the very next day. Pryor had a talk with her, in which he said he played out his right bower, — told her we were looking at another place. They came up together, and we had a long talk over repairs and all that.

"Well," she said at length, "I am going away for a year or so, and want to get rid of the house; but it cost twice that sum. It is really giving it away, and I might better have done this soon after Mr. Cassel's death. Take it at your own price, then."

Eve suddenly turned pale. I think she just realized the responsibility she had assumed.

Arrangements were made for the business to be settled the ensuing week. We sent word to Mrs. Harwood, and then lived in a curious state of expectancy, in which we felt that any thing might happen to snatch away our coveted prize. Every day we went to look at it. There was a spring-like tenderness in the air, and a purplish tint to the swelling buds. A bluebird now and then made a swift dazzle across the sky, and the waysides came to have a peculiar softness under the dead browns and grays.

No misfortune happened. Everybody came to hand, we paid away our precious money, and the house and nearly two acres of ground were transferred to us. Mrs. Harwood made up the remainder, and took a mortgage for two thousand dollars, and a note for three hundred. I must confess that I had some misgivings about the wisdom of staying at Athens on forty-five dollars a month. But the die was cast.

Athens was very much surprised. It was extremely amusing to hear the comments. Two different parties professed to be dreadfully disappointed. If they had suspected the place would go so cheap, they would have purchased it. Two or three others considered it dear at any price, and were sure one thousand dollars would not put it in good order. But we were the happiest of the happy.

"Still, we have enjoyed our nest up among the eaves," said my sister, "only it would be too hot for comfort in the summer. And now we really begin life. The past, with me, has been merely playing at it."

I felt the responsibility of a large debt on my

shoulders. I wondered how I would ever get used to it.

We had a very great surprise a few days after this. Uncle Lennard was in New York, and came over to see us. He was looking very well; but the mining business had not turned out quite as prosperously as he expected. He was getting up the company now, and hoped in a few years to be a rich man. Aunt Carry would spend the summer at Cleveland. Helen, he believed, was engaged, or there was a prospect of it. He was going to Long Branch, to look up some belongings of the ladies, and would have Eve's piano boxed and sent.

We kept him all night. How restless he was! how full of schemes and hopes and plans! Money, money all the time! Yet, when I said good-by, all his old kindness rushed over me, and I felt that I loved him like a son.

About a week later, Eve received a kindly little note from him, enclosing a check for one hundred dollars. He had made some money by a fortunate speculation, and wanted to send Eve a little gift; though he wished he could afford to add another cipher to the figures. Dear uncle Marvin! you had a generous heart. Had you been a millionnaire, you would have made people rejoice on the right hand and on the left.

"Now," said Eve, "I shall pay this directly on the house. Isn't it just lovely?"

I demurred at this. "You ought to keep something for yourself. And there will be house-furnishing, and repairs and papering"—

"And lions and lions," laughed Eve. "You are certainly Mr. Ready-to-halt and Mr. Faint-Heart in one. Dear old Bunyan! How well he knew the souls of human beings!"

In spite of my arguments, she went and paid it. Mrs. Harwood thought she had better keep it, but Eve was resolute. Then her friend asked her to go out shopping, and she purchased two pretty summer-silk dresses. At parting, she put one parcel in Eve's hand.

"This is for you, my dear," she said; "and with it my best wishes. But do not wear yourself out too fast, saving and working. There is nothing so sweet as youth, and that is the season for pleasure."

"How lovely she was!" exclaimed Eve. "I should have valued any little gift, and I wasn't expecting any thing; for somehow I have always fancied Mrs. Harwood a very close woman, though she has a good deal of upright common sense, the kind that is just and earnest. And, when we get settled, she is coming over to pay us a visit. I do seem to be in luck. I am getting all the things I want."

"You seem to want very little."

"You didn't think so when I first proposed a house," she said archly. "And, Adam, the girls are coming over, lots of them. We shall have the gayest sort of a summer here in this sleepy little town. Everybody will be amazed."

We resolved we would be in no hurry to get in. It was comfortable where we were while fires were needed, and we would take our renovating by degrees. I found the roof needed a little repairing, the leaders were choked up by leaves and dirt, and the dining-room chimney had a small leak. I had a man come, who, with my assistance and planning, did the mending, and all the leaders were freshly painted, at a cost of seven dollars. The outside of the house needed painting badly, but that must wait. Then a woman came, and cleaned the attic and the second floor in one day, at the very moderate price of a dollar and a quarter. The next thing was to paint the woodwork.

"Aunt Carry and I painted down at Long Branch," said Eve; "and why isn't it just as sensible as painting innumerable plaques and panels? There ought to be a practical side to art, when people need it for real use. Now, I am sure you and I can paint it to our liking. I want some pretty delicate tints. I shall have blue rooms and green rooms, and dainty bits of coloring. Why, Adam, it will be the most delightful thing in the world! I have wished that I could get into the business of house decoration, and now I can try on ours."

We purchased some household paints in various tints, and a can of white, to lighten if we needed. We had ten pounds in all, and by that quantity we purchased it for eighteen cents a pound. I bought seventy-five cents' worth of brushes, — one quite large, two small; and, after settling upon our colors, we went at the two small rooms. One was in a delicate lavender; the other a pale gray, with lavender alternations. Eve took the sashes, and I the doors. There were four doors and three windows. I must confess that Eve would have made good wages if it had been piece-work at a fair price. She was so quick and deft, so neat as well. Now and then I had to run down for a train; but we finished both chambers, and they looked very inviting.

"Do you know," said Eve, "that I shall paint the floors? The rooms are small, and painted floors will be cleaner. We can lay down rugs, and that will be cheaper," with a bright laugh.

That evening she "dreamed" out her color, she declared. The bay-windowed room was to be hers. By skilful manipulation, she made a lovely tint, neither green nor blue, but an indescribable medium, and, with the least bit of gray, softened it to perfection. The other was in parti-colors again, — buff, with a bit of dull blue. We finished both the same day, and found we had not used all our paint. The parlor down-stairs had been trimmed in black walnut; and the mantel was of the same wood, very pretty indeed. The hall and stairs were grained to match; but it looked now as if suffering from some eruptive disease, so many bangs and rubs had it received. The dining-room was pine, oiled originally, but looking badly now.

"A coat of varnish will help it," I said. "And the graining must be mended and varnished."

"That will be a labor long drawn out, if not of linked sweetness," she said humorously.

Then we discussed papering. There really was nothing else to do with the chamber-walls.

"And when once done, it lasts for a long while," Eve continued. "We can do it ourselves."

But we decided, while we were about it, that it would be the part of wisdom to paper the ceilings as well. Then we could go on for years without much fuss of house-cleaning. We went down to Northwood one morning, and looked at "odd lots," finding many really beautiful remnants that the dealer was glad to sell at any price. One piece took Eve's fancy particularly. It had four stripes in the width that were exquisite.

"You see," said Eve, with an eye to economy, "this will make beautiful bordering at a very small cost. I am not going to have it put on in the usual regulation way, but try how much harmony and effect I can get in it."

We spent for paper, nine dollars and fifty cents, and had enough for the chambers and the dining-room. I had a man come one day to paper the ceilings: the rest we did ourselves. There was a little deep red in the dining-room paper; and we touched up the woodwork at the edges of the moulding with Pompeiian red, and the effect was excellent. The hall and stairways had painted walls, also the parlor. They were not in very good order; but being clean, we decided to let them go until a more convenient season. The kitchen had a wainscoted dado with paper above, but we resolved sometime to paint it. I must not omit to state that Eve painted the floors of the small chambers in Pompeiian red, and was well satisfied with her experiment. We found it to be a most excellent and cleanly proceeding.

We had now spent for labor and material twenty-four dollars and fifty-five cents, and had the inside of our house in very fair order. For this we used our March surplus and the fifteen dollars we had saved before. We would have enough to live on during April, but I insisted that Eve should keep her forty dollars for the present. So far, — it was then about the 10th of April, — the weather had been decidedly cold. Not much could be done in farming.

We had entertained ourselves by reading up all kinds of farm and garden literature that came in our way, and we could get plenty of it at the library. We laughed over the failures and mistakes: we marvelled a little at some of the wonderful stories.

"The best way," said Eve sagely, "is to strike a golden mean. Since we have a garden and some time on our hands, let us try to make it profitable. If we could pay the interest with our sales" —

"O Eve!" I interrupted, "don't dream of that. In fact, don't dream of any thing. This year will be just an experiment."

"But we must avoid what has proved unfortunate in other people's experiments, and adopt the best. What is the good of all this wisdom of years and years, if it does not teach you to do something?"

I took a serious survey of my garden one sunny morning, and began to trim the trees. There were three .quinces that looked quite promising when pruned into shape. Just back of the house was one large pear-tree, and at the south-west corner a cherry-tree. At the side near the street was a large oblong of grass, — lawn, I suppose I ought to call it. Back of this were two rows of pear-trees going up to the barn, eight in all. One in each row I found was dead, but the space was better for those that remained. Beyond this there were the quince, two apple-trees, one more cherry; and there had been peaches innumerable, but they were nearly all dead, though some promising young ones had grown up. The ground had a frontage of two hundred feet on Oak Avenue, and was three hundred feet in length. Over on the west side at the dividing-line was a blackberry tangle that *did* look hopeless. I found currants, gooseberries, and raspberries. The two former were set between the pear-trees. Certainly, there had been an abundance of fruit when the place was in order.

I trimmed and trimmed. I dragged my dead and useless branches to the barn-yard, and decided that we ought to have a fireplace in the house, that we might enjoy the blaze thereof. It seemed to me an endless task; but I went over the ground thoroughly as far as I did go, and was amazed at the improvement. There would be a large space for gardening, and we discussed what our vegetable venture would be.

"Pease and sweet corn," said Eve, "and radishes and lettuce and tomatoes. Oh, we ought to plant the seeds in boxes! And cucumbers — and — every thing."

I laughed.

I was leaning on my own gate-post resting, when one of my neighbors came along. This was a Mr. Montgomery, whose son, Dan, cast tender glances at Eve. Mr. Montgomery had owned all this end of the township, and been a prosperous farmer, some fifteen years before. But when the mania for improvement overtook Athens, he cut up his farm, laid out the two avenues, Oak and Montgomery, and sold off some plots. Then came the great depression. Much of the land had lain waste since then. It would hardly pay to fence it in, so it had been allowed to grow bountiful crops of weeds. His money he had been compelled to live upon, and found himself now in very straitened circumstances, and leading a kind of aimless life. There were four girls and three boys in the family. The eldest son and daughter worked in the hat-factory at Springdale, the next station above. Dan was about twenty, and was clerk in the principal grocery-store at Athens. The next daughter had just set up as a dressmaker, and the three younger ones were at home.

"Well, young man," began my senior, "I suppose you think you are going to do quite wonders here,— set us all an example;" and he gave a good-natured but rather derisive laugh.

"I do not know about the example," I returned.

"I am rather new to this kind of business, and I may need a little advice."

"Well, I suppose you've lots of book-learning on the subject, and let me tell you that isn't worth a rye straw. What you want is practical knowledge. And then, this kind of work doesn't pay hereabouts. Bermuda and the South are sending in every thing: there isn't any profit in gardening, or farming for that matter, unless you go West. If my wife was willing, I'd start to-morrow."

"Yet," I said, "people on Long Island, and, indeed, in every direction from New-York City, do make gardening pay. There seems a continual demand."

"Well, you don't get any returns. The best prices are gone, and you come in at the fag-end. Wasn't calculating to do that yourself, I hope?"

"Not at present; but I shall raise a little to try my hand."

"There's no use bothering with it. You can buy it for half of what it will cost you. Now, do you know what I'd do with this place?"

"What?" I inquired.

"Well, first of all, I'd hustle up that great patch of blackberry briers. They are the worst things to get in the ground: you have to fight 'em out every inch of the way. I had 'em several years, then I cleared 'em out root and branch"

"But what do you do for berries?"

"Oh! plenty of 'em grow wild about here. Wife and the girls often go out of an afternoon, and pick a lot. Everybody comes over here."

"If I should tear them up, they wouldn't come. That might be an object."

Mr. Montgomery looked rather curiously at me. "Well, you'll be sick enough of 'em," he said. "Cassel just had a few set out along the fence, and now look where they've gone."

"But you *can* sell blackberries," I returned.

"Well, — what would you get? Not enough to pay for picking," rather contemptuously. "Cassel, you know, had every thing put in that money could buy; but late years it's gone to rack and ruin."

"And if I take up the berries?" I suggested, rather amused.

"Well, I'd get a man to come and plough up the whole thing. Then I'd have it seeded down. 'Twould look neat and nice, and be no trouble; and 'most any one would cut it for the grass."

"And how much would this cost?"

"Well, — two days' work, say, — about ten dollars. Ploughing, harrowing, and seeding, you know, take quite a little time."

"And give my grass away?"

"Well, you might hire it cut, but you wouldn't

more than pay expenses if you sold it. Just as broad as it's long," and he gave a chuckle.

"I do not believe gardening can come out much worse than that," I ventured.

"Well, you'll see. Fellows like you think they can do wonders, but you'll find book-gardening doesn't amount to much. However, if you want to spend your money, that isn't my affair. Maybe experience is the best teacher after all," and he nodded in a kind of satisfactory manner.

I had to run for the train, and my chance for further practical wisdom was lost.

CHAPTER VI

MY TRAMP

We were spending the evening with the Corwins, when I happened to repeat the sage advice of Mr. Montgomery.

"I suppose we will have to call him a pessimist," said Mr. Corwin. "According to his view, nothing pays but a salaried position or weekly wages. He cannot understand that a certain degree of pleasure in an undertaking is a reward. He will die a comparatively poor man; and I have heard people say he was a very brisk, prosperous farmer. Now he raises a little corn and potatoes and vegetables for the family, and keeps declaring that you can buy them much cheaper. His once beautiful and productive farm is half waste land, filling the world with a crop of all kinds of weeds. A neighbor of mine wanted to take a three-years' lease on some lots next door to him; but no, Montgomery was sure to sell them in a year's time, and they are not sold yet. When I think of all the unproductive land lying about these little towns, and the people who might have gardens and fruit, it seems such a waste! Of course, Mr. Montgomery's taxes are much higher than if his property was still a farm; and it will eat up half his substance in the end."

"And, Miss Thurston, don't ever allow yourself to be inveigled into going after wild berries of any kind," said Mrs. Corwin. "They are small, full of seeds, half green if you do get them, because the children pull them so soon. Many a time I have picked enough of my own in ten minutes, and just gone down to the foot of the garden. But I shouldn't wonder if you were overrun with children this summer, they have been so used to roaming over the place."

"I shall keep a dog," I said.

"And I shall be frightened every day and hour lest the dog goes mad," responded Eve, at which everybody laughed.

However, by the middle of the month, a gentleman came up to Athens to look at the plot of ground next to me. It had just fallen to his wife by inheritance; and she had resolved to have a country-house built, if the place was at all desirable. We walked through his ground and then mine; and I think he was very favorably impressed, for the next day he brought up his wife. They were a Mr. and Mrs. Wilbur, and had five children. They wanted a plain, roomy house, just for summer living, with plenty of out-of-doors, and some shade. On their plot stood two magnificent old apple-trees and some chestnuts. That seemed to decide the lady at once, and they concluded to go at the building immediately. So we would have a next-door neighbor in the summer at least.

I was casting about for some one to assist me in my labors, when an incident occurred that enabled me to do a good deed as well. Going down for the noon train, I saw a ragged tramp sitting on a step at the end of the freight-room. After the train had gone, he shambled along in a downcast way, watching me wistfully. He was not more than twenty, but a pitiable object; still, I had seen so many poor, half-starved railroad lads, that my heart went out to him.

"Well?" I said in a tone of inquiry, as he halted within speaking distance.

"Then, you don't know me, Thurston?" and the pale face flushed, partly with shame I think.

As I studied him doubtfully, he said with some hesitation, "Crawford. I was down at Great Mammoth Beach two summers ago."

"Not Joe Crawford!"

The tears came into the poor lad's eyes.

Twenty months ago I had parted from a nice, bright, rosy-cheeked lad, who had been but two years in service. Now he was pale, gaunt, sodden as to complexion, and his eyes showed traces of dissipation.

"I've seen awful hard times this winter," he said; "and I have a promise of a place in Jersey City the 1st of May. I've been staying a week with Jim Turner at Field's Landing, and he passed me on, — if the boys hadn't been good to me" — and the poor fellow broke down.

The old, old story. Jim Turner was good-hearted, and a first-class man when he was sober; but once a month or so he would go on what he called a "tear." Likely he and Crawford had been drinking together.

"When did you leave Jim?" I asked.

"Last Friday. I've tramped since then, and begged. I heard some one say you were here. — Thurston, I haven't had a crust since noon yesterday, and I crawled under a shed last night. I can't see why some boys should have such bad luck."

"First, then, you want a good square meal," I said. "Come into the station. I am living here."

"Oh! you're married."

"No: my sister is with me," was my brief reply; and I was rather glad Eve was up at the house.

He followed me in. There was a little fire in the stove, and he went close to it with a sigh of relief. How wan and wretched he looked, — a travesty upon youth, and the health he used to have!

"Sit down, and rest yourself," I said, "and I will hunt you up something."

I was to take some lunch to Eve, who was busy with closets, painting the shelves and floors, and did not want the walk just then. I prepared a bountiful plateful for Crawford, — cold beef, biscuits, and a great slice of cake, — and then put up ours.

"Now," I said cheerfully to him, "you eat this; then take this cushion, and curl up in the corner, and go to sleep. I'll be back in about an hour and a half," for I did not want to alarm Eve by any prolonged stay. "Make yourself at home. You're used to a railroad station."

"You're such a good fellow!" he said gratefully.

I locked the door of my office as usual, but the waiting-room was always kept open.

Eve and I had our lunch, and then went on with our work. Hers was finished presently, but I had to leave mine with the same hopeless aspect. I should not get over to the berries before midsummer. Against Farmer Montgomery's advice, I had spaded up some ground, and planted pease.

Going down, I told Eve of my tramp, and what I knew of him. I had met him first at the beach. He was a country lad, an orphan, and had learned telegraphing. When his married sister went West, he floated out to the great city, to add one more to the waifs and strays.

"Poor fellow!" said Eve pitifully.

"If they would not spend their money for drink!" I returned, rather impatiently.

"Yet you have said, Adam, that you could hardly blame them, either, when their lives were so hard."

I sighed. There was and is a great wrong somewhere, when destruction is set in the way of thousands. And I remembered the first time I had seen Joe Crawford drunk: some of the boys had done it as a joke. He was very sick for a day or two, and very much ashamed; and I had taken him in hand.

He was asleep now, curled up in the corner-seat, with the cushion back of his head. He looked pallid in the extreme, and his lips were a kind of purplish blue. Deep shades of the same tint were under his eyes. His rusty felt hat was pulled down over his forehead; but his nose was fine, and his chin had a certain character and determination, as if he might overcome evil if he once resolved earnestly. I remembered my own turning-point.

Eve was busy about housewifely matters up-stairs. She was employing her time in the manufacture of marvellous lambrequins and curtains and chair-covers. Trains came and went. I wrote a little and at six Joe was still sleeping.

"We shall have to keep him all night," said Eve; and then she glanced in dismay at his rough and soiled attire.

"Well, he can sleep anywhere: the trouble with such lads is often where to find a place to sleep."

Joe started then, roused himself, and flushed redly.

"I've had such a splendid nap!" he began. "Why, it's never that late!" glancing at the clock. "Well, I suppose I must tramp along," regretfully. "I'm obliged to you, Thurston, for this good rest and my dinner."

"Were you going anywhere in particular?"

"Well,—no;" and his face was scarlet. "I must tramp out a couple of weeks somehow."

"Then, I think you had better remain here all night," I said quietly. "We can make you a bed."

"I ain't fit to stay with — with decent people," he blurted out on a half cry.

"You can make yourself a little better. You would feel ever so much improved by a nice wash, and I can hunt up a clean garment or two."

Joe Crawford did not speak, but winked his eyes hard; yet, in spite of that, some tears rolled down his cheeks.

"Come," I began cheerfully, "we'll fix you up so that you will hardly know yourself. I have a nice little corner up-stairs, and I'll get some warm water."

I had manufactured a screen out of an old-fashioned clothes-horse, that shut my room off from the stairway. I consulted Eve, and she found an old suit of underwear and a shirt laid by for charitable uses. I filled a pail nearly full of warm water, brought towels and soap, and spread down an old mat. Then we retired to the office, and left him free from any danger of interruption.

"I wish you had some clothes that would fit him. See here," said Eve eagerly. "He is just about Mr. Corwin's size; and Mrs. Corwin was complaining a few days ago of the old clothes around, and declaring she would have to make a rag carpet in self-defence. I'll just run over, and see what I can raise."

She returned in about ten minutes, breathless, with a great bundle in her arms, — two pairs of trousers, a vest, and a coat.

"Take them up to him directly, and see how they will do. I didn't actually beg them," declared Eve, with a bright laugh, "but I made a bargain. Mrs. Corwin wanted some of that red curtain trimming, and I promised to send her some of *your* cast-off garments for her carpet."

I waited until the splashing of water had nearly ceased, and then went up with my arms full.

"I haven't had any thing so good for a month," said Joe in a quivering voice. "And these soft, clean clothes! Thurston, old fellow, may I just stick mine into the fire? They are rags and shreds, and not fit for any one to touch."

They were all that, and they did go into the fire.

Nothing could exceed his gratefulness for the suit of clothes. He brushed up his hair, and looked really well, though thin and haggard.

Supper was quite late; and Joe seemed, indeed, a new creature. Eve went out,—she was helping with some church matters. I must confess, that, since the talk of our purchasing a house, a good deal more deference had been paid us both. The old, old story of the gold ring and the fine apparel. It is always, "Friend, come up higher."

While she was away, I had a long talk with Joe. The same quicksands that wreck so many,—drink and bad company. Yet there is so little besides for thousands. Too often, if they attempt to cross the dividing-line, they are pushed back. I wondered secretly, if I had been a drunkard, whether any hand in all Athens would have been stretched out to save me.

Yet Joe was not innately vicious. Given a pleasant home and surroundings of interest, and he would have been quite satisfied. There was no evil longing for the sins that were dragging him down; but he was right in the midst of them, and it was so hard to swim against the current. How much of virtue and goodness consists in surroundings, I think the great world little realizes.

The poor lad had lost two places through the winter from drink and neglecting his business. I drew from him the fact that he had been drinking with Turner, who then procured a pass, and sent him farther down the road. Who would employ him in such disreputable attire? A friend in Jersey City had written to him that there would be a vacancy about the 1st of May; and on this slender hope he was going there, into new temptations and pitfalls Could anybody save him? Would not the evil forces so in the ascendency sweep him to destruction in the end?

We made him a bed down-stairs on the lounge. The next morning he looked like a new creature. He was so simply grateful, and he followed Eve about with such adoring eyes, that I was fain to smile.

"Why couldn't you keep him for a few days?" said she. "He might help you clear up the place. You know you were talking of hiring some one for a while."

The same thought had entered my mind the evening before. The poor lad was homeless and without a penny. And I might hear of something for him that would be less dangerous than the great vortex of the city.

I suggested the plan to Joe, and he caught at it eagerly.

"I'd do any thing for you, Thurston. I'd like to pay back a little of your kindness. Yes, I'll work at any thing. And I know a good deal about such work too. Oh, how lucky you are! I wonder — but I don't suppose I shall ever have a home of my own," and he sighed. "I've often thought how nice it would be."

"I was no nearer it at twenty than you are now," I made answer. "And there is a long stretch before me ere I can call the home really mine."

"And you have your sister. My sister was so much older than I, and married, and somehow never took much interest in me. I'd like to marry" —

"Do not marry until you can care properly for a wife," I said, almost sharply I am afraid. "It is a shame to drag any woman through want and hard work."

"I wasn't thinking of such a thing until I could afford it, Thurston," he answered humbly.

"And until you can love and honor her, and endow her with *all* your earnings, which will be little enough."

Joe hung his head in abasement, and I felt sorry. Then I added in a cordial tone, "What is the decision? Will you stay? I can't afford to pay much besides the living."

"I'll stay gladly, and do my best. I have been paid beforehand."

Certainly Joe did his best. He had an aptitude for this kind of work. He was cheery and obliging, and he followed Eve about with the devotion of a true knight. Our garden flourished under his ministration. We went at the famous blackberry tangle, armed with old gloves. and old clothes and sickles, and cut a long, straight path through. Then we dug up the roots, trimmed the dead branches out of the rows, and made it look quite business-like. It seemed as if Joe improved every day. Regular sleep and nourishing food took the haggard lines out of his face, his weak and bloodshot eyes cleared up, — they were a soft hazel as to color, — and his voice grew strong and ringing. He could sing well, and we passed some entertaining evenings.

After the berry patch, we cleaned out our cistern, and then we felt that we could move in almost any time. We had tried our heater, and found it excellent. There was a good deal of garden to make, — for I had put in only pease and potatoes, — and the chicken-house to remodel, for Eve had the poultry fever. She had already bought two dozen eggs, and had two hens sitting in the barn.

"I'll get you some fancy ones," said Gordon Pryor one evening when we had been discussing the business from the amusing as well as the profitable point. "I have a friend up on the other side of the river, who makes money out of it, — does it with an eye to profit. I should like you to go up there sometime, Thurston. I'll get a horse and carriage some day, and we'll go. Crawford can keep the shop?"

Joe nodded.

"Westfield, — you know the station, Thurston, though this is a mile or two from the railroad. Vanduyne is my friend's name. He was very much out of health some years ago, and went to Florida, meaning to stay, but didn't like it. Then he started a chicken ranch. He keeps all of the fancy kinds, and sells eggs for hatching, raises prize birds, and all that. It is a sight, I tell you. But he is the most discouraging fellow to talk business that I ever heard. According to him, you want a fortune to start, and you want knowledge enough to run the Government of the United States, or settle the Indian question. Now, it never struck me that a hen was such a very abstruse subject."

"Unless you had her for dinner at a boarding-house," said Joe dryly; and Pryor threw back his head and laughed.

"I'll get you some white Leghorn eggs: they are all the rage. And the hens are warranted to lay two eggs a day."

"Oh, dear! what will I do with the eggs?" said Eve in comic dismay.

"Sell them at a dollar a dozen for hatching; and drop four out of every dozen in boiling water."

"But why?"

"To keep the species from increasing too rapidly. Eight chickens are about as much as one can reasonably expect out of a dozen eggs."

"Yes," replied Eve soberly. "I'll remember that."

Joe giggled.

"Then, when your hens are laying bountifully, and eggs are cheap, you pack them in lime and something, and bring them out as fresh eggs when the price goes up to sixty cents."

"Is that the way your friend does?"

"His methods are past finding out; but he has loads of eggs when prices are high, and hatches chickens in an incubator, to put on the market about the middle of February. But, as I said, he will talk you into believing the thing impossible before you have listened five minutes. Still, I have an old lady friend at Springdale, who doesn't keep a very large flock, — from fifty to a hundred, — and makes a clear hundred dollars every year."

"I should like to see *her*."

"But she hasn't any method. And she thinks any one can do it."

" I have often wondered," I said, " why people in general advise you against the business they are in. Mr. Montgomery insists that no kind of farming or gardening pays; people who try poultry, for the most part pronounce that a failure; and so with many other things. Then, Watson told me the other day that I'd be sick of my house in a year or two; that I could rent for half the sum interest and repairs would amount to."

"Half the world is very depressing, the other half over-sanguine," commented Pryor dryly.

"And the medium class go on and succeed," said Eve. "I have often heard people argue that real estate did not pay; but Mrs. Harwood at thirty-five was left a widow with two small houses in New York, and now is a rich woman. She has bought and sold, owns considerable property, and has money out on mortgages. Everybody cannot work on a large scale; but a good many can do their best in a small way, if they will."

"You will do it, Miss Thurston," Pryor said admiringly.

If Eve ever thought of failure, she did not allow it to herself a moment, I am sure. I used to stand still with a sudden fear, but I meant to do my best. Her efforts, I resolved, should not shame mine. And, as spring advanced, I came to the conclusion that there were few places more beautiful than Athens. The long, gradual swell of land up to the highest point, broken here and there abruptly, as well as in a picturesque manner, clothed with verdure in the innumerable shades of tender green. The river winding along, a blue ribbon under the skies of faultless blue. The ascent on the other side dotted with little hamlets, — for they could hardly be called towns, — and here and there a handsome residence perched on some eminence like a castle. The fresh, balmy air, the grassy fragrance, the twitter of birds, the long, tender notes of the wood-robin, filled my soul with a peaceful exaltation. It was as if I had come out of a confused, hurrying struggle, and just begun to live. Indeed, I had secured time to live. It might be dull if one had no resource but a small railroad station, and no companion: I had both. What wonderful pictures Eve and I studied in our walks, what tones of color, what tenderness and breadth!

"It makes me wild to paint something higher than flowers," said Eve longingly. "I wish I had some friend who was a true artist, who could feel and see and worship; and I should ask her to come and stay weeks with me."

CHAPTER VII

JOE'S FALL FROM GRACE

Eve went to New York for the day. Joe and I worked steadily all the morning; and after lunch, I sent him down-town, as the business part of Athens was called. He was to leave a message with Pryor also.

After an hour or so I began to wonder why he did not return. I went up to the house, but he was not there; busied myself a while, then came down at four, as an up and a down train passed about that time. No Joe yet. It seemed odd: then I bethought myself that he might have gone riding with Pryor.

At five he came sauntering up on the platform. I knew in a moment what had happened. I was hurt and mortified. I had made no comments on Joe's unfortunate weakness; and it seemed unpardonable in him, under the circumstances, to drink at some other person's expense, to bruit abroad the secret I had kept.

He delivered his message in a voice that was a little thick, and his eyes avoided mine.

"Joe," I said, "you have been drinking. How could you?"

He turned and straightened himself, as if to brave it out, then suddenly collapsed.

"O Thurston!" he cried, "I'm a fool, a beast! And when you've been so kind, — and I resolved I'd never touch another drop! Shake me off, and let me go to ruin! I'm not worth saving."

Those few words, "let me go to ruin," pierced me to the quick, though he had not uttered them upbraidingly. In that great bond of human brotherhood I was in some degree answerable for him. I went and put my arm over his shoulder, and drew him into the office. Then he broke down and cried, as a half-drunken man is very apt to do.

"I shall not shake you off without another chance," I said quietly. "But I am so hurt! You might have cared more for me and my sister."

He started up. "Let me go somewhere and hide. I'm not fit to meet her sweet eyes. O Thurston! what devil did possess me? I'm fated. There's no use trying. I've signed the pledge three times, and that doesn't help."

"No," I said, "nothing will help until you resolve to help yourself. Now I am going to make you a cup of good strong coffee, and that will sober you up some. Miss Thurston can not be home until six.

Come up-stairs," for I did not want to leave him alone.

He stumbled along. "I'm a miserable wretch to treat the best friend a fellow ever had in this world in this manner. You had better cut me adrift. I shall never be good for any thing. Thurston, you don't know the awful temptation, the want that is so much stronger than yourself! I have tried over and over again. No, I never can! I'm a weak, miserable idiot!"

I had put the kettle over the fire, and it was singing already; and in a few minutes more I poured a little water on the coffee.

"Will you tell me whom you have been drinking with?" I asked.

"No one. At least, — this is the solemn truth, Thurston. While I was in Pryor's, he had a bottle of lager, and I took a glass. It stirred up all the devil of longing in me. I started to come home, then I went down the street to a saloon; but I said I wouldn't go in, and I went past it, and on down to the boat-house. There is a little place below there" —

"Yes." A low den it was too. There had been strenuous objections to having the man's license renewed, but somehow it had worked through.

"I went in, and had a drink of whiskey, and then

my brain was all on fire. And I took another drink. I had only a quarter."

"Where did you get it, Joe?" I had been very careful not to give him any spending-money, and a horrible reflection on his honesty flashed through my mind.

"Miss Thurston gave it to me. Oh, what a vile, thankless creature I have been! I've carried that quarter since last Friday. Kick me out, Ad, dear old chap! I'm not worthy of shelter and kindness."

He began to cry again, and sprang up as if to go. I forced him back into his chair, and poured the coffee, which was black.

"Here, drink it!" I exclaimed. "Then lie down on my cot, and take a nap."

"I will never touch another drop, I swear I will not, Thurston! That is the last of the devilish stuff. Oh, what a good, good friend you are! Do believe me, do!" he entreated.

"We will talk it over to-morrow. Now lie down." I led him to my bed, over which I had thrown a blanket, and went down-stairs. Eve did not arrive in that train; but there were several of the business-men I had come to know pretty well, and we chatted a bit. The next one was in at six-forty. I gave out some express parcels, looked over my accounts, and whiled away the time, half expecting a telegram, though none came. But she stepped out of the next train, and gave a careless nod to the polite conductor.

"I am quite late," she began eagerly. "I hope you did not worry, and that you and Joe have had some supper. I have done such lots of things, and seen such crowds of people! and, oh, it is so lovely to get back, even to a railroad station!"

We were in the waiting-room by this time. I had her satchel and parcel in one hand; and the other arm I put around her, drawing her to me in a tender embrace, as I kissed her. She seemed so especially dear.

"O Adam! we might pass for lovers!" with a curious little thrill in her voice.

We went up-stairs, she talking rapidly; and then she threw her hat and mantle on the bed. I had set the dishes on the table, and the kettle was again boiling.

"Where's Joe?" she asked, as she lighted the lamp.

"We had some coffee a while ago, and, as he was rather used up, I sent him to bed."

"He is not ill?"

"Oh, no! rather tired out," I replied carelessly.

I had resolved that I would not let Joe Crawford go; and this secret, if kept between us two, might prove a bond.

"I have had two dinners, or luncheons, or whatever they may be," she said gayly, "and a treat of cream, and some bananas; but I brought the last home to you and Joe. And now you must have some supper."

I went out, and found Joe sleeping heavily as I expected.

Eve poured my tea, and sliced the cold meat, dished out some jelly, and then leaned back in her chair.

"You will laugh when I tell you all," and her face was radiant with mischief. "I have nearly furnished my house, and I have boarders and boarders!"

"O Eve!" I exclaimed reproachfully.

"I will begin at the very first. I went in to see Mrs. Harwood; and she grows sweeter and sweeter, with just spice enough to keep her from spoiling. She proposes to come over the first two weeks in June, and stipulated that she should be received as a boarder. She wants to go out driving every day, and it will be your business to hunt up the quadruped and the vehicle. Then I went to the Browers's, for she told me they were going away. O Ad! some people *do* have a lovely side to their misfortunes, after all. You know Mr. Brower failed in February; and of course he gave up every thing, but that only paid thirty per cent. And now, through some friend, he has a situation to go out to a great fruit-importing house, at Zante I think it is, and he will take the family. Living is very cheap, and he has a good salary. Mrs. Brower is just wild with delight. Of course, she is charming any way; but I couldn't help thinking that they never really suffered in any misfortune. They are selling off their furniture at private sale: that was *hers*, and the really valuable has all gone at a fairly good price. Next week they break up. Mrs. West will go to Tennessee to her other daughter's to live. That lady is coming on just after Fourth of July, when they will go to Saratoga, and up to Canada. Meanwhile Mrs. West must board somewhere, and she is very fond of the country. I don't know just who proposed this; but I am going to have some household goods, and Mrs. West will take it out in board. She is the dearest, sweetest old lady, and will make very little trouble."

"Upon my word," I said laughingly, "it is a clear case of barter! Eve, you are setting the improvements of political economy at defiance. It is only in the early stages of civilization that people trade in this manner."

"I always get tangled up on political economy, but I *can* make bargains. She pays eight dollars a week,—a pretty good price, I think; and there will be eight weeks,—sixty-four dollars. For that I get a really pretty cottage suite, springs and mattress, lots of odds and ends of carpets that will make over into rugs, and some beautiful glass and china, odd pieces that are not salable. In fact, I think I shall have a good deal for my trouble and small expense."

"But — and you are to teach music and painting, and keep house, and every thing! You will wear yourself out."

"I shall have a handmaiden. I had partly bargained for her. Then, in July, six girls are coming over for a week. I am so afraid I shall get lonesome in the country," and she made an amusing face. "What makes you look so grave?— does the prospect frighten you?"

I smiled then. "It is not the girls," I said, "but the one girl dearest to me. You seem to be doing every thing; and I cannot make a dollar more, try my very best."

"But you save it, you see," with her bright look, which certainly *is* inspiriting. "Do you not remember several of the neighbors said it would cost at least one hundred dollars to put that place in order? We have only had it a month yet, and see what has been done at a trifling cost. And next week we must move in. The goods will be up on Tuesday, and on Friday Mrs. West is coming over. I am so glad Joe is still here, though I suppose it is not very profitable for him. But he is so handy and willing."

We had finished our supper by this time, or rather I had. Joe was still asleep. Eve stood the tea on the back of the stove, and deftly put away the dishes. I sat there, growing angrier at myself that I was not in some business where I could keep her a lady. I hated to have her always planning how she could make a little money. Yet, with all the incidents of the day, she had been to look at a new picture that was creating unusual interest, and her vivid description seemed to place it before my very eyes. She was fitted to adorn some higher station. How could she be so delightfully content!

I roused Joe presently, and sent him to his own bed. But afterward I lay awake a long while, pondering the grave question of another's moral salvation. I should have been glad to go to Mr. Bradford, and ask his help; but I could see that there would be no sympathy between the two. Joe would shrink into himself, and seem ungracious, stolid; and Mr. Bradford would drop into platitudes. They would not meet at any vital point. Yet why should not the salvation of *any* soul be an important matter with him?

Eve was bright and stirring the next morning: I was about to say bustling, but that word never applied to her. She always moved with such grace and ease, and looked so truly the lady. Joe was up early, swept the office and waiting-room, and was out on the platform before I came down. He looked rather shamefaced, but his dissipation had left no other trace.

"Did you tell her?" he asked in a whisper.

"No," I answered; and he wrung my hand.

We decided at breakfast that it would be best to take every thing we could spare, and let Joe sleep in the new house. The piano had been there several days; but it was still boxed, and no one knew it had come. We packed baskets and boxes, and Joe moved on a wheelbarrow, making a good deal of amusement out of it. They put up window-curtains and lambrequins, hung pictures and brackets, and placed some pretty vases and ornaments around. My cot was put in one of the small rooms, and a rug laid in front of it. There was a pretty curtain at the window, bordered with a soft, dull red; a wall-pocket we had manufactured to hold odd papers; two bookshelves arranged bracket-wise; and when the chairs and washing-stand came up, it would look cosey enough.

Joe and I had no chance for a talk all day; but Eve went down to the choir-practice with Ruth Montgomery. She had been asked to join them;

but for various sensible reasons had declined, though her voice never failed in the congregation.

"Thurston," Joe said, after a long silence, "you are the best fellow I ever knew. I acted like a fiend yesterday, didn't I? Was I very — much" — and the poor lad faltered with shame.

"You were not quite out of your senses, I am thankful to say. But, O Joe! how could you?"

"I don't know. I'll take the pledge again."

"What good will that do, if you do not mean to keep it?"

"But I *do* mean when I sign it. Only I'm so awfully weak when the temptation comes. And the desire is so strong — you don't know, Thurston. You've never been there."

"Joe," I said slowly, "I have been there: to my shame and sorrow I confess it. Yet it was not from any real love for liquor, but rather the jolly companionship, and the most horrible indifference. I can't say that I ever longed for it. And to burn up one's blood and brain and health, to throw away character and capability, does seem so senseless."

"What did you do?"

"I resolved, and then I kept steadfastly to my resolve. I said my strength should be stronger than the temptation."

"I have tried," he returned complainingly. "I

thought the pledge would help me, give me some strength; but it did not," and he sighed.

"No," I said, "you do not try to the extent of your strength. You rather try the extent of the temptation. You keep looking at it, and longing for it; and you take yourself to the door of the saloon, and then you topple over, and say you can't help yourself. Suppose yesterday you had come directly up here, and not tempted yourself further? Suppose you had said, 'I will not do this thing,' and walked resolutely away. Then you would have tried your own strength. I do not believe God ever made any soul so weak but that it could put forth *some* strength. You and I, who were born of sober, healthy parents, cannot plead the excuse of the poor wretches who have been born of generations of drunkards. So God has already helped you in that way."

"Ad," he said, in a low, awed voice, "are you religious?"

It was not the first time in my life that I had wished I dared say boldly and bravely that I was. I did not understand the great and awful mystery that some can make so simple, and others so complicated and well-nigh impossible.

"I have never quite decided the matter for myself," I answered slowly; "but if I cannot do *all* the things I consider right, I can at least refrain from some I know to be deadly wrong. And this matter of drinking is one. If the taste of it fills you with desire, then you must not drink at all. I think I would make a resolve for six months, at least. It has been the cause of all your troubles so far. It keeps you at poverty's door, it throws you out of situations, it loses friends and trust and respect. It may not kill you speedily, but you might better a thousand times be dead. And your example acts upon others. You encourage them every time you drink. Some younger lad may lay his sin and weakness at your door."

"I never thought of it in that light. Oh, I wish I *could* stop! God knows I wish I could stop!"

He was walking up and down, his voice in a great tremble, that meant earnestness now, even if evanescent.

"You *can*, Joe. Just think as strongly and surely that you can, as that the temptation has so much more power than your own will and your own soul. What you want is real backbone. All the resolves in the world will not save you. It is a great fight with the powers of evil, and God *will* help you; but he doesn't keep you in spite of yourself. You *must* act. Nothing saves you against your own self. If you are looking for that, you may as well hurry to a drunkard's grave at once."

"But, oh! what *am* I to do?" he pleaded.

"You are to begin in good earnest. See here, you are not quite twenty-one yet. I suppose you have been drinking three years or so. How many situations have you lost in the last year? What have you gained except to add to the prosperity of the liquor interest? You have gone in rags, you have suffered with hunger and cold, and the man who sells you rum laughs to himself to think what a silly fool you are."

Joe's face flushed deeply.

"It *is* idiotic when you come to think of it in that light. It is shameful all around. See here, Ad Thurston, I will never drink another drop as long as I live, so help me God!"

He stopped right before me, and put out both hands. I took them in a strong grasp.

"Make that promise solemnly to God," I said; "but give me your *faithful word*, that, for the next six months, you will neither buy it for yourself, nor allow any one to treat you. Tell me this every Saturday night. When you are away from me, send a postal or telegram. Giving an account so often will keep it fresh in your mind. And never think you *cannot* do it; always believe that you can by going away from the temptation, not looking and longing after it. And now," I continued, "I am going to give you Miss Eve's quarter back again. Think that you spent *my* money, not hers. You see, it isn't any *trust* when you know a fellow *can't* do a certain thing. I know you have the money to get a drink, but I trust you wholly for my own and my sister's sake. I know you mean to keep your word this time."

"Yes," he said just under his breath, and began to walk up and down again.

I had learned before this that long sermons were useless. There was such a thing as talking away the strength of an argument in cases like these. One's own reflection and resolves must count for a factor, or the work is in vain.

After the train came in, we went down for Eve. Pryor was there; and we all walked back together, and had a pleasant little chat about our moving.

"Do you know," said he, "that I am half sorry? What jolly evenings we have had in this little office, and what famous talks about every thing! I never enjoyed a winter more in my life, though of course I've had gayer ones. I can just imagine, though, what a paradise you will make of that place up there. You have taken hold of the right end, and you'll succeed too."

"If we shouldn't stumble over an apple," returned Eve, her eyes alight with humor.

"An apple!" he exclaimed in amaze; but Joe caught at the joke, and giggled.

"Oh!" and he laughed. "It will be Adam and Eve in a garden. And who is to play serpent?"

"Some designing Lilith, who will set her cap for Adam. But we have made a league, offensive and defensive; and we shall allow of no third person until Paradise has been paid for in hard cash!" Eve exclaimed resolutely.

"O Miss Thurston!"

Pryor looked at her so steadily that he almost had his heart in his eyes.

"Yes," she resumed, in a tone that was friendly to a point of frank meaning. "It is hard, I know, — for the girls. Ad *is* nice."

"But you" —

"Well, I've brought him into this trouble, almost against his will, and it would be cruel not to see him through. So I shall have to put up a card over the hall-door, 'All hope abandon, ye who enter here.'"

"You *are* cruel," he said. "That was not the way the flaming sword was used."

"But, you see, we do not mean to have any falls from grace until the five years are ended."

"Pryor is more than half in love with your sister," Joe Crawford said that night.

CHAPTER VIII

THE HIGH STUDY OF ECONOMY

On Monday morning we began to pack up our bulky articles. The smaller ones had gone in the manner in which Pip was brought up, — "by hand." I had hired a wagon of a neighbor; and after breakfast, we made ready, and moved. Joe and I put the kitchen-stove in place, and the fire was kindled. Joe and Eve put the matting down in the two chambers, and the furniture was placed in proper position after some moving about. Eve had chosen the room with the bay-window, and it furnished very prettily. Indeed, the bedroom suite had never looked half so pretty in the big room over the station. Then she prepared the dinner; but we were compelled to have it in the kitchen, as our conveniences were of that sort, and extremely limited.

"The first thing to-morrow morning we must go down to Northwood, and buy some more matting, a dining-table, and chairs. When we get rich, we can have some carpets. I have just fifty dollars."

"Which you ought to spend on yourself."

"As I mean to;" and Eve nodded complacently. "The 1st of June I shall have ten dollars more. The 1st of July thirty dollars; and if the class in painting gets together, — I have offered to give a class of ten girls twelve lessons for five dollars apiece, just half price; but having them all at once makes the difference. That will be fifty dollars, you see," triumphantly.

"You seem to coin money," I said jocosely. "I shall have to look well to my ways."

"Oh! this is a sort of summer harvest," she laughed. "But I do hope to go on with the music; and now I have my own dear piano for aid and comfort. For fifty dollars we must furnish our dining-room, and cover our parlor-floor."

"Well, you know how to work miracles," I replied.

Then we went out in the garden. The grass was looking green and lovely: there were some daffodils in bloom, and here and there a crocus. The rose-bushes had been trimmed: there were indications of tulips, and great mounds of day-lilies. We could think how lovely it would be when the fruit-trees came out: the cherries were showing white, and the peaches were in a haze of pink, but nothing really open. We had discovered a great lilac, and several bushes of syringa.

"I can hardly wait," she declared; "and yet I wish

the days were twice as long, there is so much to do. Why, I never knew time to go so fast."

We were to sleep in our own house that night, and Joe was to take the lounge down at the office. He insisted that I should not come down for the first train but I knew I should be awake. I spent the evening taking the piano out of its coffin, as Eve called it. The packing had been well done, and it had not suffered a scratch; but it needed polishing, and, no doubt, tuning. We decided where it should stand; and, as soon as we had the matting down, I would get some help to lift it.

The stairs and hall we resolved to leave for the present, or, at least, until my pay came. We discussed the feasibility of purchasing our parlor furniture on the instalment plan, just the articles that were absolutely necessary. Somehow· we could hardly resign ourselves to the idea of retiring to bed, every thing seemed so strange and unreal. And long afterward my brain was busy wondering how the house, and all we desired to have therein, would ever get paid for.

We left Joe to keep the station the next morning, while we set off in search of adventures. Matting we found was comparatively high, it being early in the season for it; but we saw some very pretty, not quite as good a quality as I preferred, but the man lowered his price in consideration of our taking the whole piece and a remnant besides, as we needed forty-eight yards. That came to fifteen dollars and thirty-six cents. Then we looked at furniture, — the expensive, the beautiful, and the cheap. We found one man whose stock was good, and reasonable in price, and who was very anxious to secure a customer, either cash or on instalment. We turned into a block presently where there were four auctioneer's flags flying.

"Let us go in," said Eve. "Mrs. Toodles never wanted a bargain any more than we do."

They were selling some very handsome furniture in the first place, but the bidding was quite above us. We watched for a while, and then went out, regretting our inability to have a voice in the matter. The second was an intensely common establishment, filled mostly with Irish women; and the confusion of tongues would have done credit to Babel. The next was quite thinly attended. They were selling some excellent carpet very cheap. Then two suites of bedroom furniture, followed by a handsome dining-room suite in walnut. It went cheaply enough, but quite above us.

Then an ash table, buffet, six chairs, and a small side-table, were put up. People seemed languid. A small, Jewish-looking man started it at twenty, which the auctioneer scouted, but took reluctantly. I added a dollar, so did he.

"Let us consider how high we can go, and fix our limit resolutely," whispered Eve.

"Well?" inquiringly. "Do you like it? How high will *you* go?"

"I had not thought of ash, nor a buffet;—bid again while I consider."

I did, rather reluctantly it seemed. The Jew scanned me eagerly.

"Thirty dollars," concluded Eve. "It is all we ought to spend. The man is a second-hand dealer."

A woman put in the next bid, then the Jew again. The two had another bout. Then I bid. The woman turned away in disgust. Two or three people went out. Then the Jew bid half a dollar, and I followed suit. It was up to twenty-nine dollars and a half; and we half turned, for we knew it was lost to us. The Jew was watching us closely. At the last moment I touched my limit.

"We shall not get it," I said in a whisper; and now I felt disappointed.

"Going," said the man of lungs,—"going,"—a long, long pause of almost breathless silence,— "gone!"

I was so utterly amazed that I looked questioningly at the Jew.

"You haf a goot bargain. I buy him to sell again, and cannot give so mooch," shaking his head.

Eve and I glanced at each other in a curious manner.

"Well, it *is* a good deal for the money," said she; "and it is pretty — neat and solid-looking — yes, I like it. Let us be content."

We paid for it, and I found an expressman who took it to the station for seventy-five cents. On our homeward way we laughed a little, and felt quite uncertain. When we reached Athens, we found our other furniture had come, — a chamber suite, two extra chairs with fine rush seats, but a good deal defaced, and two packing-boxes.

"I think here is quite a large bargain also," laughed Eve.

About four o'clock our city traps came up, and the load was moved over to the house. In all it made quite a show. And when we had the furniture set out in the dining-room, it looked very well indeed. The buffet, though simple, was very pretty, and the chairs excellent.

"Yes, I *do* like it," declared Eve positively. "It wants cleaning and polishing, and it furnishes admirably."

I thought so myself. In fact, though we had been rather surprised into bargain-making, we were not dissatisfied. I took the covers off the boxes, and we had a good laugh over the contents. There were several pieces of partly worn carpets, a pair of blankets, odds and ends of almost every kind, some pieces of elegant china and glass, some kitchen utensils, a pair of pillows, shades, brackets, and two or three pictures.

"I thought the stair-carpet would do a while," said Eve, surveying it dubiously. "The edges are good, and we can have the middle covered. And there will be enough of our up-stairs matting for the hall — until we get rich," laughingly. "We must believe ourselves at Lake George, or at the seaside, in a furnished cottage, and it will look all right."

The next day we put the matting down in the parlor and dining-room. The latter appeared very pretty and summery. The piano was set up; and we brought in the odd chairs, and looked quite at home.

"I shall not have a parlor suite at present," announced Eve. "You remember those lovely Turkish lounges in French cretonnes for ten dollars, — I want one of those and some lounging-chairs, cheap folding ones, and no end of rocking-chairs. Those things will come by degrees. Now let us enjoy ourselves, and be content."

The stair-carpet looked fairly well when it was

down. Two breadths of matting — all we had — were put somewhat in the centre of the hall-room. The spaces at the edges were to be painted red. Those at the hall-door and at the rear were quite wide, and a rug could be laid in both places. Two of the Brussels remnants we had purchased in the fall, harmonized admirably. The room up-stairs was put in order, and the work seemed almost done.

"So, you see, we will not need to run in debt, after all," said Eve triumphantly. "Indeed, the furnishing has come much more easily than I expected. And Mrs. West will be pleasant company to keep me from longing after the delights of Egypt, as I sojourn in this wilderness."

That night Joe said to me, "Thurston, should you mind if I did a little work for the new people at the building? They are short-handed, and the man is hurrying them dreadfully. They offered me a dollar and a half a day."

"Why, no!" In fact, I was rather pleased. "Do as much as you can — anywhere."

"It is so strange they don't send up for me!" and Joe knit his brows anxiously.

"Something may come to hand presently," I returned, in a more hopeful tone than I really felt. I had written to Jersey City, and the reply was, that Joe Crawford was not very steady or reliable; but when the rush came on, and they were short of hands, he might find a place. Already the poor lad's bad habits stood in his way. Yet he was so willing and good-tempered, ready to do any thing with all his strength. I had been casting about to see whether I could keep him a while longer; but, with all I had on my hands, I could not pay him wages. He had taken express packages the last week, and earned himself a new hat; but he did need a suit of clothes.

He, it seems, was thinking of the same thing. "If I could earn a suit of clothes," he said. "I could get one for twelve dollars. And I could do a good deal for you nights and mornings."

"That's good of you, Joe."

"Well, I ought to make up my board. Oh, I wish I could stay with you always, Thurston! I never liked any one half as well as you and Miss Eve."

She was playing on the piano, and we went in. Oh, how delightful and homelike it was! I was one great throb of thankfulness. My cup seemed running over; but I had a fear that it was too fairy-like, and would vanish.

Joe was up at five the next morning, and delved away in the garden for nearly an hour, when he insisted that he should go down to the station. Eve made biscuits: we had radishes and fried eggs, that were done in a manner known only to Eve, and were simply delicious.

"I have bargained for four more hens," said Eve. "They want to sit, and Mrs. Banks doesn't want them. The way she does, is to kill them off as soon as they begin to cluck. She was going to sell these to the butcher. She says they are of no account after you let them sit once, as they only lay six or eight eggs, and then want to sit again. But she says a late hatched pullet will lay all summer through. I shall treasure up all these bits of chicken-wisdom. And that reminds me that I ought to have some young chicks to-day. After breakfast, let us go out and see."

Surely enough! In one nest we found four, and in the other six. What lovely, cunning balls of down they were! I do believe Eve kissed the one she held up to her cheek. Joe had made two coops of lath; and now we put all the chickens and one hen in one, on the floor of the barn, and the eggs under the other hen. We brought out a saucer of water, and some crumbs of bread; and two black-eyed chicks knew by intuition that eating was the great business of life. I could hardly tear myself away, so fascinating were the little midgets in white, yellow, and brown.

"To-night Joe or you must go after my new hens.

Mrs. Montgomery is to let me have two dozen Brahma eggs, and Mrs. Clark a dozen Plymouth Rock. You see, I am going into the chicken business in good earnest."

"I wonder what next!" I retorted gayly.

Joe ran up home to breakfast, and then went off to his day's labor. They were digging and carting dirt, and laying the cellar-wall. The house was to be quite large, much on the plan of ours.

Mrs. Brower and Mrs. West came over about noon, accompanied by a large trunk. Mrs. West was a pretty little woman, with a soft, wrinkled face, blue eyes, and silvery hair that was a mass of natural waves and stray ends, and just the sort of tender voice that one would expect. She kissed Eve, and called her "My dear;" and the ladies walked up together. Eve had her dainty luncheon almost prepared. The weather was still chilly, and we kept just enough fire in the heater to diffuse a comfortable warmth. Mrs. West was delighted with the appearance of the house, and Mrs. Brower admired every thing in an almost effusive manner. Her pretty enthusiasms were not really insincere, but they evinced no discrimination whatever. She was just as content in the thought of going out to Greece, as if it was a fortune left to her, and quite certain that Mr. Brower would prosper. A happy disposition perhaps, but one that was never weighted with care or trouble.

In the afternoon she returned, and at supper-time I found Mrs. West and Eve as cosey as possible. She had, from her husband's estate, an annuity of about seven hundred a year, the rest having been spent by her children long before; but she was so content and sweet, so simple in her tastes, that it seemed a fortune.

"It is all settled, just what we are to do," said Eve, as we were walking down to Mrs. Banks's, who was our colored washerwoman, but an extremely nice body. "Mrs. West isn't coming down to breakfast. She likes a cup of coffee, an egg and some toast, about nine o'clock; and that will be taken to her room. Then, she prefers her heartiest meal in the middle of the day, which seems to be our habit just now. She is extravagantly fond of reading, so our books from the library will come in play. There certainly will be no trouble about entertaining her. It seems to me that I shall pay this debt easily."

"And the handmaiden you spoke of?" I inquired.

"Oh! that is Letty Banks. She wants to take lessons on the melodeon, as they have a very fair one; and she wondered if she could not come and work it out. So, you see, other people understand 'barter,' as you call it;" and Eve laughed. "She will come to wash my dishes every evening, and all day Saturday; and I am to give her two lessons a week."

"You certainly *are* brilliant in managing."

Eve laughed gayly.

Mrs. Banks received us in a quiet, pleasant manner, took me out to the hen-house, and the captured hens were too sleepy to say a word. I packed them in my basket, and tied down the cover. Letty, bright-eyed and trim, about fifteen years old, had a little talk with Eve while we were gone. After vacation commenced, she would be willing to come regularly. Now she was going to school.

We took our hens home without any misadventure. Joe had made nests for them in a dark corner, and Mrs. Banks told us to keep them shut in for the first two days. We put in the eggs and the hens, and left them to settle themselves. Our other mother had eleven little chicks, but we concluded that she had better remain where she was for the night. Joe had gone down to the station for the nine-o'clock train, pretty well tired with his day's work, but very cheerful.

The weather was lovely the ensuing week. Gardening began in good earnest. The fruit-trees displayed a wealth of bloom: lilacs scented the air, that was sweet already with the varied fragrance of spring. The little belts and clumps of wood the hand of improvement had left standing, put on their bravest greenery. I never tired of studying them; and it seemed as if I had never understood before, how beautiful the world was. Surely, one would go far, to find a lovelier place than Athens.

By Saturday night, Joe had four dollars and a half for his three days' work, and another dollar for delivering parcels. He handed it over to Eve, with the utmost pride, declaring that she must be his banker. As we were walking down to the station, he said, —

"Thurston, they had some lager at the building to-day. One of the men treated."

"Did he treat you?" I asked quietly, but with inward fear.

"No: I kept my word. You know, I was to report every week how it fared with me. It wasn't as hard to refuse as I thought; but I was thirsty, and I went up to the house for some water. Miss Eve gave me some splendid cold tea, about half milk; and then I didn't seem to care for the lager."

"I hope I shall hear just as good an account of you every week, my dear Joe;" and I put my arm over his shoulder. "I know you *can*, but there will be some hard times."

"I don't mean ever to drink again. I ought to help myself, when you and Miss Eve are so ready with your kindness and sympathy."

Eve did not go to choir-practice that evening. I found her playing and singing to Mrs. West; but I had hardly settled myself, when Pryor made his appearance with a small parcel.

"There are a dozen white Leghorn eggs," said he, laying it carefully down on the table. "I used some strategy to get them. Vanduyne is still selling eggs at a dollar and a half a dozen."

"I hope you didn't give that;" and there was a touch of remonstrance in Eve's voice, as she wheeled round on the piano-stool.

"No, no. Set your heart at rest. I told Vanduyne I was going to bring you up next week. What day can you go? It is a sight, truly, and you will be amazed."

"I have no hen," said Eve, glancing at the parcel, and not heeding his query.

"Beg or borrow one, then. These are too valuable to have for breakfast. Now please reward me with a song. They missed you at church."

"I am so much farther away now."

"But I hope that is not going to keep you at home?"

Eve turned over some songs, and we three sang

together. At ten Mrs. West quietly withdrew, and presently Eve stopped playing.

"I suppose I must be going," began Pryor regretfully. "It doesn't seem half as gay and cosey as when you were at the station. I suppose I ought to suffer for having persuaded you to buy a house."

"Yes," replied Eve piquantly. "And now you compel me to buy a hen. Where all this extravagance will end, the future only can tell."

Pryor rose. He was in the mood when he longed for a word or a look to persuade him to stay; but Eve was dignified, and I had promised to play watchful dragon.

"Good-night," lingeringly. "I shall be so glad when it is warm enough to sit out of doors."

"Good-night," we said in a breath.

We all went to church in the morning, except Joe. Mrs. West enjoyed it very much. In the afternoon we took Joe with us, and rambled through the woods, bringing home an armful of wild-flowers.

I found the next week, as I surveyed my garden, that I had some things planted pretty well in the shade. I had hardly supposed the trees could reach so far. But there was still quite a large space over at the back. I put in more sweet corn and some for the chickens, then squash and pop-corn. Already I found weeds were beginning to grow apace, and I realized that eternal vigilance was the price of many things besides liberty. Still, I *did* enjoy the work. A garden, I learned, always offered fresh entertainment, and Eve's two families of chickens were our delight.

On Wednesday morning, Pryor drove up to the station in a two-seat wagon, and insisted that we should go at once for Eve. He had bargained with Joe the evening before to keep the station while we were away. He had to "see a man," and would leave us at Vanduyne's, while he was doing some business.

Mrs. West insisted that Eve should go. She was not timid about staying alone, as there were workmen on the building next door.

It was a perfect day, and birds were singing their love-ditties in a maddening manner. Could it be possible that the bleak and bare world of a brief while ago was smiling in richness and bloom? Surely, this in itself was a miracle. And, oh, the long wafts of sweetness! Would I go down to the sand and the glare of the great beach, and live in the hurrying rush for the little difference in money? It seemed as if I should never love a city again.

I had seen chicken-farms at the West, larger in extent and numbers than this place of Mr. Vanduyne's, but nothing in such perfect order. It was like turning the pages of an illustrated poultry-book. The owner was a fair, still delicate-looking man of six or eight and thirty, very affable in manner, and with a trained voice, that bespoke familiarity with the world of society as well. He received us courteously, and, as he was not especially busy, attended us himself through the different departments. Every thing was arranged as compactly as possible, and in a manner to save time as well as to prevent waste. There were three large houses of young chickens, old enough to be without mothers: there were broods with hens, broods with artificial mothers, and one incubator was still full of eggs. There were young chickens being prepared for market: there was a house with all the appliances for packing eggs in large or small quantities, and it seemed then as if it was half full at least. Every kind was labelled; but, on a close inspection, even an unpractised eye could detect the difference in shape and color. Then, of the same kind, there were three sizes, — large, medium, and small. Evidently Mr. Vanduyne had not reached the secret of compelling every hen to lay a large egg.

As for the show-pens, they were truly marvellous. I never saw any thing more nearly perfect. Every feather was as true as if it had been painted on the fowl. But the clouds of white Leghorns were like snowdrifts. The brilliant red of comb and wattles, the rich yellow of their legs, made them dazzling. They really seemed to know they were handsome, and to enjoy it. There were immense Brahmas, snowy white as well; others with their beautifully pencilled collars and tails, and dark ones that were not less striking. There were all kinds of fancy breeds and magnificent games, down to tiny Seabrights not much larger than birds. One could have studied them for a week.

It was as Pryor said,— Mr. Vanduyne gave away no hints, or bits of knowledge. Eve was at her best and brightest, and did surprise him into several admissions; but he soon covered them with a doubt. He could keep his hens laying all winter: he could raise hundreds of chickens without getting disease among them, and he evidently was making it pay. But he laughed satirically at most of the methods in vogue, and was doubtful of the success of ordinary people in the attempt to make it profitable.

Pryor was gone less than half an hour; and I began to feel that we must not trespass upon Mr. Vanduyne's time, and neither must I waste my own. We had already consumed nearly two hours. So we expressed our obligations, and he cordially invited us to come up again.

"Well," began Pryor, when we were seated in the

wagon, "were you paid for your trouble? Have you learned any thing, Miss Thurston? I was very glad you never suggested the ownership of a hen, or he would have drawn into his shell at once."

"It is all very elegant," replied Eve. "It has taken time and money to perfect all this, and is like the wonderful fruit-farms. But sometimes a peach or a pear off your own tree may have as fine a flavor, and one of your own hens may lay as fresh an egg for your breakfast. I picked up a few words of wisdom," and she laughed. "You see, every thing that is not perfect is taken out of the choice flocks, so their faults and failings are not propagated. But, after all, some old woman summed it up: 'A good hen ought to lay twelve dozen eggs a year; and at twenty-five cents a dozen, she earns three dollars, and eats up one.' Now, the profit is, making her eggs bring in more than three dollars; and keeping her good and warm in the winter — hot food, with pepper and spices; plenty of fresh warm water; when she cannot find worms or bugs, give her some meat."

"You have it quite down to a business point, Miss Thurston," Pryor said with admiration, as well as amusement.

"I strive to bring every thing to a business point," she replied sententiously. "I have started out to be a business woman, and to make the eight hundred dollars that I am justly entitled to."

"Eight hundred? Why just eight hundred?"

Eve laughed merrily. How pretty and dainty and bewitching she looked, though I had remarked of late she had not put on her sweetest ways for Gordon Pryor.

We explained about the money.

"See here, Miss Eve; wouldn't it be a stupendous joke if every man and woman should set out to get his and her share, and the children as they grew up? By Jove! what would become of the millionnaires? You certainly have discovered the great panacea, the secret of equalizing the crooked and unjust things of this world."

We all laughed.

CHAPTER IX.

A PASTORAL IN HENS.

Joe added six dollars to his store the next week. He wanted his clothes so badly, that Eve proposed to lend him the rest; and we went down to Northwood, while she kept station with a big boy at hand. Through the winter she had added to her other accomplishments the train-signals, and quite a knowledge of telegraphy, and could manage very well; though, when I had occasion to leave her, I always made certain that Frank Barr would be about. He soon became one of Eve's devoted admirers, and I think she wilfully encouraged him. I know there were times when Pryor wanted to kick him, out of pure jealousy that a smile should be wasted on a cub of thirteen.

I never saw a happier lad than Joe this morning. He seemed bubbling over with a wholesome, grateful joy. We found a very nice business-suit for fourteen dollars, and his shoes were three and a half more. It left him just five dollars in my debt. We went into the library to change some books, and then sauntered up the busy street, somewhat disfigured, I must own, by saloons. The blind-door of one opened, and a young lad not more than eighteen staggered out. I saw a hot flush go over Joe's face: then suddenly he broke away from me, and threw his arm over the shoulder of the boy. I walked on slowly. Perhaps the good seed had taken root when Joe desired to save some one else.

"I couldn't help it!" he exclaimed, as he rejoined me, his eyes full of tears. "I thought of the wretched object that I was when I came to you, and how good you were; and I wanted to say a word. He has a mother and two sisters — oh, why must he break their hearts! — and he told me where he lived, — 19 Cross Street. Maybe it isn't true. Oh, why can't they shut up these dens and holes that drag boys and men down to destruction!"

Why not, some of them at least? I counted five on one side of the block, four on the other. Two or three young men dropped into one, even as I counted. If they cannot be strong for themselves, has Government no duty towards its citizens?

Eve declared herself very proud of Joe in his new clothes. He went to church with us on Sunday, though he insisted on sitting in a far-back seat. Now, why should not some one take him by the hand in a friendly manner? I had begun to like Mr.

Bradford a good deal, in some sermons; but it seemed to me that he took himself and his religion too far off, and, when he called you to follow, he was out of sight. If you could walk side by side; if you could feel and believe that it was not the system that was so dear, but the human soul it might snatch from the ways of destruction!

One of the sweetest and bravest things was Eve walking right over to Joe when church was out, and taking him under her protection by the cordial smile and inclination of her head. There were three or four others, and no end of girls: and Joe, blushing like a peony, fell back to me; but she had given him that fine, brave recognition before them all.

"Will you be surprised to hear that my painting-class is an absolute fact?" Eve inquired, a few evenings later, as we sat at the supper-table. "Josie Morrison was in here an hour ago, and the last girl has joined. They are to begin the first week in June, and come every Tuesday and Thursday afternoon. I shall transform this room into a studio, and range my girls around the dining-table. Just fancy me!"

"My dear," said Mrs. West, who had succumbed entirely to Eve's fascinations, "how can you find time for so many things? You will work yourself to death."

Eve laughed gayly. "Why, do you know that I thrive upon it! I am absolutely getting fat, and I never was better in my life. But"—retrospectively—"I don't know that I am much busier than I used to be, only it *is* different. Why, some days I have run half over town, made dozens of calls, gone to a "tea," to the theatre, and then to a dancing-party, and come home two o'clock at night, aching in every joint, and by ten the next morning started on another round. I don't work half as hard; and there is not the awful rush and worry, and wonder as to how you will get gloves and ribbons and gowns, and running all over to find cheap goods—no, I mean elegant goods—for a little money. Why, I think it idiotic!" and Eve straightens herself up. "It makes me laugh, from its sheer ridiculousness. Fashionable girls have to work very hard when they are poor, and want to seem rich."

"And you know how to do so many things! Where did you learn them? What a treasure you will be to your husband!" and the sweet old face is solid admiration.

"That depends—on the kind of husband. I have resolved that I will never make believe rich for any man's sake; and I cannot help thinking that a great many men are just as fond of appearances as women are said to be. They would not be willing to keep house in two rooms, — except Adam, here," and she nods at me; "and that heroic virtue is due to *my* training. If we had not lived over a railroad station, we might never have owned a house. And how many young husbands would like to admit their wives did not keep a servant? It is about an even thing, dear Mrs. West, though we women *do* get the blame."

"I do not believe you will go begging for a husband of the right kind."

"Well, they are scarce;" and Eve drew her rosy lips down solemnly.

She had found time, with all her other work, to do some parlor ornamentation. We had framed several pictures, and made a pretty standing frame, or almost easel, for a plaque that had been given Eve a year or so before, and was a very good painting. This was done up in ebonizing and gold paint. Then we had invested in a steamer chair, which she cushioned with satine, and tied with bright ribbons, and made a very attractive parlor reclining-chair. We had plans innumerable for tables, easels, and bookcases. There did not seem any time to get at them, what with the garden, the chickens, and daily duties.

I bought some cheap odd lengths of lumber, some lath and chicken-wire, and remodelled my hen-house and yard. From our first eggs we had hatched twenty-three chickens, and lost one. We put them in the loft of the barn, tying the hens in corners so there should be no unnecessary jarring. The chicks grew apace. They were all kinds, — odd lots. We fed them table-scraps, scalded meal, and cracked corn, as soon as they were able to eat that. I kept a supply of gravel and bits of grass-roots: they had plenty of sunshine, and throve finely. Of our two dozen Brahma eggs, we only hatched twenty-one chickens. Our next hen brought off nine, which we divided between the other mothers, and set her again, on some white Leghorn eggs from a neighbor. A few days later, another hen came off with nine, when we placed the new eggs under her, and let the other have the chickens. If she was surprised, she said nothing, but went on with the pertinacity of a hen. Eve was quite wild over her little flock.

Certainly, the place began to look like a veritable garden of Eden. I wondered now how it could have stood empty so long, and I began to feel afraid some untoward accident would deprive me of it. The vines were reduced to order, — honeysuckle, wistaria, and Virginia creeper. The trees bloomed magnificently, but two of my pear-trees showed signs of decay. One blossomed but never leaved out, and I cut it down. The other was very scrubby, and, later in the season, showed indications of pear-blight;

so that wended its way to the woodshed. Certainly, I would not have to buy kindling-wood very soon.

Joe worked on our next-door building a good deal, though he insisted that a certain amount of labor was due me for board. He paid his debts, and replenished his wardrobe; and a prouder lad I never saw. His thin figure filled out, and took on the ruddiness of health: he was bright and cheerful, and I began to feel that he might yet make a man of himself.

With a little training and oversight, our young handmaiden did very well. She came about four; washed up the dinner-dishes for Eve, prepared supper, often doing some sweeping and cleaning, in between. After the supper-dishes were washed, she practised half an hour, for visitors rarely came that early; and sometimes she remained an hour or two.

Mrs. West we found the perfection of boarders. She certainly was one of the loveliest of old ladies. Pryor hit upon a delightful scheme. He purchased a horse, and took a carriage from a friend who had no use for it, and invited the ladies to drive out with him. Eve was charming, frank, sisterly, but always showing that matrimony was a long way off in her plans. Couldn't Pryor see?

If April was delightful, May was enchanting.

The fragrant air, the fields and woods abloom, the gardens with their tidy paths — even the fields of weeds look lovely now in their soft greens. My two long rows of blackberry bushes came out in a perfect snow of blossoms, and I resolutely kept the paths clean. I had to go over my raspberries again, and trim out many more dead branches; but there would be enough.

Our first-fruits were radishes and rhubarb, — the lovely thick stalks in a coat of beautiful red. We had sauce and pies, and the latter were simply delicious. Eve could make a pie with an under crust as light and flaky as a cream biscuit.

Our choice Leghorn eggs brought out ten cunning chicks, and we changed hens again. One other one brought out the whole twelve, — the first hen that had done so well. We had now eighty-four chickens, but Eve declared that she should not stop short of one hundred.

"But what will you do with them all?" I asked in amazement.

"Broilers," replied Eve, with a droll smile. "And now eggs are only twenty cents a dozen. They are quite cheap enough to transform into chickens. I came across some funny Houdans the other day; and the woman has promised to save me some eggs, and lend me a hen."

"You will have the ranch presently. But we must not overcrowd."

Everybody had predicted that we would find them so troublesome; but thus far they had not interfered with my garden. They had the barn-yard enlarged considerably; and I threw into it pea-pods and plantain, which I soon found they were very fond of. I made a covered run for rainy weather, by stretching some cheap unbleached muslin over a framework, and covering it liberally with linseed-oil. It kept the runs light and dry, and answered admirably. We gave them red pepper, kept a little iron in their drinking-basins, and used the utmost cleanliness. The refuse I showered on my garden as a top dressing.

Mr. Montgomery seemed rather resentful that I had not "seeded down" the whole thing. "I'd get tired enough before I was through; and as for chickens, they always ate their heads off. Women folks were continually fussing about them; and it would be cheaper to buy all the eggs his family used, than have them about." He was quite interested in selling off some of his property, now that a new house was being built in his vicinity, and, as a preparatory step, put up all his prices.

I liked what I saw of Mr. Wilbur; and one day his wife came up and paid Eve quite a visit, staying to lunch. They compared notes about cities and theatres and summer resorts, and found they had some mutual acquaintances. The house was being pushed rapidly. It would not be completely finished before another season, but Mrs. Wilbur wanted to bring her family out by the middle of July.

As for ourselves, we did not suffer from dearth of friends. There were many nice people in Athens, but they wanted shaking up. They had settled into dreamy grooves. They looked too much through the eye of faith, but they saw only the evidence of things in the far distance; and though they might be hoped for, there was no real substance to them. But when Athens was so beautiful, healthful, too, in all the higher parts, why should it not be prosperous? Why should not people come here as well as to go to places that had not half its attractions?

"Lots of boarders go up to Truro," said Pryor. "There is a hotel, besides two large boarding-houses. To my mind, it is not half as attractive as this; but they do have good times, — dancing-parties, moonlight-drives, and all that. This place is so stupid, so inert! though I do think your sister will manage to infuse a little life if any one can."

One evening not long after this, we had an influx. It was a moonlight night and very warm. Ruth and Dan Montgomery came first. Ruth had taken a great liking to my darling Eve. Then Mr. and Mrs. Morrison, the Corwins, Pryor, and after this about half a dozen young people,—girls who were to be in the painting-class, and their brothers. It was absolutely funny when they came in. Eve was equal to the occasion. She set them to acting proverbs, and we had a good deal of amusement. Then she played, and actually made them all sing. As soon as the first bashfulness was worn off, we had quite a concert. Everybody enjoyed it immensely. Then they all wondered that there were so few good times at Athens,—so little fun, as some one phrased it; and the affair ended by the party being invited to Mrs. Morrison's the next week. Eve promised to go.

"You do manage to make the most pleasure out of every thing," said Pryor admiringly, as he lingered on the porch.

"Perhaps it is because I have been brought up to pleasure," returned Eve with a laugh. "It does not answer for you to be dull in a city, or you would be dropped out without any mercy. You must bring your share of wit and entertainment to the picnic."

"Still, I do not believe there is another girl in the whole wide world like you, Miss Thurston."

We watched him down the path. "I wish he didn't care quite so much," I said.

"I try to be careful. I have never given him *that* kind of encouragement. Adam," and her voice was suddenly inspirited, "I mean to have a diversion. I shall train Ruth Montgomery to catch him. She is pretty and sweet-tempered, and could be a bright, entertaining girl. It will give me something to do."

"You idle girl!" I cried laughingly.

"It was very pleasant," said Mrs. West. "See how much I have gone past my usual hour. My dear, you are a marvel."

"If I'd had cake enough to go around," said Eve dolorously, "or lemons to make lemonade, or figs, or nuts, or cream, consequently we had to season it with our wits. Quite a surprise party!"

We put out the lights, and went to bed.

And what shall I say for June? The world was full of flowers, the air was fragrance that stole into one's very soul. Such skies, such views, such pictures, everywhere; such a heavenly completeness, that my heart went up in gratitude continually. Was it from the glad consciousness that sometime I might really be the owner of this bit of land, and this house, growing prettier to my eyes every day? I had always been amused by the enthusiasm of people concerning their own houses or their first baby. I am afraid, now, that I began to have exalted ideas of the possessorship of land.

Pryor dropped in at the station a day or two after.

"Thurston," he began, "will you allow me to bring some one up to your place to see what *you* have done? Maybe I can sell the Moore house. There was a man over here looking at this very place last summer, but he thought it rather discouraging, and wanted more ground. His health isn't very good, and he has two sons to step into his business in New York. He wants to buy a place where he can have a nice large garden, and chickens, horse and cow, and all that. Yesterday he stopped off a train and talked about it; but he is almost afraid to try Athens, there is so little enterprise. I thought, if he could see your place and the Wilburs's new house, he might not consider us quite so benighted."

"Why, of course," I answered.

"Wouldn't it be jolly now, if I could sell the Moore place? And, you see, that would tend to improve the value of yours as well. Who knows, Thurston, but that your coming may be the start of prosperity for this forlorn coast?"

We both laughed. The man, a Mr. Randall, came to hand. He was little past middle life, and did look very poorly; but he proved pleasant and entertaining, with a good fund of common sense. Pryor was right. He was caught by the wonderful improvement we had made. I had almost forgotten how forlorn and unpromising the place had looked. He examined the fruit, the garden, the chickens, the house, and then we went over to inspect the new one. Afterward we went up to Moore's, which was only a short distance above us, on the same avenue.

The house was a large, attractive one, with a hall through the middle, three bay-windows, two large piazzas, a fine, long arbor, with a variety of grapes; a large barn, and numerous sheds, and three acres of ground with considerable fruit. The land, like ours, lay on a gentle slope, was dry and sunny. For two years this house had not been tenanted. The price was seven thousand dollars. Mr. Randall did seem quite impressed.

"If I could do as well as you have," he said to me, "and if my folks would be content. Still, it is easy getting to the city, and we do go away every summer. We are talking about it now. It *is* a big expense," and he gave a low whistle.

His family consisted of himself and wife, one single son, who would live at home, two daughters, a niece, and a grandson and his widowed mother. There was plenty of room. We could see that he was "very much taken," as the Athenians expressed it. He did not even demur at the price.

Two days afterward he was over again, and questioned me closely about my plans and methods. He had been brought up on a farm.

"But matters have changed so much since that time," he said, with a brief, amused laugh. "Now it is all scientific farming. People make as much off of an acre of ground as my father did from three or four, and do it easier too. I don't know why, but a man does have a hankering after a country-place as he grows older."

I am afraid I *was* enthusiastic. I may as well say here that Mr. Randall took the place, the owner falling five hundred dollars in his price. After some repairs, the family came over the first of July, and so far they have not regretted it. We found them very agreeable neighbors. Pryor was delighted with his success, and sent Eve two veranda-chairs in red, that certainly were ornamental to our front porch, as well as useful. Accompanying them was an amusing note, in which he quoted the old adage, that, if a visitor brought his chair, he might be sure of a welcome.

Then Eve was appealed to for a home. Mrs. Wilbur wanted to find a boarding-place at Athens for a few weeks, as they had been promised some rooms by the middle of July, in their own house. Eve scoured the little town, and was much entertained by her experiences, as well as entertaining us.

Up above us, there was considerable boarding: indeed, Truro was quite a favorite. But among those who could take so large a family, — for there would be eight in all, — most of the householders seemed to feel afraid. Several days after, when Eve's hopes had fallen to zero, since she could not suddenly enlarge our house, one of our neighbors, a Mrs. Ten Eyck, some of the old aristocracy, came in, and, after considerable apologizing, wanted to talk the matter over. Her husband was dead; her father and mother lived with her, the former partially paralyzed; and she had one young son who went to the city on business. She confessed reluctantly to Eve, that their income was very small; and she had been thinking of this business for several years, but did not know how to begin.

Eve set the matter before her in a sensible and attractive light. She must make a business of it, but in a pleasant way; and she would find many little bits of satisfaction, that would quite repay her for the sacrifices on the other side. She declared that in any difficulty she should come at once to Miss Thurston for advice.

"My dear," she said to Eve, "how have you learned so much? And you are so young!"

"I have always thought I'd like to know Mrs. Ten Eyck," Eve said afterward, "she is so quaintly formal and delicate. But I am almost afraid of the five children, though Mrs. Wilbur is a very sensible mother."

Mrs. Harwood was to come the middle of June. Meanwhile Joe and Pryor struck a bargain about the horse, with my consent; though later on I resolved to join them. Joe would keep the horse clean, and in good order, for the use of it an hour or so a day. His parcel delivery had so increased, that it took too much time to travel on foot, seeing that he was in such requisition at the new house. I offered the stable, and also to pay half of the keep to have it one-third of the time. We were to agree about our "time" amicably, and not have arbitrary days or hours. So Mrs. Harwood's carriage was provided without any difficulty. Pryor had been paying twelve dollars a month for rather indifferent care. There was a good deal of the time that he was busy about other matters, so this arrangement suited him admirably.

"Really," exclaimed Mr. Corwin, as he sat with us on the porch a few evenings later, "I am not sure but the ruling spirit *has* appeared at Athens! Or the goddess of good fortune, shall I say, Miss Thurston? I have never known people so stirred up since I have been here. Montgomery has nearly doubled the price of every lot he owns. And the young people have broken out in parties and *musicales* and painting-classes, and are planning picnics."

"Two or three people like Montgomery are enough to stamp out every gleam of prosperity," declared Pryor in a vexed tone. He did not monopolize the chairs, but generally took the step of the porch, so that he could face his audience. "See here, Corwin, don't you want to join me in a scheme? If you will buy half the Wallace shore property, I will chip in for the other half. I happen to know that Wallace has hard work raising money on it. Athens has such a wretched name that people are wary. He would sell it cheaply, but we'll offer him a fair price. I know some parties who would take it inside of two months. What they want to do with it, is my affair; but they are not coming here if they have to pay a big price. It would be a good thing for this three-cent town. But if I hinted it to Wallace, he would be like Montgomery. Come, join me, and make a few hundred dollars. We can pay a small amount down, and the balance in a year, say. I wish you could join, Thurston. You see, I do not like to shoulder the whole thing, for Wallace would set me out as a thief and a scoundrel. But the matter is sure."

"How much down?" asked Corwin.

"Not more than a thousand."

"And you are certain?" he asked slowly.

"Sure as the tax-gatherer or the man with the scythe," and Pryor laughed.

"I will think about it. We'll walk down after supper to-morrow evening, and look at it."

Then we talked nonsense.

CHAPTER X

EVERY-DAY IDYLS

Mrs. Harwood came over the middle of June. We were almost buried in flowering shrubbery. I thought I had trimmed and pruned, but there was no end to it still; and there were some lovely roses among other things. The syringa perfumed the air up and down, and every room was sweet. We had still some cherries, currants were in their glory, and raspberries were just ripening. I found there were several kinds, two of red and a palish-yellow one besides the blackcaps. As I cleared up my chicken-houses, I distributed the fertilizer as a top dressing; and now with the horse I felt that I should be quite rich.

Mrs. Harwood was delighted. She admitted that she had made allowance for Eve's enthusiasm, but that it had not been overdrawn. Eve had arranged her room for our new inmate, and taken one of the smaller ones. We found Mrs. Harwood very bright and entertaining. She had a dry kind of wit that amused us all, and seemed to fascinate Joe. I think she really loved Eve as if she had been some connection; but how could she help it? She was quite suspicious of Pryor at first; but Eve insisted that for the present, matrimony was out of her thoughts. She also took a great fancy to Joe, who was growing handsome by the day. I would hardly have believed the transformation. His eyes were so clear and merry, his complexion fresh as a rose, even if a little sunburned, and his voice had a manly ring as if he had come to be proud of himself. He had bought a new light summer suit, that gave him a very "natty" look; and he had begun to save a little, which he handed over to Eve to keep for him.

I hardly know how Joe did put in so much in the way of work. He was quick, and he could fit one thing in with another most admirably. I began to think that holding out a helping hand to Joe was one of the best deeds of my life.

Every day the ladies went out driving; and Mrs. Harwood enjoyed the lovely winding roads, the bits of wood, the peaceful river; and farther out, there were some actual farms, one quite celebrated for its Alderney cattle. Then they paid a visit to Mr. Vanduyne's chicken-ranch, and took several short journeys by rail. Sometimes it was all three of the ladies, at others Eve and Mrs. Harwood, or that lady and Mrs. West. Every evening there was a houseful of callers.

"I really do not think you are likely to die of loneliness," Mrs. Harwood said to Eve. "And I am so glad you have sense enough to take your pleasure as you go along. Though where or how you find time to get meals, is a mystery to me. You ought to keep a hotel."

Eve laughed at that. "I am thinking about an addition to the house," she answered merrily.

As for the meals, they were a mystery to me. Eve and Joe could concoct something in the least space of time. We had chickens and eggs, not very many of our own, but they were cheap; we had fruits; and many were the dainty dishes we had served up under high-sounding French names, but they were better than French admixtures. I thought her strawberry shortcake was perfection, but she could make with raspberries and cream a shortcake equally nice.

Meanwhile Mrs. Wilbur came over with five children, a nurse, a housekeeper who at present supervised the whole family. Mrs. Ten Eyck was quite dismayed at first, but Mrs. Wilbur was one of the most agreeable of women. She spent about half of her first week with us; indeed, all summer she was Eve's shadow; but she had such pretty and engaging manners, that she never seemed intrusive.

Pryor and Mr. Corwin bought the plot of ground, a

kind of point jutting out into the river. There was in some places quite a wide strip between the road and the river. A few dilapidated boat-houses and saloons, and several old factories, in which some of the most wretched of the Athenians, black and white, lived, disfigured the shore.

Pryor engaged part of it first, then he made Wallace say what he would take for the whole. Once he decided to back out. "Very well," said Pryor indifferently, and seemed in no great heat about negotiations. Then Wallace came to terms, and sold, receiving a thousand dollars down, another thousand at the end of six months, and the balance at the year's end. Then Pryor interviewed the factory people who wanted it, and found their offer to be just one thousand dollars higher. It was to be an establishment for weaving wire cloth, as the lease of the place they were in could not be renewed on favorable terms.

It was a source of great amusement to us all, when the property was resold, to see the manner in which Wallace took it.

"If I'd had the slightest idea that the factory people would have come to hand, I'd made them pay roundly for it! Why, Pryor, you've given the land away,—fairly made them a present of it! I didn't think you were such a short-sighted fool! If I had that land back again, no such money would get it from me!"

Mr. Montgomery bewailed the matter in much the same manner. If a few more such sales were made, Athens would become a laughing-stock of all the towns around. Such men as Pryor were enough to ruin any place. No one could stand out for decent prices if property was to be given away in that style!

"What idiots!" Pryor said angrily. "Now, these men will bring in quite a number of new people, and find employment for many others. There must be houses for them to live in, and all that; they will trade at the stores; and this factory being here, may start up others. Wallace had a fair price for property that hadn't paid him a penny for twenty years; and we have made a little, — enough to pay us for our trouble. Only I wish, Thurston, it had been you instead of Corwin. Not but what he's a good fellow, only I would like to give you a lift. Well, better luck next time."

Mrs. Harwood went away reluctantly. She wanted to take Eve to Lake George with her for a week or so, but a crowd of girls were coming for the Fourth of July. However, she insisted that Eve should be her guest at Saratoga a week in August, and that she should spend some time with us in the autumn. Besides her board, she insisted upon paying six dollars for the carriage-hire, and made Joe a little gift that surprised him greatly.

"Take good care of my girl," she said to me at parting. "I can't have her getting faded and worn, no, not for twenty houses."

"I should be rich enough to keep her a lady," I answered with a regretful sigh.

"Eve Thurston could never be any thing but a lady," she returned rather sharply. "And if she willed, she might be kept in luxury."

The next thing was Mrs. West's departure. We had become so attached to her, that I think even Joe shed some tears with his good-by. Her daughter, an elegant, middle-aged woman, came over for her, and expressed not only gratitude but delight that her mother had fallen in such good hands. It was a sad parting, and they exchanged promises of writing.

But for Mrs. Wilbur I think Eve would have been quite depressed by the loneliness of the house. I wondered what we would do when winter came. But she had to get in order for the new influx. Letty was ready to come now; and I was glad to have Eve relieved of some work, though she did not look as if her care had weighed heavily.

The 1st of July was Saturday. Five girls were coming, and on Sunday two gentlemen. The rooms were freshened and put in order, and made sweet with flowers. Mrs. Wilbur came up. She was much amused at what she called a " hen party."

Certainly they were the gayest crowd. The two Brooke girls, a Miss Fisher whom I had met at aunt Carry's, Bel Lane, and Kitty Travers. The sixth would arrive on Monday.

We asked Pryor to come up to tea. I needed some one to keep me in countenance. We had broiled chicken, fried potatoes, raspberry shortcake, and custard. But the merriment was beyond any description. I thought them the wittiest lot it had ever been my fortune to meet. Sadie Brooke was the drollest and most winning — shall I say the most audacious? — flirt that I ever saw.

I had to go down to the office, and Pryor had to see the inevitable man. Sadie and Kitty Travers walked down with us, and then strolled on to the river, where I overtook them, and escorted them homeward. We met Mr. and Mrs. Wilbur, who swelled our procession.

"I couldn't rest until Mr. Wilbur had looked in upon you," declared his wife. "But the party seems to have increased," and she glanced rather amazed at the new additions.

Saturday night had become a kind of reception evening with us. Two of the Montgomerys were in,

Charlie Wharton, Mr. and Mrs. Morrison, and their daughter. I was very glad to have the Wilburs meet some of their neighbors.

The party talked, half a dozen at a time, and laughed in chorus. I do not know who first proposed a picnic, but Mr. Wilbur took it up enthusiastically.

"See here," he began. "I shall have to spend the glorious Fourth in these classic but unpatriotic shades. Generally I manage to take my wife off somewhere; but, as this cannot be done, I ought to have some compensation. Is there a respectably level ground, with the proper degree of shade, where a quadrille can be danced, and the exhausted participants loll around afterward, without danger of getting freckled or sun-burned? For one, I am choice of my complexion. Ambrosial Balm is excellent, but dear. If you can find this favored spot, and will promise to let me dance with all the prettiest girls, I will pay the piper."

"Excellent!" exclaimed Sadie. "Mr. Wilbur, I hope you want to dance with me?"

Everybody laughed.

"There's Terry's woods, you know," Dan Montgomery made haste to announce. "It's cleared pretty well, and it isn't far."

"Capital place," declared Pryor. "If only those

who contribute will be allowed to dance, I beg to be placed on the cream committee at once."

It went on taking shape; and before one would have imagined it, the matter was arranged. The picnic was to open at three punctually, at Terry's woods, unless it rained.

"If it rains, we will have to adjourn to my new house. I will see that they get all the floors laid on Monday," said Mr. Wilbur.

"Or we might take the station," appended Joe. "There ought to be one jolly frolic down there in remembrance of old times."

"I think of engaging it for a dancing-school next winter," said Eve sententiously.

It came out that there were some amusing associations connected with it; and Mr. Wilbur insisted that, as new-comers, they were entitled to a fair share of knowledge concerning their neighbors' affairs. Eve went briefly over the story of our housekeeping, setting it forth in a most entertaining light. Mr. and Mrs. Wilbur laughed heartily. The clock struck eleven; and our guests started with guilty consciences, beginning to make excuses for such late staying.

"The picnic is a true fact, as my little girl says," announced Mr. Wilbur. "No backing out. I shall be there promptly, with a fiddler; and every pretty girl will be there, so we shall know in what esteem the truants hold themselves. Miss Brooke, I shall open the grand entertainment with you. My wife will provide her own partner, and look out that there is no poaching on her manor."

"Yes, girls," said Mrs. Wilbur laughingly, "you may all pull straws for him after the picnic is fairly under way. Good-night, good-night."

They dispersed, rather reluctantly I thought; and we talked on for a good hour, I am sure. In fact, I heard laughs all the remainder of the night.

Sunday morning was splendid, but rather warm. We all went to church, and Athens seemed to be amazed. The afternoon we spent up in the chestnut-grove with cushions, blankets, hammocks, and books. Some of us went to church again in the evening. Pryor, Mr. Bradford, and the inevitable Dan walked up with us, and we had some very good singing. Sadie managed to give Mr. Bradford an invitation to the picnic. Miss Travers's admirer, a Mr. Dane, and Frank Gaylord, had been added by the evening train; so we all walked down again to see them off, and both declared they would be up on Tuesday.

Pryor was in early Monday morning. Eve was to give herself no uneasiness about the cream, and if there was any thing else —

"We are going to make biscuits, and boil a ham,"

returned Eve. "Miss Ruth is going to supply some cake; Mrs. Corwin and Mrs. Wharton also. There will not be much for us to do."

"Couldn't you go for a nice row late this afternoon? The river is so lovely, and when the heat of the sun is over"—

"Oh, enchanting!" interrupted Sadie Brooke, coming forward. "We always row at Lake George. Come, let us hurry with our biscuits and things. If only we did not have to eat, how much time we might devote to other matters,— fun, for instance!" and her eyes were brimful of dangerous light.

Instead of biscuits, she and Kitty Travers went off to ride with him. I was busy at the station, and in my garden picking berries. We still had a plentiful supply of delicious currants, and the raspberries seemed never failing. We really were the envy of some of our neighbors, who couldn't see how we could get so much out of that old, neglected place.

There came up from New York a basket of choice fruit and a box of confectionery. Eve declared the donation party had begun. By night, several cakes had been sent in. We went for the row, and it was most delightful; the sky full of soft, fleecy white clouds, that now and then hid the sun, though that was fast dropping behind the hill. It was such a lovely, drowsy river, with its reaches of shade, and open spaces, and a few little settlements. One of the towns made quite a pretence to business, with its docks and several factories at the water's edge. But the soft golden and hazy lights, the faint breeze stirring the sedgy grass, or the trees higher up, and rippling the waters, made it a perfect picture. Some one repeated Tennyson's poem of "The Lotos-Eaters." Another gave us Robert Browning. Bertha Brooke contributed bits of pathos and audacity from Owen Meredith. Coming home, everybody sang in the soft summer twilight. Even now that seems one of the fairy touches of existence. Had I ever truly lived before? I glanced at Eve with her lucent eyes and soft-tinted cheeks, and knew she was enjoying herself to the uttermost.

There was a plain little supper for us, arranged by Letty, who somehow entered right into the spirit of the affair, and served us with a kind of cheerful delight. Before we were through, the guests began to gather again, and we had a merry evening.

Joe was as full of pleasure as any one else. Sometimes when I looked at him, I could hardly believe him the same lad who had come to me in such dire distress. Every day he seemed to grow larger and handsomer, and his manners were really refined, delicate. Had Eve worked this change? Oddly enough, Pryor was less boisterous in certain ways;

and even Dan Montgomery was coming to have a gentlemanly air. Was it not the contact with real fineness of breeding? Eve, with all her nonsense, had such a gracious, charming refinement. She never lowered herself to people, but, in some curious fashion, met them on her level, drew them up to some better height. But it did not seem as if these few months could so have transformed either soul or body.

We had our wish, and it was a tolerably fair morning; though we all agreed it would rain before night, as it always did on Fourth of July. Joe and Mr. Pryor went up to the ground to clear up, and arrange some seats; while the girls dawdled around after the pretty, graceful fashion of girls of leisure. Mr. Wilbur took them all through his new house, though Mrs. Wilbur declared they looked at a great deal of it with the eye of faith.

Athens made a show of patriotism by now and then firing off a pistol, or a squad of boys congregated about a pack of fire-crackers. Some of the larger towns around had processions and speeches: even our solitary and forlorn Brass Band went out of town. But there was quite an influx of visitors, and trains ran full: indeed, there were some extras. Joe insisted that I should go to the picnic, and promised to run up once or twice between trains.

Dan Montgomery came over with his father's wagon, and offered to help carry up the "creature comforts," as Pryor dubbed them. Our house seemed to be the meeting-place, and we formed quite a procession when we started. It was over the hill above us, something farther to the north, a kind of natural clearing in the strip of woods, — oak, hickory, hemlock, and chestnut. The short grass had been raked and swept. There was quite a pretentious table, two long plank benches, some camp-seats, several hammocks hung, and three colored musicians.

Few especial invitations had been given out: there had not been time. Frank Gaylord had brought a young Cuban up with him, who was employed in the foreign correspondence of his uncle's business-house, — a very gentlemanly young fellow with a rather handsome face and fine manners.

"He seemed so lonely, and did not know what to do with himself," explained Frank to his sister and mine. "You see, he only came to New York last March, and has not made many friends; but he's first-class, and I was telling him how jolly you all were out here."

"Take him around, and introduce him to everybody," said Helen. "It may not be fashionable; but we are in country-wilds, and it does make a stranger feel more at home."

Frank obeyed the behest. Manuel Estradura seemed a trifle abashed at first; but Sadie Brooke and Mr. Wilbur took him so cleverly under their mutual wings, that he almost became the hero of the occasion. His rival was Mrs. Wilbur's cousin, a Mr. Palmer, eight and twenty perhaps, and charming enough to be remarkable at a fashionable watering-place. Sadie declared privately that she felt utterly eclipsed and maddingly jealous.

The music struck up, and the dancing began. Pryor was supremely happy with Eve for a partner; while Dan Montgomery looked on in a rather surly fashion, resolving, I dare say, to acquire the art at the very first opportunity. In the Lancers that followed, Eve had Mr. Palmer, and Sadie the Cuban; but in the next set Sadie was supremely content with the tall, distinguished stranger.

They danced, they chatted and laughed. There was the quickest of repartee, the merriest of *badinage*. It was a picture out there in the woods,—a Watteau-like scene that harmonized admirably. Joe was wild with delight when he came up. They were just about dancing again; and he took Ruth Montgomery, rather to my surprise. I thought of Eve's plan of attracting Pryor thitherward, but in my heart of hearts I knew it would not work.

It was a happy time with youth and delight. The

moments flew too rapidly. Never did music sound sweeter, never did sandwich, cake, cream, and lemonade taste better. Is there any zest like that of the freshness of youth and the piquant unconventionality of such an occasion?

"There will not be any thing quite as charming at Lake George, I know," declared Sadie wilfully. "I have half a mind not to go."

Palmer looked up quickly.

"Are you booked for Lake George?" he asked. "I am to start next week with a camping-out party, and spend a fortnight. Are you going with a party?" and he gave a mirthful glance around.

"I am always in a party," declared Sadie. "I abhor solitudes and sages, and enjoy being 'in the midst of alarms.' Yes, my sister, Miss Fisher, Miss Lane, and Miss Travers, go with us. I only wish I could coax Eve Thurston to join, but she has spent one whole summer there."

They compared notes about their respective locations, and found they were not going to be very far apart. Mr. Bradford, who had come up an hour or so before, found himself quite supplanted, and had to comfort his soul with Bertha. Was he really attracted to Sadie Brooke? I could not imagine him choosing such a gay society wife; but he was in no wise devoted to young women.

On the homeward route Mr. Palmer was her escort. The young Cuban seemed curiously attracted to Eve. Mrs. Wilbur now informed us that she had made all arrangements with Mrs. Ten Eyck for our party to have supper there, and Mr. Wilbur had laid in a liberal supply of fire-works. There was a little demurring, but Eve was speedily overruled.

There had been quite a number of Athenians who had strolled up to Terry's woods, rather curious to know just what was going on. We had made several of our friends and neighbors very welcome, and the breaking up was characterized by expressions of delight and good feeling at their venturing to trust our hospitality.

"Why, we might often have pleasant little times like this," said Charlie Wharton. "Athens has been the stupidest place; but if we only can get in some new people with a little vim and brains above a Sunday-school picnic, where you are in fear of children breaking their limbs, or tearing their best clothes!"

"They are well enough in their way," rejoined his sister-in-law, "but the older people might enjoy a pleasure on a different scale. And I do think we owe a debt or a vote of thanks to Miss Thurston for stirring up the Rip Van Winkles."

"Yes," declared Pryor. "Thurston, you will yet

be the light and regeneration of Athens. When we come to get some business and some new people" —

"And a hotel," interrupted Sadie. "Put Miss Thurston in as business manager."

"And I will do my best toward filling it," said Mr. Wilbur.

Eve, Joe, and I paused a few moments at the house. Joe was to do the chores. I ran down to the station, and attended to the up and down trains. When I reached Mrs. Ten Eyck's, I found Pryor and Mr. Bradford had both accepted the invitation. Indeed, it was quite a party. Mrs. Wilbur was mistress of ceremonies, and we did have a gay time. Afterward we went out on the porch. It was quite cloudy, so it was considered prudent to have the fireworks at once, as the children were eager for them.

So we ended with a patriotic glorification. Our day had been a great success. Frank Gaylord and Estradura were going on the train, but Palmer had accepted Mrs. Wilbur's invitation to remain a few days longer. We saw the travellers off, with declarations on their part that they had found Athens delightful.

The next morning Joe and I were very busy, and the girls had the house to themselves. But in the afternoon they all went off driving with Palmer and Mrs. Wilbur. Indeed, they were so late that Letty and Joe had supper all ready when they came home. Mr. Bradford and Pryor were both up that evening.

Mr. Wilbur's house was progressing so rapidly, that they had decided to get in before it was all finished, and resolved to move about the middle of the month; though Mrs. Wilbur explained the case more fully to Eve. They had some friends who would like to board with the Ten Eycks, but who wanted to get out in the country by that time, and Mrs. Ten Eyck would be pleased to have them come, — a married couple with a son and daughter. The Wilburs did not intend to furnish very elaborately. Most of the floors were hard wood or stained, and Mrs. Wilbur promised herself much pleasure talking matters over with Eve. Both husband and wife had taken an immense fancy to Joe.

Indeed, Joe developed such a multifarious genius that I was sometimes quite amazed. He was like a woman in the "short cuts" he took to accomplish his object. If he did not get a satisfactory result one way, he used another. Some of his suggestions were so excellent that Mr. Wilbur placed the arrangement of the grounds and several other matters in his hands. A nice barn was to be built through the fall, and next year they would keep a horse and a cow.

Already Joe had begun to save some money. He

had bought a nice, inexpensive summer-suit, and was paying for a watch on instalments. His parcel business was considerable, and the regular expressman of the town looked sourly at him. He had also made a contract with several ladies in Athens, elderly people, to take them to drive now and then, bring them to the station when they needed to go to the city, and take them home. His prices were so low, that Pryor quite laughed at him at first; but when he made seventy-five cents on some days, and had the pleasure besides, he felt quite elated.

"Thurston, next year I'll have a horse, you see if I don't," he said confidently to me. "I've made up my mind that *I'm* going to see if I can't get my share of the world's wealth that Miss Eve was explaining to me one day. It looks like a big thing, to set out for eight hundred dollars; but I dare say if I hadn't stumbled over you as I did that day, I should drink up that amount in ten years; so I just said to myself, 'If you can afford to drink up that sum in beer and rum, you can afford to save it.' And money *does* help you to make money. O Thurston! I can never be grateful enough to you and Miss Eve," and Joe's eyes were limpid with tears.

Certainly, even this was worth doing. And it seemed, with a helping hand now and then, that Joe might be a success for himself. Cities were full enough of young men crowding each other for bread, and even here Joe was making more clear money than in any position he was likely to get. The thought of his future troubled me now and then, — whether, indeed, this was a good business discipline for the man.

Thursday was crowded full of pleasure. The girls were to go back on Friday, except Miss Gaylord, who was to rejoin some relatives at Long Branch on the first of August. Now she proposed to spend the intervening weeks at Athens.

"It will be very pleasant to have her," said Eve. "I have been so used to some society and companionship, that I must be let down easily;" and she laughed gayly.

Mrs. Brooke sent an invitation for Eve to accompany them to Lake George, and remain a fortnight; and Sadie insisted that she should consent.

"Indeed, I cannot!" said Eve. "I must finish up my painting-class and some music-lessons, and make some fine attire. Then I am to go to Saratoga to Mrs. Harwood."

"Then you can surely come. We will never, never forgive you if you don't!" cried the chorus.

Eve did partly promise.

There was a rather amusing dispute at the last. Eve had arranged it with me that the girls' week should be considered a visit. They had not intended that, but Eve pluckily held her ground. The girls gave in presently, and were so agreeable, that I felt quite certain they had settled it among themselves.

We were all sorry to have them go. Mr. Palmer had remained, and joined them on their return-trip. Mr. Pryor and Mr. Bradford both found an important errand to take them to the city. The girls insisted that there should be another splendid week in the autumn. Gertie Fisher, we knew, was to be married. Her lover was buyer for a New-York house, and was now abroad; so there might be one less.

It seemed quite lonely that evening, for, strangely enough, no one dropped in; but we had the inexpressible pleasure of going to bed early. In fact, we had been dreadfully dissipated.

Frank Gaylord had written to ask if he and Estradura might come over on Sunday afternoon, and Helen had replied in the affirmative. So we were not likely to be utterly deserted. The quiet Saturday was a real pleasure. We looked after our young chickens. I trimmed and tied up vines, and took account of stock, as one might say.

On Monday, Eve had an express parcel with the jolliest of letters signed by the whole five girls, who had endowed her with enough table-napery to last a lifetime, or furnish the hotel. They strongly suggested the latter.

We liked Miss Gaylord very much. She and Frank were the youngest of a large family, all married and scattered, save these two, who were still under the guardianship of an uncle, who had been like a father to them. Helen had a small portion of seven thousand dollars well invested, and was about twenty; not quite such a madcap as some of the others, and a very pleasant companion. Frank was two years younger, a bright, smart business fellow. When we came to see Estradura again, we were much pleased. He was a fine musician, read French and Italian beautifully. I had half a fancy that he was smitten by Miss Gaylord, at which suggestion Eve smiled a little.

CHAPTER XI

SUMMER AND SENTIMENT

Our next excitement was getting Mrs. Wilbur's house furnished. I wondered why everybody, old, young, middle-aged, or between, came to Eve for counsel, suggestion, and approval. Mrs. Wilbur carried her off to New York two days to help her select furniture. Every thing was to be light, airy, cheap, she said, but not as Eve and I counted cheapness. There were willow, bamboo, splint chairs; rugs; bed-room suites in maple and ash, and they were plain. The furniture was not to be removed in the winter.

For compensation Mrs. Wilbur insisted that Eve should take her dressmaker for two days, and this was a wonderful relief. The painting-class met again, and Helen was much interested in it. She was delicately helpful in many ways. Mr. Pryor was their gallant, of course.

I found a great deal to do in my garden. Weeds grew apace, though Joe had a curious knack of exterminating them. As my raspberries ceased bearing, I cut out the old canes, which made quite a thinning, and trimmed back young shoots. I cut out a multitude of young currants, and made a new bed of them in a rather shady place, to see if I could root them. Our chickens throve nicely. We had been culling out the cockerels, and using them up, and very nice we found them. The horse, too, proved a great satisfaction. I gave the stable, and Joe the care; for we used it the most, I found. The food we supplied by thirds; and it proved not at all onerous, as she was an easy keeper.

We heard from the girls. It was very jolly at Lake George. Mr. Palmer's camping-party was just magnificent. If Eve *could* only be there! couldn't she, wouldn't she, come? Then Mrs. Harwood wrote. She would be ready for Eve on the 10th of August, and would like to keep her a fortnight.

"That falls in right with the painting and every thing," said Eve. "Some of the music-scholars will stop now; but after all, I seem to have about as much pleasure as work."

"You make pleasure out of every thing," I replied.

Then a new application surprised us. Mr. Estradura came over one day to beseech Eve to open her hospitable home, and take him in. A friend was to spend some months in New York to learn the language, and perfect himself in American ways; and they desired to board together in some pretty country-place for six weeks or so, and he had seen nothing he liked so well as this place and the woods up beyond. His friend was something of an artist, and he would be delighted with the scenery, the home, the quiet; and if they might have the horse a little now and then. His friend had some fortune, and was willing to pay for all the comforts and pleasures, and the piano would be such a treat.

Eve was quite amazed. We talked it over in a sort of family conclave. I saw she had a leaning toward it.

"But you must go away," I said. "You shall not toil and moil the whole summer."

"That is all the bother. As for the rest, they will have their breakfast, and go to the city, and I shall see nothing of them until evening. I shall not be expected to provide entertainment for them all day; and as there will be two, they can be company for each other."

"You have worked enough for one summer."

"Well, I am not much worn out," and she laughed. "I have had a good time so far. Then, the first of August the Wilburs are going away for one or two weeks, and I *may* be lonesome. No, to tell the truth," and her gay expression settled into soberness, "I *do* think of the money. There will be quite a sum to meet in the fall, and I should like to keep Letty. If we were alone, it would be too great an indulgence."

"I hate to have you thinking of money all the time!" I declared warmly. "You, of all others, must not grow mercenary."

"Fancy me at the most successful of watering-places, balancing the purses of my admirers, and using all my ingenuity to learn which is the heaviest! There is nothing mercenary about that!"

"I shall come to hate the place"—

"No, you will not, Adam;" and her soft arms were about my neck. "Every day it fascinates you more and more. Every shrub, every blade of grass, every berry, and even the potatoes, are dear to you, and have a flavor that no others could ever have. There *is* something exhilarating about one's own home. While I am young and well, I ought to help; and I love to have people about me. I was not formed for solitude."

"I may as well give up," I said. "You will talk me over to your way of thinking; but go to Saratoga you shall. It would be ungracious to Mrs. Harwood."

"I shall surely go. Set your heart at rest. I will see if I can figure out the other matter."

Estradura was very much in earnest. He came again one evening to announce that his friend had arrived. They were to go to Manhattan Beach for several days, then take a brief trip to the Catskills, and wished to settle themselves as soon as they returned. He and Eve looked at the rooms: they would have to content themselves with one large one and a small one.

"That will be all right," declared Estradura. "I will have the small one, and we can sit in my friend's when you do not want us down-stairs. You are so happy and gay, Miss Thurston, and every thing is so pleasant, — the whole wide out of doors as well. My friend will be charmed."

Eve explained that she was engaged to go away for a week or two. Could they get along in her absence?

"We shall miss you, of course," and he smiled flatteringly; "but even that will not keep us away. We shall count on having you afterward."

So they settled it at length, giving me no voice in the matter. They would come the last week in July. Then Eve engaged Mrs. Banks to superintend Letty during her absence.

On the top of this arrived the most amusing letter from Sadie Brooke. Mr. Palmer was to spend about ten days in New York on business, and then return to Lake George on the 5th of August. They had commissioned him to bring Eve, and five days later she could come down to Saratoga. Mr. Palmer had been bound by all manner of solemn promises, threats, and warnings, not to venture into their presence without her; and they would all be dying to see Mr. Palmer. See what a great commotion a little obstinacy on her part would create!

It was very funny, to say the least. Every thing *did* come together. Eve consulted Mrs. Wilbur, who only made matters worse by declaring they would take that for the commencement of their journey, making it all the pleasanter for Eve.

"And if it will be any assistance," declared Helen Gaylord, "I will stay a week or so longer, and see that the house is not shrouded in gloom for your absence. Long Branch will keep."

It was extremely good of her. Somehow the matter did get settled harmoniously. Helen moved into Eve's room: and the two others were garnished and changed about for the new-comers, who were prompt to the day, though a note announced them. Mr. Estradura's friend was rather smaller and slighter than himself, but extremely pretty,— you could apply no other adjective to him. He talked very broken, and was much embarrassed by his mistakes, flushing like a girl. But that evening they sang some Spanish songs that were enchanting, and altogether it was delightful. After a few days they began to feel very much at home, and really troubled no one. Indeed, they rather entertained us with their exquisite foreign ways.

Every thing went along smoothly. Mr. Palmer was over at the Wilburs's, who were quite settled already. Eve was extremely busy, but Helen helped like a sister. No evil befell us: it did not rain on the appointed day, and the travellers started off in high spirits. Eve had given everybody charges. Mrs. Banks promised to come when needed. Joe declared that he could run the house himself, if it were necessary.

But, oh, how lonely it was! I wondered how I could ever live without Eve again. There seemed so much time for every thing. I looked after the chickens, though Joe was much more deft when it came to finishing their earthly careers, and preparing them for the cook. My blackberries were ripening magnificently. The Wilburs had engaged two quarts a day; also, Mrs. Ten Eyck, who liked her new people very well; and several others had spoken for some to make blackberry brandy, which I thought I should try myself.

Meanwhile the new-comers had begun with their factory, and in one little spot Athens seemed quite awake. Mr. Corwin decided to build two pretty cottages on his ground, either for sale or to rent; and we all had a hand in the planning. He found he could raise some money easily, after he had them started, as he was resolved not to mortgage his house.

Miss Gaylord did splendidly, and declared that she needed no one besides Joe and Letty. I was getting to be quite a housekeeper myself, and tried to remember Eve's charges. We heard from her nearly every day; and every thing was just splendid, with no end of fun. She was afraid Saratoga would not be half as nice.

However, she went on the appointed day, and was conscience-smitten that she had fancied she might not be happy. Mrs. Harwood was delightful. There were rides and sails on the lake; parties and parlor-dances and hops; and she staid two whole weeks. Even then Mrs. Harwood would have kept her. Pryor had gone up and spent one Sunday, and came home rather fractious, I thought.

Miss Gaylord went away the week before Eve's return, on account of some festivities, at which she was needed. We did miss her immensely, but we managed very well. I had a half feeling, that, if there were no Eve in the world, Pryor might turn in that direction. He did promise to spend a Sunday at Long Branch.

I went down to New York to meet Eve. Was she really prettier than ever? — bright, arch, and vivacious; her cheeks like a peach, her eyes lucent as water-blown lakes.

"And with all the fun and enjoyment, I am so glad to see you," she confessed. "I have had at least one wish every day to be at home. Oh, how have you managed? and are the Cubans disgusted?"

"Not a bit," returned I. "What with easy-chairs out on the lawn, and the hammocks, and the horse, I do believe they fancy themselves in clover. Letty has not given notice, neither has Joe gone off; and we have had pears and peaches, and all the luxuries of the season."

"Oh, how lovely it looks!" she exclaimed, as we walked up the hill. "O Adam! *do* you remember the splendid walks of last autumn, and how we coveted just this particular house? Why, I never had such a happy, satisfying, pleasure-crowded year in my life."

I was glad to hear her say so. She flew into the house like a child, and could not rest until she had peeped into every room, seen Letty and Joe, and run over to the Wilburs's. The place was suddenly transformed. She looked like a sprite dancing about the garden, inspecting the chickens, and patting Bess, who seemed to give her a most cordial greeting. Yes, she was a part of every thing, and mine.

I was just selfish enough, in that hour, to rejoice that no one had any claim upon her.

Mrs. Banks had come over every afternoon to see about the dinner. The breakfasts, Letty and Joe managed admirably; though I dare say Mrs. Banks had planned them out the night before. And now she insisted upon Miss Thurston finishing her holiday; so Eve disported herself in her white dress, with adornings of cherry-colored velvet, and ate peaches to her heart's content.

There had also been a harvest-apple, which had not done as well as its wealth of blossoms promised; but we had enjoyed it nevertheless: and now another was ripening, from which we had pies and sauce.

I believe the Cubans enjoyed Eve's home-coming the least of anybody. They seemed at first rather embarrassed, and went out after dinner, to walk up the road, and smoke their cigars. Pryor, fortunately, was out of town, so I had her to myself; and we looked over the household books which I had kept; and I related the few ups and downs, while she entertained me with the delights of her sojourn.

"Do you know," she said, "that I am inclined to predict a conquest, though I don't just know which will win the crown? But Mr. Palmer is hard hit with Sadie Brooke, and very much in earnest. Mrs. Brooke admires him extremely. And if one *could* tell about Sadie; but I think she is more in love than she would like to have any one suspect. Mr. Bradford is very — what shall I say? — deeply fascinated. Indeed, it will be well for the other girls when she makes her election: they can have some sort of chance."

"Even Pryor went down to her, I suppose?" I asked meaningly.

"No, he did not. I wish he had. I was — well, hateful to him; and I am ashamed of it. But I don't want him to ask me, and I am afraid he will never be disenchanted any other way."

"Then, you may as well have it over with," I advised.

"After all," said Eve the next morning, "Athens *is* beautiful, — not wild or grand, but comfortably beautiful. I am sure I could live here all my life, and take my tours elsewhere."

After a few days we settled down into the accustomed routine, and then it seemed as if the Cubans suddenly woke to the fact that Eve was a charming young woman. They coaxed her out on the porch; were fain to give up cigar-smoking for her sake. They taught her Spanish: they sang to her and with her. Mr. Cassimera played deliciously on a guitar; and really, one might have fancied them half in love with her.

All this was flame to Pryor's passion.

"See here, Thurston," he exclaimed huskily one night as he walked down to the station with me, "have you no care or thought for your sister? What do you know about those fellows? They are both head over heels in love with her, and they may be frauds and humbugs; and I dare say they don't really mean any thing with all their great fuss."

"All the better for them if they do not mean any thing," I answered. "I do not think my sister's heart is lightly won. Society women are used to making themselves agreeable, and receiving attentions that in a little place like this would naturally be more serious. They are very gentlemanly."

"Hang it! I don't care what they are! You have had opportunities to know about me, Thurston. You must have seen — have understood" —

"Don't, Pryor," I interrupted. "I would save you any pain that I could. Use your own eyes. What has she done to encourage more than a friendly regard?"

"Well, I love her. It is out now. And you have a good deal of influence over her. She feels bound to you — about the place, I mean; but if she were quite free — and I like you so well, Thurston, that no brother could be dearer. Why can we not all pull together? Come, do not stand in my way. Heaven knows I would lay down my life for your sister if she needed it! Give me a brotherly speeding in this matter."

I had tried hard to shield Eve from an occasion like this, but I had never imagined the sweet old story might be told to me in such a desperate fashion. What *would* Eve do if she were here? What if she had an underlying strand of tenderness for him? Yet it seemed as if I knew her heart.

"I am afraid it is of no use, Pryor," I said; and I felt heartily, deeply sorry for him. "So far as I am concerned, I could give you a brother's welcome any day, or a God-speed; but I think it *is* hopeless. Eve doesn't care to marry. She likes a young girl's good time. She has not" — how should I say it without hurting him? — "she does not mean to encourage *any* one." Then the past came into my mind like a flash. Would it help her here? "There was something in her life a while ago — it is her secret, and I have no right even to hint at it; but I may say it will keep her from all such matters at present. They would be distasteful to her."

"But I would wait — she is not engaged, tell me that!" and his voice trembled with fateful anticipation.

"She is *not* engaged, but as little will she desire to listen to lovers at present. If you *must* try your fate, Pryor, I will not stand in your way; but I warn you it will be hopeless. Watch her closely. If you can detect the slightest sign of encouragement"—

Pryor sighed. We had reached the station, and the train came in. Then I locked my office.

"There never was such a happy time as last winter," he said, with a lingering intonation that pierced me. "I have never seen anybody that I liked so well. Thurston, I can't even bear to say good-night to you; for you are so near and dear to her, that, if I did not love you so well, I should hate you bitterly. But in all truth you could not be so false-hearted as to influence her against me"—

"No, no!" I cried. "Test her yourself. If you win any thing beyond a friendly recognition—"

"Good-night!" he exclaimed abruptly, and plunged down the street.

I walked slowly homeward. Eve was in the hammock; and the two young men were singing, with a guitar accompaniment.

"Isn't it delicious?' said Joe from a seat on the terrace-grass.

They dispersed presently with a kindly good-night. We sauntered around in doors.

"Eve,' I began, "have you been taking lessons of Sadie Brooke?'

"I am afraid there was some one before that, and

then long before that," she answered with a laugh. "After all, why shouldn't we enjoy ourselves? Summers are fleeting. I do not want them to fall in love with me — and I try in certain ways — O Adam! *do* I flirt? I sometimes feel as if I were getting cross and old-maidish — when Pryor is here. I wonder — oh! what makes you so solemn? I will shut myself up in a convent, I will put on a cap and glasses, but *you* must love me and be tender."

"It is about Pryor," I said. "Let me tell you."

I drew her to the corner of the sofa, and repeated nearly all of the conversation. For a moment or two she was silent.

"Oh!" I cried, "*could* you care for him, love him in time?"

"No: I do not think I could love him dearly, could *want* him for my husband; and it ought to be the strongest of all preference. I like him, I could be good friends if it were not for this regard that now keeps me all the while on the defensive. I am *so* glad you told him. Life is delightful with you, Adam, and you are so good to me."

"Still, when you *do* love, you must not let me stand in the way."

She gave me a tender kiss, many of them indeed.

The next day, Pryor was called to a neighboring State by the illness of his mother, and was gone over a week. Still, there was no lack of visitors to sit on the porch during the lovely summer evenings. And so August drew to a close, and September came in.

One day — it was the first week in September when a curious incident happened. The 3.10 train came up from the city, and there were only two passengers to get off. One was a common, middle-aged man; the other a rather slim, compact-looking young lady, in a soft gray dress, a gray straw hat with a great cluster of nasturtiums on the brim, hanging about on their long, light green stems. We had a large mound of them in all colors, and these looked as fresh as the real ones in our garden.

She walked down the platform rather slowly. I thought of Joe, and wondered if she would like to ride. I came along behind her; and just after the steps, she turned.

"I wonder," she began in a soft, cultured voice, — how I remarked all these little things now, — "I wonder if you could tell me where a Miss Thurston lives, — a Miss Eve Thurston?"

"Yes," I answered. "Turn straight up this street."

I walked along — not right in range, but at a "respectful distance."

This was some one I had not seen before. Eve had mentioned several new acquaintances made at

Lake George and Saratoga, and one especially, a youngish married woman, who had begged permission to visit her. This lady might be two or three and twenty, certainly not older. There was something very interesting about her, though she was sweet and gracious rather than beautiful. Her eyes were a clear blue, a color seldom seen out of childhood, large, serious, frank in certain respects, but with a steadiness that impressed you. The complexion was clear and somewhat pale; the hair of a rather flaxeny brown, instead of golden tints, and abundant if one could judge by the great coil worn low down in the nape of her neck.

She made a little halt. "Is it far?" she asked.

"Oh, no! just above, on that hill."

She glanced up toward it.

"How odd, to call a little village like this, Athens!" and she smiled.

"We have the old names in the New World."

"And Mount Ida, and shepherds with their crooks, and their sheep browsing — or I believe it is goats that browse. When I was a little girl, I was taught that sheep nibbled; and it seems to express their fashion of eating."

I laughed at the conceit. I don't know why, but I was glad to have her a friend of my sister.

"Goats still seem to be in fashion," I said; for just

then we saw two tethered in a small patch of ground. "But we have no shepherds."

She halted a moment, and half turned. There was a polite inquiry in her face. Was she wondering why I followed her?

"Fortunately, my sister is at home this afternoon," I announced, congratulating myself on so bright a thought.

"Your sister? Is Miss Thurston your sister?"

My evil genius prompted me to reply, "Madam, I'm Adam;" but a kind of astonishment seized me, that she could have met Eve, and known her, and not have heard of me. My brotherly vanity was wounded.

"Yes," I answered, opening the gate.

She seemed to hesitate. I was sorry that Eve was not on the porch in her soft white gown. I invited her within; and she came slowly, casting questioning glances around.

"I will sit here," she said, pausing in the wide hall, our reception-room. "Tell Miss Thurston a lady, a stranger, wishes to see her."

I obeyed her behest.

"Oh, goodness!" cried Eve; "you do not think her an agent or a canvasser, do you?"

"No," I said positively. Then I laughed. "She is artistic."

"And æsthetic. Green gown and all that?"

"Gray gown. Heavenly blue eyes. Not quite as tall as you."

Eve threw off a kitchen-apron, and stood arrayed in white. Giving some charges to Letty, she passed through the rooms. I went out to the barn, for I was patching up my chicken-house to make it good and warm; and Joe and I had made plans for a greenhouse. We had been gathering stones to lay a wall, and the mason had explained to Joe how to make mortar for laying them. It really would not be much more than an extensive cold-frame, sheltered by the barn.

Of course I thought of Eve's visitor. She had not gone away when train-time drew nigh. Joe was going down with the wagon to meet a passenger.

CHAPTER XII

A TOUCH OF ROMANCE

THEY came out to the garden in a strangely familiar way. I wonder what I would have said or done if I could have seen what those two girls were to be to each other in the years to come!

They walked up towards me. I brushed the *débris* off my clothes.

"My friend, Miss Hildreth," announced Eve. "My brother, Mr. Thurston."

Miss Hildreth smiled and bowed, and we plunged at once into an amusing conversation.

"Come and find me some nice peaches and pears," said Eve. "I see some lovely ones that I cannot reach."

I obeyed. We rambled around and talked. I felt like quite an old friend, since Eve was so informal with Miss Hildreth. We discussed flowers and fruit and locations, and drives about the country, and sunsets; and then, looking at her watch, she declared that her time was up, and her train would soon be *en route* for the city.

"Adam will go down with you," my sister said. "And you will be sure to come over for the day, — let it be early next week, — and we will have a most delightful drive about the by-ways and hidden nooks."

I put on my "other" coat, and escorted Miss Hildreth, put her on board the train. In fifteen minutes the up-train was due, and the rest of our household would arrive. I was all curiosity to hear about Miss Hildreth, yet there was nothing but patience.

Estradura and Cassimera leaped lightly from the train. They were such agile, graceful, well-mannered young men. I had some parcels to look after, but Joe came; and I hurried up home just in time for the dainty dinner, which certainly was as well served as that of the first Eve.

One event after another occurred. It was ten o'clock before I had Eve a moment to myself.

"It is too utterly funny," she said. "You are dying with curiosity to know about Miss Hildreth. I can see it in every line of your face. She is an artist, and has a studio in New York; paints pictures, gives lessons, has one brother — isn't it queer, there are only two of them, and two of us? But he is in South America, making a fortune; and I have you here safe and sound, and shall never, never let you leave me." With this, Eve clasped her arms about my neck, and kissed me tenderly. "Well, where was I? Oh!—this is the oddest—is there a curious kind of fate or presentiment? She, Miss Hildreth, was going up the Hudson one day early in July, and there was a merry party on board that interested her extremely. Once they were sitting quite close together; and they were talking about Athens, the beautiful walks and drives, and wishing they were artists. They mentioned Eve Thurston, and she thought it such a peculiar name; and she gathered from their chatter that they had been staying with this Miss Thurston, so she imagined it was a delightful old country-house where boarders were taken in the summer; and she fancied Miss Thurston one of those fascinating women of about forty, who always attract young people to them. Think of that!" and Eve laughs merrily. "But, you know, she only heard snatches, and not a coherent conversation. It lingered in her mind, and she resolved to hunt me up. She has orders for two landscapes, 'Autumns', one about a month later than the other, and one with a river. So she came over to-day, and found me, and actually said ' My dear child' to me. That was simply delicious," and Eve laughs again. "Well, the end of this marvellous and improbable story is, that we like each other, and she is coming over one day next week, and we will drive around to hunt up cosey nooks. How I shall tease the girls!"

I was silent, revolving Miss Hildreth's strange entrance into our world.

"She was very nice," continued Eve. "She gave me some references in a quiet business way, as if she was not afraid. She boards with a cousin of her mother, a charming elderly person whose description suggested Mrs. Harwood to my mind. And I must say I like her, although I do know there are frauds and adventurers in the world."

"She is no fraud!" I declared indignantly.

"Then, she impressed *you* favorably. I am glad of that, for you ought to be wiser than I, Adam. Still, we will — why, we will trust her, unless she tells some awful story, or does something very naughty. Now we must both go to bed and dream about her. Would it not be funny if she never came again?"

We both laughed heartily at that.

I do not think I dreamed of Miss Hildreth, but I thought of her a long while before I fell asleep. I could see her large, clear eyes through the dusk, and the very atmosphere seemed touched and penetrated with her voice.

We talked of it the next day, and somehow it had a very incredible air.

But we were busy enough planning and considering. There was fruit to can and preserve. We would have more pears than we could use, and more peaches; but we found ready customers in the Wilburs. Joe was laying out their garden, and had reduced their blackberries to order. My currant-slips had rooted nicely, so we gave them a row of currants, and, later, were to transplant some of our over-abundant shrubbery. Mr. Randall came down to ask my advice. The neighbors about us seemed to think we had such a wonderful garden. How did I do it, one and another inquired; and even Mr. Montgomery ceased to sneer at book-learning and experiments.

Miss Hildreth sent a card, specifying the day of her visit. The weather was still warm; but there had been a little rain the evening before, and the roads were in an excellent condition. I found myself watching eagerly for her train. The acquaintance had a flavor of the unusual in it, a touch akin to the occult. That she should have hunted up Eve and Athens just because the names had taken her fancy!

We found her quite as charming as on her first call. I say *we*. I escorted her up to the pretty house, where some late wistaria and Chinese honeysuckle were in bloom, and no end of salvia and foliage-plants. Somehow, every thing had grown so abundantly with us. I could hardly convince myself that it was the neglected old Cassel place.

"How beautiful it is!" Miss Hildreth said, pausing. "Mr. Thurston, you should be a gardener or florist. You have the divine inspiration."

"I think much of the credit due my sister," I answered. "She has the exquisite ideas."

"If I were not an artist, I should want to be a florist. The height of my ambition is to own a greenhouse."

I smiled. Eve came out to welcome her friend. Joe had the carriage ready. They were to go in the morning, as Joe had an engagement to drive two old ladies out at two o'clock.

They had, it seems, a delightful time, and were hungry enough when they reached home, allowing Joe just ten minutes' grace. We had a merry luncheon, then Miss Hildreth inspected the farm with Eve, and they went over to Mrs. Wilbur's. I had to pay attention to business, but I took one little walk with them down to the river's edge. Miss Hildreth was very fond of sailing or rowing, — was quite handy with the oars herself. We coaxed her to remain to dinner; but she had promised to be back by dusk, and we were forced to exchange a reluctant good-by. She was such an agreeable companion. While she had decided views on many points, she was so gracious and liberal-minded; and the girls found that their tastes in reading were much alike, though Miss Hildreth had gone deeper in the classics. Music she knew very little about, but was extremely fond of it.

"Still, I understood that I could not do every thing," she said. "I wanted to take care of myself, and I did have a decided talent for all kinds of art-work. I shall probably never be very famous, but I shall try to make myself happy with what I can do."

"We are wonderfully alike," declared Eve afterward. "Miss Hildreth and her brother have planned to live together, and he is so fond of country life. His ideal is to have a pretty country home. He went to South America three years ago, with a friend; and they thought, in five years, they would make quite a fortune. But somehow their plans have not worked; that is, they are not very rich yet. Miss Hildreth wants him to come home. She is quite enchanted with our plans, and the way we are managing. Wouldn't it be funny if they came to Athens to settle? And, O Adam! she wants to come over to board for a fortnight or so. Her aunt owns a house in New York, which she rents furnished, reserving some of the rooms, and taking her meals with the family. She is going away for several weeks. You see, we will have to come to the hotel;" and Eve laughed.

"You are so attractive."

"I let people pretty well alone: I think that must be it," she answered gayly.

"Have the Cubans said any thing about going?"

"Not a word. They are sure to stay all this month. Mrs. Harwood was to come. And, O Adam! the tax-paper came in. We must look over our assets and liabilities."

I sighed.

"Well, we have had a good time," was her consoling rejoinder. "And, Adam, I think we have done a little good. I am so proud of Joe, so pleased about him. Have you any idea how much money he has saved?"

"No," I answered.

"He set out to put by two dollars a week, just what he thought he would be sure to drink up under other circumstances. And he has done better than that. He has over forty dollars, and a very creditable wardrobe. He wants to buy Bess of Mr. Pryor. She cost seventy-two dollars."

"She would be a good bargain for that, but Pryor believes in making money as well. Bess is an easy keeper. I don't know whether Joe would find her profitable in the winter."

There was a soft, wistful light in Eve's eyes.

"I suppose," she said slowly, "that there are a good many boys and young men who might be saved and made useful members of society. And I wonder how many young men in Athens have saved any money this summer?"

"Dan Montgomery hasn't, for one."

"And a good many of them are idling about. Why can they not take up life in real earnest?"

"I think it may be because they haven't you standing right behind them," and I laughed.

Eve blushed brightly.

The third week in September we went over our business for the last six months, counting assets up to the first of the month. It stood in this manner:—

My salary for six months	$270	
Eve's painting-class	50	
Music-scholars	110	
Paintings and fancy articles sold	17	
		$447
Mrs. West's board	$64	
Mrs. Harwood	16	
Miss Gaylord	20	
Estradura	40	
Cassimera	40	
		$180

To this we were able to add $16 for fruit sold. It made a total of $643. Out of this we had spent

$92 for furnishing and repairs. Then we went over our chicken account. We had bought ten hens and nine dozen eggs; and three dozen eggs had been given to us. Out of one hundred and seventeen eggs, we had raised one hundred and three chickens. The food that I had bought had cost me $26, making a total of $33.25. We had had from our hens, after raising their broods, thirteen dozen eggs, which, at the prices averaging, had been worth $3.25. We had used fifty-seven chickens and two of our hens, which at forty cents apiece, a low estimate, would have cost us $23.60. Our forty-six young chickens and eight hens now stood us in $6.40. If we could make them lay through the winter, then would come the profit on eggs. I had sixteen beautiful white Leghorn pullets. These I kept by themselves. The others ran together. All our cockerels had been culled out except two.

We found that after our living and incidentals were subtracted, we had just $201. The interest was $126, our tax $34. Then, at the 1st of September we would have a balance of $41 in our favor.

I glanced up at Eve. "That is not getting rich very rapidly," I said rather ruefully. "At this rate, we shall get our house paid for — when?"

"We have done a good deal of furnishing this year, remember. We can save at least a hundred dollars on that next year. And there have been repairs" —

"And the house must be painted by next spring. It *is* very hard to get ahead on a little money — a low salary. What a pittance forty-five dollars a month really is!"

"But you have done so much besides. Why, the house and grounds are improved beyond compare. And we have lived — well, quite stylishly."

At that Eve bridles up, and gives me her most bewitching smile. Still, I can hardly be appeased.

"I don't know when we will get the house paid for," I say disconsolately.

"There *is* one thing — I think we can always sell at some advance. See how much Athens has improved in a year. We *did* buy cheaply; and, O Adam! we have had a delightful home."

"My dear girl, you are better than gold," I say with a tender kiss. "But think of the money you have earned!"

"And think of the pleasure I have had. Saratoga, Lake George, picnics and every thing. And now I have begun with four new music-scholars, and I shall try to do some pretty Christmas work. There'll be no class to take painting-lessons, I am afraid, but I will manage some way. Dear Adam, don't get blue or discouraged. It seems as if we had a good many blessings. We are *not* rich, and perhaps never will be; but we will get all the joy we can out of life."

A few days after, Eve and Mrs. Wilbur went down to the city, and called on Miss Hildreth. She shared a studio with a pleasant, middle-aged woman, a Mrs. Raymond, who painted china, tapestry, plush, and satin, and had some exquisite work on hand. Indeed, they were quite fascinated with the latter.

There was no question but that Miss Hildreth had told the truth about herself, curious as the episode appeared. Eve was delighted, and had actually agreed for her to come.

"She insisted upon taking the little room, if Mrs. Harwood should come," said Eve. "And she thinks she will stay a month. She likes October in the country. O Adam! I wonder if we cannot get one or two rooms finished off up-stairs by another summer? I wish the house was twice as large. I should keep it full all the time. One turns the fruit and vegetables right over to profit, — the chickens and every thing."

Eve certainly was a happy housekeeper.

I must put in a word about our hand-maiden, Letty. She was absolutely bewitched with Eve, and she was an ambitious girl as well. Music she seemed to have in her soul, as well as her finger-ends. She did not mean to go back to school, and she did want to stay with us. Her mother desired her to learn dressmaking. However, it was presently settled that she was to remain with us through the winter at low wages, go on with her music, and Eve was to teach her somewhat in sewing.

Mrs. Harwood managed to get round to us the last of September; and three days later, Miss Hildreth was to come. The Cuban friends were to remain through October. Eve put Mrs. Harwood in her room, and we rigged up a comfortable bed in our attic for me, while Eve was to take my room.

And now I must relate the march my dear Eve stole upon me. She borrowed Joe's money, — forty-five dollars it was then, — and ten from Mrs. Corwin, and took up another hundred dollars on the note. I felt almost angry when she confessed it.

"See here," she began in her pleading, charming fashion. "I am going to pay Joe two-months' interest on his money; and by that time, my music-dues will come in. The other small sum I can soon return. Our expenses are not going to be fearful this winter. You will see me coming out in a new plush suit, maybe a seal coat. Oh, I dare say I shall try your very soul with my extravagance!"

Well, there was no use in scolding. Indeed, Mrs. Harwood was so enthusiastic; and she took such a fancy to the Cubans. She was very fond of young men. It was growing cool in the evenings now, though it had been summer up to this time; and every evening we made a fire in our grate in the reception-room, burning logs that gave out an odorous fragrance. We had put up hooks for two hammocks; we had a pretty, light couch that we could roll around; and, with the easy-chairs, we looked lazily luxurious. Every one *did* enjoy it. When Miss Hildreth came, her delight knew no bounds.

Joe took Mrs. Harwood out every day. He was still busy for Mr. Wilbur, but they were soon going in town. The two elder children were already there, attending school. Next spring the house would be put in good order, all the finishing-touches added. Joe was to work at the grounds.

"That young fellow should be a landscape gardener," said Mr. Wilbur. "I have been surprised at his ideas; and he does his work so thoroughly. I have just been paying him ordinary wages; but I mean to give him a nice sum in the end, for he has saved me dollars and dollars, and he is so willing to change any thing. I want you to overlook him a little. We have the matter all planned out, and I think he can get the grounds in good order before every thing freezes up. I shall be over every now and then."

There was a pretty oval lawn, the carriage-path

going up and winding around the house. The bed of this had been made with stones of all sizes compactly laid, and covered with dirt, then gravel. There were some spaces for flowers: shrubs, bordering, hardy plants and trees, had been set out, and fertilizers of various kinds brought. Joe had sodded the lawn and the terrace in a beautiful manner, and it was to be covered presently.

I was very much pleased with Joe's success. He was equal to Eve for putting in the time; and the thought of one day owning something, inspirited him thoroughly.

Indeed, I am not sure but October was as delightful as any other month. Only the Wilburs *did* go away, and we missed them sadly. Then Mrs. Harwood said her good-bys, though she overstaid her fortnight. Eve demurred at considering her in the light of a boarder, after accepting her generous hospitality.

"My dear child," she said, "do not look at matters in a wrong or distorted light. I am a rich, elderly woman: you are just beginning life, and it would be the quintessence of meanness for me to take of your slender store. I could make you a present, you know; but I approve your business methods, and just now the money is best."

It was true enough. We liked Mrs. Harwood so sincerely and well.

But I think we were both bewitched over Celia Hildreth. She was such a nobly sweet girl, so friendly, so ambitious to do well, so generous to all others. She would have Eve paint a little, and praised her with rare judiciousness.

The Brookes, Gertie Fisher, and Mabel Lane, came over one day. There was so much to tell. Miss Lane was engaged, Miss Fisher was to be married, and so was Kitty Travers.

"And the clique will be broken up," bewailed Sadie Brooke. "We have had the loveliest time for three years, and now you are going to spoil it all."

"It *is* a great pity, since *you* are never likely to leave the charmed circle. Eve, she flirted shamefully with that elegant Mr. Palmer; while any of us would have given our two eyes for him."

"And thrown your lovers overboard? Not a bit of it!" declared Sadie.

"You will flirt once too often — won't she, Eve?"

Sadie colored curiously.

Of course they had to hear the romance about Celia Hildreth. It was very curious, they all agreed.

"So you may know we did not slander you terrifically," laughed Bel. "The passengers must have thought us crazy that day."

"Where is Mr. Palmer?" Eve asked.

"Gone off, — nobody knows where, — to some Western ranch," answered Sadie, with assumed unconcern.

Did she care for him?

Oh, what a lovely autumn it was! After all, I had been prospered wonderfully; and I sometimes asked what there was, short of a fortune, that could make me happier. For I could not undervalue money. I was learning the worth of it more and more every day. Was it not as noble for Joe and me to strive for our small share of it as for some great millionnaire to rejoice when he doubled his thousands? We were wronging no one, we were defrauding no man, but striving honestly and heartily for our little share of the world's wealth.

With the first of November our happy household dispersed. Cassimera was going back to Cuba, Estradura to return to New York for the winter; but he insisted that we were sure to see him early the next summer, and begged to be allowed to come in a friendly way occasionally. They had enjoyed themselves so much. They had been so happy; and to hear them, one would think they had sojourned in Paradise.

Miss Hildreth remained a week after they had gone. She had secured two music-pupils in New York at eighteen dollars a quarter for Eve, who now was sure of going to New York twice a week, and one day she must be able to come in and paint.

Then Mrs. Wilbur came up with some wonderful news.

"Would you believe," she began, "that Royal Palmer is actually engaged to Sadie Brooke? They had a half engagement, and quarrelled, of course, as all true lovers do; and last evening it was made up. He only came home yesterday morning. Quick work, wasn't it? She is a charming girl, but I predict for them a stormy time. And, O my dear Eve, I wish it had been you! I wish I had an unmarried brother, or Mr. Wilbur possessed one; and I should demand you out of hand."

Eve laughed. "I felt almost sure of it at Lake George," she said. "And I think it a splendid match."

"And Roy is a splendid fellow. But, oh! what are you?"

"Splendid too," declared Eve, standing up to her tallest.

"You are sure neither of those Cubans took your heart away?"

"Oh, quite, quite sure!" and Eve laughed gayly.

CHAPTER XIII

ATHENS IS ROUSED

I REMEMBER one evening, Joe and Eve and I sat round a fire of blazing corn-cobs, and talked over our plans and our gains — shall I say? Joe was very happy, very proud and triumphant. When Mrs. Harwood left us, she had added ten dollars to his store; and now Eve had paid her borrowed money. He had bought a really handsome new suit of winter clothes, and had sixty-four dollars to his credit. He had talked over the horse with Pryor, who seemed loth to part with it, yet he had not positively declined.

I think Pryor was beginning to understand that my sweet Eve could give him nothing warmer than friendship. He did not stay away, but there was a slight difference in his bearing toward her. He was very busy just now trying to boom Athens. The wire-factory was to begin operations the first of December. Mr. Corwin had rented both of his houses to the overseers of the different departments; and the probability was, that he would sell one at an advance of about three hundred dollars over the cost.

"It is not very much," he said, "but it releases my money for me to work with again."

Indeed, he and Pryor were planning some cottages, considerably smaller, on a tract of land the latter owned; and a paper-mill was negotiating, through him, for a desirable piece of water-front. This would bring in a number of new people.

I was feeling quite cheerful over my garden. Its products very much surprised Mr. Montgomery. I had five bushels of potatoes, after using from the last of June. We had sundry other vegetables, and thirty bushels of corn on the ear. I had planted a splendid variety of sweet corn — "Giant," it was called — that had yielded beyond any thing; the ears being both long, and containing a large number of rows. It was delightful table-corn; and, though we had supplied some of our neighbors, still a great deal had hardened; but the chickens were crazy over it, so I found it no loss; indeed, I thought it the most profitable of any. I felt another year I could do better still, with a judicious amount of fertilizer. Then we had no end of canned-fruit, and two bushels of pears laid away to keep, though I found they ripened up rather fast. I also tried some experiments with grapes, of which we had an abundance, though not so many that bunched handsomely. We had made blackberry cordial, and three gallons of grape wine.

Our pullets were coming on nicely. Three or four of the white Leghorns laid at five months, and some of the mixed ones. We had about ten beautiful light Brahmas, and began to average six or eight eggs a day. We had a customer in New York for all our white Leghorn eggs at forty cents a dozen for the season. Of our old hens we had but five left, and they were good for another year. We resolved to force them all to their utmost, and see what we could do. The front of both houses was nearly all of glass, and had a southern exposure; was good and warm and dry.

Joe had not quite finished his work next door, but he was still kept busy. Indeed, on a rainy day, Joe and Bess were in great demand at the station: then, there would be employment about the new buildings, so it did not seem worth while to go back to telegraphing. And I began to mistrust that Joe *was* dreaming of a home and a somebody, as he had once suggested. He was always escorting Ruth Montgomery somewhere, and it seemed as if she was not averse. Joe *was* too young and too poor to think of such a future; but, after all —

"No, don't let us interfere," Eve had said. "If

she should like Joe, she will wait; and I begin to think she will not do for Pryor. He needs a more stirring wife,—a kind of stylish society girl, who will help him get rich."

"And Joe needs a wife to keep him poor," I laughed.

"No: Ruth might help *him*. There would be so many little ways, and he would make her very happy. Oh, what nonsense! Well, let us neither make nor mar."

I looked at him now, and the honest manliness shining in his eyes touched me.

"This is solid comfort," he said presently, with a long breath. "When I have a house, I shall have a grate or a fireplace."

We had started our heater, but so far had not needed much fire. This in the reception-room was a luxury. We had settled again in our regular sleeping-rooms, though we all declared ourselves ready to vacate at the appearance of a crowd. But the girls were very busy with approaching weddings. Even Sadie Brooke's had been set down for Christmas Eve.

We were very happy, even if life had narrowed. Indeed, gay, laughing Eve seemed inclined to a little halt, especially as now she went to the city twice a week. We returned to regular reading; and, by odd spells, she painted quite industriously. Our greenhouse experiment was a source of great interest. We had put in our plants; and, though we would have no fire, we trusted to keep them alive. At least, we had some splendid blossoms now.

Eve had another odd entertainment. From papers that one and another sent us, she cut out items of various kinds, and put them in scrap-books. She had collected quite a variety of chicken wisdom, of the care and culture of flowers, besides what she called her house-book, — a very useful volume. We were all interested in experiments. Some we found useful and judicious: others we laughed over.

Besides our out-of-door's garden, we had our dining-room window quite well filled. Miss Hildreth had sent Eve some lovely roses and bourvardias.

Joe sprang up presently, and said it was train-time. He was so good about this matter, though sometimes I felt conscience-smitten. Indeed, it was quite delightful not to have to go all the time.

"It almost seems as though we ought to move back to the station," declared Eve. "It was so easy and pleasant, with everybody dropping in. However, it will not be bitterly cold before January; and then three months will pass rapidly."

There was a step on the porch. "That is Pryor,' said Eve.

Sure enough. He had our evening-mail in his hand, — three letters for Eve.

"Oh, how charmingly cosey you are here!" he exclaimed. "I never *did* see people get so much good out of life," and he looked as if he envied both of us."

"Oh!" said Eve. "Helen Gaylord is coming over for a few days. And on Sunday, Estradura wants to dine with us, if it is not too great an inconvenience. So our friends are not quite of the butterfly order. The first cold snap does not freeze them up. I was just saying to Adam that we would have to go back to the station, for fear no one would want to climb the hill."

"I do not believe you will be left much to your own devices. Still, it was the jolliest thing! Do you know, Miss Eve, I have wondered many a time this summer how you had the courage to do it? Some people would have been buried: you flashed out a star of the first magnitude. And Athens has been coming to the front ever since. Ad, I have a scheme on hand myself. You know those lots on Elm Street?"

I nodded.

"They are one hundred and fifty feet front. I can build six nice cottages of five or six rooms, every two houses being joined together, and leaving a pretty open space between the alternate ones. Corwin thinks it worth the doing. I can rent them in the spring. Don't you want to help me plan? Miss Thurston, I want some of your ideas."

Eve was interested at once. We brought out pencils and paper, and had an amusing time drawing cottages. Eve's plan was the best, we had to admit. She managed to put in more closets, to arrange windows so the house would furnish nicely. Then she sketched out pretty fronts, so they should not all be just alike.

"Corwin has sold one of his houses; and the probability is, that the other will go. I am going to try for two hundred advance on mine; and, if I can get that, I'll turn my money over. Though they will pay fair interest in renting. You see, the two new mills are going to stir up matters."

I ran it over in my mind. If Pryor could make twelve hundred on his houses in one year, it would be quite an addition to his income.

"What is Joe going about?" he asked, rather abruptly. "Isn't Wilbur's place finished?"

"Yes, all that can be done now."

"Joe is a nice fellow. If he should not care to go away, we can keep him busy. Do you know, Corwin and I have been talking of a lumber-yard? If building should have a boom, it wouldn't be a bad thing.

I should like a trusty, honest fellow, such as Joe is going to make. Yet I did not take much stock in him at first."

"Joe is my *protégé*," said Eve, rather proudly, and in a tone that forbade any doubtful remark.

"O Miss Thurston! adopt us all. There is not a soul of us who doesn't envy Joe. And all the young people are talking of what we can have this winter. Now, couldn't we form some kind of a social club, and have a little dancing and music, and now and then a regular supper that the gentlemen should provide? Think it over in your brilliant brain. Why, I would even meet up in the station. The best cup of coffee I ever had in my life was there."

Eve laughed gayly.

"Come up to-morrow night, and help me entertain Miss Gaylord," she said, as he was going away; and he replied that he should be happy to.

Joe did not come in until ten; but he wore a rather shy, mysterious expression, that I think we both connected with Ruth. We told him of Pryor's visit and the prospect.

"How good of him!" exclaimed Joe, with unaffected pleasure. "Do you know, I think the old Garden of Eden must have been here, and a little of the goodness is left to leaven everybody? I shall get along just splendidly."

We had been reading Warren's entertaining book, "Paradise regained." Eve had been training Joe in elocution; and he had such a nice, fresh, earnest voice, that it was a pleasure to listen when his turn came around.

Miss Gaylord reached us the next morning, and found a warm welcome. Mr. Wilbur came over in the afternoon, and had a long interview with Joe, paying him his back wages.

"And you could not guess," said Joe, when I entered the station. "I never would have believed such wonderful luck possible. He said"—and Joe winked hard to keep the tears of joy and gratitude from his eyes—"he said I had been so faithful, and worked so well, and actually saved him money, and that he had been putting by a little every week to make fair wages; and it was absolutely fifty dollars, Thurston. I did not want to take it; but he said I had been worth that, and more, and that I ought to study landscape-gardening, and make a business of it. Couldn't we get some books? And now I have one hundred and eighteen dollars, all my own, and good clothes, and am a sober fellow. I do not believe I ever will drink again, Thurston. I shall think of the health and prosperity and respectability, and, oh, the love one forfeits! Think what I was last spring! I don't know—you both have been angels to me: I don't care if I do cry a little, there!" and Joe wiped his eyes.

"I want you to be strong enough to resist the temptation everywhere, not merely in a place like this. Could you stand up against the boys? I want you to be proof against persuasion and jeers, and even that insidious little demon who whispers, 'Once will do no harm.' My dear boy," and I took his hand. He really seemed like a younger brother.

"Miss Eve," he said that night, "I ought to be paying some board. I am going to earn two dollars a day. I am to keep my hours, and still manage my parcel business, though there will not be so many people wanting to ride out. And I am going to buy Pryor's horse for eighty dollars, paying him fifty down, and the rest he is going to take out in use. And you are so good to me; but you know there isn't much gardening now, or gathering of fruit and vegetables; and you keep Letty all the time"—

"But you run down to the station, and let Adam sit at his ease at home; and you look after the furnace, and chop wood, and bring me things, and take me driving"—

"That isn't any thing," he cried eagerly. "I'm glad to do it. There is not any thing I would not do for you and Adam. I shall feel better if you will let me pay you something."

So it was settled on a basis of three dollars a week. Eve would not take any more, and Joe would not pay any less.

"You see," said Eve, "there is the next interest provided for. And now I shall indulge in a new gown, and you must have a new suit of clothes."

We made our living quite an economical matter. Meats we bought in a co-operative fashion, and divided: various other goods we purchased in large quantities. I had obliged my neighbors by ordering coal by the car-load, quite early in the season. We had obtained it a little less than cost, and had long tons; and it had proved very satisfactory. Once Mr. Wilbur had sent us fifty barrels of flour, when it had taken a tumble; and I found no difficulty in disposing of them at a small profit, that gave us the price of one, though we made sure of two. By these methods, and our store of fruits and vegetables, we kept our living at a figure that was really a source of astonishment to me. Indeed, we had quite a little co-operative society in this matter.

Pryor came up to help entertain our visitor, and it seemed as if he enjoyed it greatly. We made quite a summery picture in the glow of our wood-fire, with the hammocks up, and easy-chairs about. Two or three others dropped in, and we ended with a little music.

"Adam," said my sister a few days later, when she and Helen had been visiting Miss Hildreth, going to an art-sale, and Eve had given her lesson, "I intend to be sinfully extravagant in the way of dress. Kitty Travers is to be married early in December, in church, at three, and have a two hours' reception. Sadie Brooke is to be married in church on Christmas Eve, but goes right away, and will have a reception afterward. The Wilburs are to have an elegant tea, and I am asked to a theatre-party; and, oh, I am to pour tea myself at Mrs. Harwood's! So I shall get a pretty blue-velvet gown. I have white lace to trim it with, and black lace; and I am going to have a cloth gown, trimmed with chinchilla fur, as I have oceans of that on hand. Miss Hildreth has a friend who can get a piece of velvet much more reasonably than at retail. Indeed, I have found that my material will cost just thirty-six dollars, and my two music-scholars will pay for that. I am to have a third, I believe, at fifteen dollars a quarter; and my four here are going on. Then I am likely to dispose of some Christmas work at Celia's studio. They are going to make a specialty of sales all December, and Celia asked me to send in some things."

"Where are you going to get time to do everything?" I asked in amaze.

"Well—Helen insists that I have more time than

most people. I think I know how to take advantage of every thing. Why, I am not as busy now as I was at aunt Carry's. Some people here in Athens would be dismayed at the rush in a fashionable woman's life. So you see," she says archly, "that I have not dropped out of society."

Pryor was certainly devoted to us, or to Miss Gaylord. We coaxed her to go on staying: she was such a pleasant, wholesome girl. Estradura came up, and enjoyed himself mightily. Pryor took both girls down to the theatre one evening. I was not sure whether it was a ruse to take out Eve, — whether, indeed, his admiration of Miss Gaylord was not a blind.

The young people in Athens were so in earnest to have a circle of pleasure, with Eve in it, that finally she helped them to form a Fortnight Club. It was to meet once in two weeks at different houses, with music, recitations or reading, tableaus or charades. The lady at whose house it met was responsible for the entertainment. Dancing was also to be allowed. Refreshments were discussed; and finally they settled upon sandwiches, one kind of cake, coffee or cream. The first one who overstepped the boundary was to be fined five dollars.

Eve asked them first to our house. A gentleman who was a member could invite a lady, a lady could bring an escort. The admission-fee was one dollar, and the members limited to twenty-five. Nineteen joined, and there were twenty-seven present. Besides, we had invited Celia Hildreth, and Helen, Frank, and Mr. Estradura. We had music, singing, and dancing; and Pryor gave us an excellent Irish recitation. At ten we were to end our pleasure, but they seemed very loth to go. So our evening was a success. Mr. and Mrs. Wharton had joined, and the second entertainment was to be at their house.

I must say that we heard quite often from uncle Lennard. Sometimes he was in excellent spirits, sometimes quite depressed. But he was so eager to have Eve tell him how we were prospering with the house. This autumn aunt Carry's last daughter was married, so her soul would be no more perplexed with that anxiety.

Our weeks absolutely flew by. Sadie Brooke made us two brief visits, and it seemed to me that she grew in beauty and in fun. We laughed unceasingly when she was with us. Mr. Palmer came over one evening, and his engagement did not seem to burden him with gravity.

"Isn't it funny," said Sadie, "that I should come over here, and find a lover? Oh! *do* you remember that first gay visit to the station? and what good times we had here last summer? O Eve Thurston!

you are a confirmed match-maker. There's Gordon Pryor going the way of all the rest after Helen. He was awfully sweet on you, and jealous as a pasha last summer. *Are* you going to remain single, and laugh at your friends, as you see them floundering in the marshes of matrimony after a will-o'-wisp?"

"No," returned Eve solemnly. "I'm going to be married myself, when Mr. Right comes along."

The blue velvet dress was lovely. It seemed as if Eve had never looked so beautiful in any thing save white. The cloth was dainty and jaunty, with its soft gray-fur trimming and muff. The club, the teas, the parties, and weddings came off in their succession. How Eve found time to paint, and embroider a little, and also to take an interest in church work, really puzzled me.

Eve went down and spent the day before Christmas with the Brookes. Sadie had five maids of honor, and was bewitching in silk and lace and flowers. I went down in the evening, and escorted my sister. The church was beautiful in its Christmas adornments, and the wedding like a picture. Mrs. Palmer returned home, changed her dress, and they took the night-train to Baltimore, where Mr. Palmer's mother and an invalid sister lived, and who had begged they should come there for a Christmas dinner.

I brought Eve out of all the splendor to our own little cottage. Joe had a bright fire in the grate, and some fragrant coffee on the stove. Was she so happy, so serenely content? O Eve, my darling! I wished that night I could be a millionnaire for your sake. You were worthy of the best.

"Do you know," said Eve gayly, as she sipped her coffee, "that I have a new scheme? I shall make your life a burden, Adam, but not about an apple. Here is Joe to do landscape-gardening. Here are you who can make a dry twig grow, if you stick it into the ground; and I can make bouquets and bargains. The world is sighing for flowers. It is smothered in them, and yet, like Alexander the Great, 'it sighs for new curiosities to conquer.' We must become florists. We must go into a real garden. That is a subject for you to dream out on this blessed Christmas Eve. It has come to me like an inspiration!"

We both stared at her, the eyes lustrous and merry, the mouth daintily sweet, the cheek like a sun-kissed peach.

Then she laughed. The clock was striking.

"Merry Christmas! Merry Christmas!" she cried, and kissed me, then turned to Joe with the sweetness of a sister.

"Miss Eve," he said huskily, "you know I would

do any thing for you. I'd go round the world. You have helped to make a man of me, and, by God's help, I mean never to shame your work. All my life long you will be to me an angel holding out your hand; and if ever I should be tempted to go wrong, I will come and cling to it."

Did we need to be any happier? I forgot I was a poor young fellow on forty-five dollars a month.

CHAPTER XIV

WINTER BLOOMS IN EDEN

Eve and I went to church Christmas morning. The sound of her voice in the hymns and carols will never vanish from my heart or brain, for it touched both. We were to go to the Corwins's for a two-o'clock dinner, and to the Morrisons's for the evening, as they were to have a grand Christmas-tree. Joe was to take Ruth Montgomery down to Northwood, to hear quite a famous singer.

Altogether it was delightful. Just afterward came a cold snap and a splendid snow-storm. Joe hired a pretty cutter, and made the most of the pleasure. Certainly, the lad had a good deal of shrewdness in turning a penny, as old country people say.

Some time after this, Helen came up again. It was quite evident that Pryor was in earnest. Eve took him in hand in an indescribable manner, as if she had been his sister. It was curious, but at first it almost seemed to me as if he had offered Eve an indignity. She spoke of it one evening when they had gone out sleigh-riding.

"Having loved you, I do not see how he *could* love any other woman!" I exclaimed.

"O you foolish Adam! Could it make me any happier if he went mourning and moody? He is young, vigorous, enthusiastic, and, I think, a bright, energetic young man; the kind of person to have a happy home, wife and children, and prosper with them all. He has improved very much in a year, and the Gaylord connection will be just the thing for him. Helen was very noble about it. She was afraid at first that I might have cared; and he was brave enough to tell her that he had liked me very much, and he desired us always to be friends. Helen will love him dearly, and that is just what he wants and needs. I am glad to have it so."

"I wonder if you like Estradura better?" I said slowly, watching her with eager eyes.

"Not that way. We are very good friends."

I remembered Pryor's jealousy of him, and smiled.

"All the girls will be married presently," I continued; and I know there was a suggestion of loneliness in my tone.

"Well,— Dr. Johnson advised us to keep our friendships in repair. I have begun with Celia Hildreth. And Mrs. Wilbur is to have a charming niece come from Georgia to spend next summer with her, and, of course, *she* will fall in love with me. My poor Adam, you will never stand any chance!"

She looked so utterly bewitching as she said this, with an assumption of melancholy, that I was compelled to laugh.

"Well, I am content to wait a while. Our league was for five years, you know; and by that time we may each have a thousand dollars."

"What a dismal tone! A thousand dollars, and two thousand dollars' worth of enjoyment."

Certainly we did not lack for the latter. Some one seemed to be coming all the time. Mrs. Harwood was over and staid a week. She was not feeling very well; had been "dissipating too much," she declared. She used to lie in the hammock, with some pillows, and a bright shawl thrown over her, reading, or watching the grate-fire. We had taken to cannel-coal now, and its bright blaze pleased her wonderfully. She used to watch Eve as she flitted about. I remember this winter she wore a beautiful deep red gown, with a good deal of white lace about her neck; and, somehow, it seemed to make her look taller and slenderer.

We talked and read a great deal about greenhouses, and plants of all kinds. Our little greenhouse had done very well. We had banked it up on the exposed sides, and had a double door. The roof was of double sashes; and we covered them with matting and old carpets, or boards, on very cold nights; but on days that were pleasant and sunny we let them have the light. The pansies bloomed abundantly in February. Sweet alyssum, mignonette, and some of the hardier red geraniums, kept in flower.

Our chickens were doing pretty well,— not as wonderfully as some we read about, but they gave us a profit; while our neighbors' sat on the roost, or huddled together in some sunny corner. We gave them hot cooked food every morning. It stood on the back of the stove, and we kept our fires all night. I put plenty of red pepper in it, and we gave them an abundance of warm water to drink. In their water-kettle I generally kept a few old bits of iron that were in a state of rust. For dinner they had a light meal of wheat, buckwheat, and oats, and at night a solid meal of corn. Twice a week a sheep's pluck, and pounded or ground bone and oyster-shells. During December new-laid eggs went up to fifty cents; in January they touched sixty; February still at fifty; in March, forty and thirty-five. All our refuse vegetables went to them; and we let them run at large, except when it rained, or the snow was deep. We had forty-nine in all. In November we had three hundred eggs, and sold to the amount of five dollars; in December, three hundred and sixty, and sold to eight dollars. January gave us five hundred, and we sold to fifteen dollars. February gave us six hundred, and we sold fourteen dollars' worth; March, six hundred and eighty, bringing us in ten dollars. So up to the first of April we had realized fifty-two dollars. Now quite a number of the hens wanted to sit; so we put them in the barn, and let them begin business. Among my Leghorns I had nine splendid layers; the other seven were very indifferent, not as good as some of the common fowls; and we decided now to use up a number of the poorest layers. Several of my Brahmas were immense, weighing seven and eight pounds.

So we decided that poultry would pay. Ours had been an experiment very well attended to, yet it had proved no great amount of trouble. I felt that I would like to select some industry that I could carry on with my business. We rather inclined to the flowers. Every year they would come more into use, and the demand increase. One needed larger grounds for poultry-raising. Still, I felt, that, if I pushed it, even on my limited scale, I should make several hundred dollars a year besides all we wanted to use in eggs or chickens.

During March I accomplished the painting of my house. Pryor and Mr. Corwin bought a large amount of a new kind of paint, highly recommended for its durability; and the quantity I needed cost me thirty-two dollars. I painted all my blinds, and most of the house, hiring only ten dollars' worth of work done.

I had managed to put by fifteen dollars a month of my wages, and at the end of the six months had seventy dollars; but I found that Eve had been saving up the interest as well. We had thirty dollars of the egg-money, and feed enough now to last the next two or three months. Of course, we paid the other hundred dollars, and were very happy over it. Now it was just an even two thousand, the face of the mortgage. After all, we had not pinched ourselves. Still, I knew well, and insisted, that I could have done very little without Eve's help; and she could not have helped if she had not earned money. True, we might have gone on living at the station or in three rooms, and rigorously denied ourselves all society. But the real question is, whether the possession of houses and lands, and money in the bank, is worth the sacrifice of returning to semi-barbarism; for a life of deprivation amounts to that. We prate of living simply, and find our tramps, who go back to first principles, and pay no house-rent, intolerable nuisances. As we lop off here and there, we drop down in personal neatness and the amenities of life.

Philip Gilbert Hammerton has discussed this point with much truth and fairness.

But the fact remained, — I wanted to get my fortune faster than at the rate of forty-five dollars a month. Hundreds would have jumped at my situation. You may estimate the great army of the unemployed when you count the number who apply for any position. Not a week through the autumn but some lads stopped to question me about my road, or any thing in the vicinity. They doubtless went to others. Some were nice, honest-looking young men: some bore traces of dissipation. I felt my own poverty and inability sorely at such times, though we did often give them a good meal.

Of course, there were higher salaries than mine; but these more fortunate ones were not going to step out for *my* sake. Then, I had tied myself to this place while I had my house, and the living here was pleasant; but I wanted to be making more than my monthly stipend when I was forty.

The past six months, Eve had earned one hundred and forty-six dollars by music-teaching, thirty-five by holiday work, and our boarders had brought us in one hundred and eighty-eight dollars.

Among other things, we discussed a hotel. Pryor was infusing his own enthusiasm into some of the sleepy Athenians, — rather, I should say, into some of the new-comers. The old families like the Montgomerys could hardly have been blown out of their rut by a charge of dynamite. Strangers were coming in to look at property. The paper-mills company built a nice dock. There was one wretched little lumber-pile connected with a coal and wood yard, kept by a Mr. Van Alen, who was a counterpart of Mr. Montgomery, and who always talked as if Pryor were an adventurer, and would soon bankrupt the whole town.

Meanwhile, Pryor sold the middle houses in his row, which were the prettiest, we all thought, and rented two more at eighteen dollars a month. The one at the upper end was the least desirable, as it had no southern exposure; but, when he offered this for fifteen dollars monthly, it was eagerly snapped up: and at May, the last one was rented. Corwin had bought some other lots, and decided to build again. If I only had a little money to join them in a venture!

The Randalls were delighted with these evidences of prosperity. Some of the old houses were repaired and painted, the streets cleared of stray bushes and blackberry-briers. Two more villas were sold.

Pryor had lent out some money on property at the foot of Jay Street, and now made its owner a fair offer, that was presently taken. With the backing of Mr. Wilbur, he at once opened a lumber-yard, to the consternation of Mr. Van Alen. His affair with Miss Gaylord had progressed to an engagement. Helen had already bespoken board with Eve as soon as the first of June. Mr. Estradura proposed to come on the first of July. Indeed, Eve had applications enough to fill a large house.

Joe, meanwhile, had bought a business-wagon at an auction sale. Pryor engaged him for general factotum, and moved his office up to Jay Street, making it that much nearer the station. He also purchased another horse, and now they had a good team.

If possible, spring looked lovelier than it had the year before. One cause, perhaps, was its lateness, and our gladness to welcome it. I had kept every thing in my garden quite up to the notch, and there really was little extra work to do. Two more trees were dead, — a pear and a peach, — but there were enough left. I must say here that I saved my pears very well until the middle of January, and we found them a great treat. Our grapes did not fare so well, and we used them up, but managed to have some Catawbas yet at Christmas. During April I had not counted on so much profit in eggs; for we were beginning to use them largely, and some hens were off duty. But one day a man, who had heard the fame of our hens, came for a dozen white Leghorn eggs for hatching. I picked out the finest I could find, and charged him fifty cents; though now they were down to thirty, and even twenty-five. The next day he came for some Brahmas, and engaged two dozen more Leghorns, making no demur at the price. In April we had seven hundred and ten eggs, to my great surprise. And quite often some one wanted eggs for setting, which kept up my profit wonderfully. I sold twenty dozen for ten dollars; ten dozen for three dollars and sixty cents. We never stinted ourselves, and we were very fond of them.

We discussed seriously the plan of finishing our extra rooms up-stairs. I purchased some lath, and hired a man by the day, helping him considerably. A mason came and put on the scratch-coat, following it shortly after by a smooth coat of brown. This I painted when it was dry, and put up some pretty bordering. One room was large, and very nice; the other fair. After painting the floors, I found the whole cost to be not quite fifteen dollars. We decided to make a little change in the furniture; bought new matting for our dining-room, a new stair-carpet, and moved the others up-stairs; purchased a pretty single bedstead for one of the smaller rooms; and, with various odds and ends, furnished the small one up-stairs, and bought a new set entire for the larger one, which was to belong to Eve when the house overflowed.

Athens presented such a bright business aspect that it was quite inspiriting. Another incident occurred to increase its prosperity; though it was, in part, due to the energy of the towns above us. We were allowed four more trains daily, from seven to nine in the morning, and from four to six in the afternoon. Every room in Mrs. Ten Eyck's house was engaged by the middle of May, and one or two others ventured to open their houses.

And now occurred an odd circumstance that did depress me at first, and seem to extinguish one of my hopes. Just north of the station, there was a large tract of ground, belonging to some heirs, that had lain unimproved for years. It fronted on Rutherford Avenue, and ran down to the river's edge. Myrtle Avenue had been laid out, and two cross-streets, but no improvements made. It sloped gradually, and had a lovely sunny exposure. Here and there a cherry or an old apple tree appeared, blossoming profusely, but despoiled of their fruit by the boys.

Suddenly Athens was startled by more prospective improvements. The old Teall property was divided among six heirs. Two of them, living at a distance, placed their share at once in Mr. Pryor's hands for sale. One — a Mr. James Teall — had his surveyed, and staked off, and talked of building two handsome villas. A Miss Teall had married a gardener and florist, a Mr. Riker; and he announced his intentions of beginning gardening on a large scale. They hired a cottage in the vicinity, and started work at once, ploughing, laying out, planning for greenhouses, planting vegetables, setting out shrubs and plants.

I had not supposed that I could try such an experiment on my own place. Still, I meant to enlarge my flower-house considerably another year. But that some one else should come, armed with my idea, half broke my heart. To be sure, there were other places besides Athens; and occasionally one heard of a plant for sale, already established. I did not yield to my despondency very long, for Eve looked at it in quite another light.

"Adam," she said, "I think we may be able to learn a good deal, in case we want to take up such a business. We will watch what this Mr. Riker does, and make notes of all the ways and whys. I do think, if one could come to understand it, it would be a profitable business; and I know now, if there was a prospect, Mrs. Harwood would come forward with assistance readily enough. So we will both keep our eyes open, and learn all we can. What a lucky happening for us!"

That cheered me immensely. My fears looked so small and foolish, that I would not confess them.

Mr. Riker's ground had a frontage of five hundred

feet on both Rutherford and Myrtle Avenues. Linden Street was the first beyond Jay, and ran from the river up to the top of the hill. The next street was merely a wagon-road. The square gave him about five acres, the other six heirs had the same. Mr. Teall's property came next to this. I almost looked at the young fellow with envy, when by a lucky stroke, as one might say, he came into possession of such a beautiful plot of ground.

His wife, judging from appearances, was five or six years the elder. He might have been twenty-five, not older. Following out Eve's hint, I walked over one day to make a friendly call, as he had been in the station several times.

It seemed to me that he was undertaking too much; that his garden-truck would be in the market too late for decent prices; and that he had more on his hands than could be well attended to, unless he hired a great deal of help. But he seemed ambitious, confident, and was going to work with tremendous energy. He knew all about flowers and shrubs and soils, and quite confused me with his authoritative manner.

Mr. Wilbur came up with his wife, and planned some finishing and furnishing for the house. The family were to move the last of May, leaving the two boys to board through the week, and attend their school for five weeks longer. Mr. Montgomery looked them up a cow; Joe found them a "man," — a stout young fellow of nineteen, who had been working on a stock-farm. The horse and carriage were sent up, and it looked quite homelike at our neighbors'.

Mrs. Wilbur had not changed in the slightest degree, and was just as ready to monopolize Eve. The Palmers were coming for a week or so, as soon as matters were really settled. Sadie made the most enchanting of wives; and Bertha had a young man, a special one. Soon all the gay crowd would settle themselves to other lives.

I insisted that Eve should give up her music-teaching in New York through the summer, and she readily acquiesced. She had five pupils now at Athens. Miss Gaylord was to have our largest guest-chamber; Estradura was to take the two small ones, using one for a dressing and sitting room. When Miss Hildreth arrived, she was to share Eve's chamber. Joe and I took the smaller rooms above. Letty, who was to stay with us through the summer, went home at night. Helen insisted, that, when there came occasional guests, she should be allowed to take Eve's sky-parlor. We made a delightful family, with just enough variety to keep us all fresh and full of zest.

My garden did nicely; though I missed Joe out of the paths, and everywhere, and sometimes weeds rioted. After having my land ploughed, I did the work myself, but I put more ground in corn. This year I did not have to be economical in fertilizers.

Now, as our hens ceased to lay, we culled out the least desirable, and reduced the stock; but we decided not to raise more than a hundred chicks. This spring we did not have quite such splendid luck, but ours was better than many others. Out of one hundred and twenty eggs we had ninety-five chickens, and out of those lost five. I parted out the young cockerels, and fed them with fat-producing foods, for I knew we should use most of them.

There had grown up a very nice, friendly feeling between our immediate neighbors and ourselves. Even Mr. Montgomery did not sneer at my garden, nor predict dire misfortunes. One daughter was married, and went away from home. Dan began to see, not only the hopelessness, but the ridiculousness, of his hanging around after Eve, and devoted himself to a daughter of Athens, though I doubt if he immortalized her in a poem.

And Joe — our dear, foolish, ambitious, earnest Joe — confessed to Eve that he had asked Ruth to marry him, and she had promised.

"We are to be engaged a year," he explained.

"We want to get a little something together. I suppose I ought to wait until I earn my eight hundred dollars; but I was telling Ruth what you said, Miss Eve, and she thinks we will try it together. You see, I've a horse and wagon; and now I'm going to give you all the parcel-money to keep. And I want to pay four dollars a week for my board hereafter; but I shall do the little chores, and ease up Adam all the same. You know, I never can pay you for making a man of me. Do you know, Miss Eve, it seems like a horrid dream, — all those hateful, shameful months when I drank, and went in rags? I do not even want to tell Ruth, I am so ashamed of it. I did say, that, for a year or two, I had not been real steady. Oh! what angel induced you both to pluck me out of the fire?"

"You're not to scold Joe," Eve said to me after this talk, "nor read him any homilies, nor consider it an unwise step. Ruth will make him a lovely wife; and it will be such a delight to have some one of his very own, to have a home to improve and beautify. They will be just like two children; and he will help her sweep the house, and wash dishes, in order for her to have leisure to enjoy him. Adam, it was worth coming to Athens, just to save Joe."

It was some time before Joe had the courage to say any thing to me on the subject, though I am quite sure he counted on my knowledge of it. Certainly Joe was a lad of whom one need not feel ashamed. He and Pryor were great chums, and Joe was ambitious to learn every thing that came in his way.

"It would be odd if, twenty years from this time, Joe Crawford should be among the influential and highly respected citizens of Athens, and hearing himself spoken of as assemblyman after having held minor offices," I said laughingly.

"He may do that before twenty years."

Meanwhile our family settled itself under the roof-tree; and our happiness reached its summit one cold, stormy evening in June when we had a fire in the grate. We certainly looked Oriental, disported in hammocks, lounges, and easy-chairs. Mr. and Mrs. Wilbur, Mr. and Mrs. Palmer, were over; and Eve played all kinds of soft, suggestive music in the next room. It seemed wrong and wicked for the moments to fly on the wings of the winds, and bring us midnight.

Mrs. Harwood came over now and then of a lovely day, and every time it seemed harder for her to leave my sister.

"Is Adam never going to get married?" she asked one day. "There are so many nice girls about here, and many a one with money would be proud to take him. I will hunt him up a wife myself. Then you and I will take a long tour away somewhere, and let the young couple 'gang their ain gait.'"

Could I ever be in just the position to make marriage desirable? Had I lost the daring faith of early youth that rendered so many dreams possible? Certainly I looked more at the realities of life, — counted the cost, as one may say.

CHAPTER XV

AND YET ANOTHER

AFTER that June storm, it was the perfection of summer weather, of riotous bloom, of such waves of greenery that the earth seemed like an emerald sea. Such skies of glory, such wafts of sweetness, such heavenly calms, when, for a few moments, the toil and moil seemed to stop. A country life amid such surroundings often fills one's mind with vague wonders concerning the other world and the next life. If the best of this is but a type and shadow, what will the glory of that prove?

I stood and watched the train winding along. The hills over opposite, with here and there a house standing out; the river in the interstices of the trees; the birds with their sweet, entreating, early-evening songs, quite different, if you will observe, from the jocund morning carols, — moved me inexpressibly. Are these presentiments? I had a curious feeling that something was to happen that would alter my life and that of Eve, — that in some strange way I should always be able to connect it with this hour and the song of the wood-thrush.

There was a shriek, and the train halted. No one was going up from Athens. A number stepped out, nodding, or giving pleasant greeting, then the one I was watching for.

Her veil was down. When the noise and fuss sped off to the distance, I looked closely at her. She had been crying. Even now her lips were all in a quiver of emotion.

"Miss Hildreth"—

"Walk a little way!" she entreated. "O Mr. Thurston! my heart seems broken. Even now, to-day, my brother may be dead!"

"Your brother!" I think she loved him with a greater passion and fervor than Eve loved me.

"He has been very ill again. He had the fever the first year he was there, but then I knew nothing of it until all the danger was past. Now they say he must come home,— if he has strength to bear the journey; but I am sorely afraid. I am sure I have not heard the worst."

"No," I replied, with a poor attempt at comfort, "do not think that way. From whom did you hear?"

"He asked a friend to write. His last letter was curiously brief and disconnected, but he said he was in great haste. It seems he was improving:

then he had a relapse. A sea-voyage will be the only thing. But if he should die at sea! O Laurie! Laurie! If I never see you again, how can I live! What will life be without you?"

It was such a heart-rending cry. I felt so helpless and blundering. I should like to have gathered her in my arms, and let her cry on my shoulder as Eve did in her great sorrow. But I must leave her here and now, for I was required at the station.

"Go to my sister," I pleaded. "No one can comfort you so tenderly."

I stopped, and she paused also. "I must return," I began confusedly.

"Yes, yes. Thank you for your sympathy."

She went on so wearily! I kept looking back until I knew I had not a second to lose, and found two very angry people hammering on the ticket-window. However, they were served in time. Under the new arrangement, I could not leave until after six. How long and leaden the moments seemed! What inane questions people asked! Then Joe came in sight, bright and cheery. There were several parcels to be taken, and he was all vivacity over some of Pryor's ideas.

When I went home, Miss Hildreth was in Eve's room, and did not come down to dinner. And in the evening she had a wretched headache.

"I am afraid it *is* very bad, Adam," said my sister. "He has been ill so much longer than she has known of, and his friend does not seem hopeful. Sending him thus seems a desperate chance. And her horror is, lest he shall die at sea. She cannot change any thing: she can do nothing but wait in this awful suspense. And she loves him so dearly!"

There were tears in Eve's tender eyes. I kissed her with a passionate fervor. And we could do nothing for the other poor girl!

She went down to New York the next day, but she looked like some wandering ghost. I think I never saw such wordless pathos in eyes as that in hers.

Every one tried to rouse her hopes. No one could hurry the steamer. No one could lighten that dreary waiting.

Somehow we could not be gay, though the young people were making merry with summer pleasures. Their Fortnight Club had been a success, and was still in existence. I should have stated, that, early in May, we did have one grand frolic at the station, up-stairs. It was not so elegant; but they danced to their heart's content, with the inspiriting "viol and flute." The dressing-room was my office. The table was set in the smaller room off the ball-room, and the gentlemen were generous with refreshments. But it had been gay and joyous enough.

Now they were planning a sail up the river, and a picnic at a very beautiful and romantic place. Eve had been training them to do without her.

The days went on. There were two or three pictures to finish, a few lessons in a last course to give; and Miss Hildreth went about her task under the strain of compulsion.

"But it *is* best," she said. "I should craze myself with grief, if I had to keep still."

The steamer came in. Estradura, who was kind and gentle as a woman, went down with her. I wanted to go; but fate ruled me out, since it was not necessary. There was no person answering that description, but it was a comfort that Hildreth's name was not in the passenger-list. The mails had been sent up to the office.

There was a brief note. They had not been able to complete the arrangements in time. Mr. Hildreth was no worse, but a little weaker, perhaps. He would reach New York, positively, in the next steamer.

"If he lives that long," was Miss Hildreth's dreary comment.

Curiously enough, we go on, and take a certain interest in the every-day matters of life, even when one's mind seems wholly pre-occupied with some great pain or anxiety. Miss Hildreth's strain pervaded us all. Mrs. Wilbur's niece, a Miss Kate Leverne, came; and we found her a bright, vivacious girl. There were many other delights; but we all walked softly, as it were, as one does when there is a death in the house.

At length this day came around. Eve and Helen were going down to the city, and Mr. Pryor had some business that required attention. I saw them off. Then I strolled up to Riker's, and watched the progress being made. They were laying foundations for two greenhouses on Linden Street. We had a talk about methods and soils and fertilizers for different kinds of flowers, temperature, and appearance. The young fellow had a great deal of pride in his knowledge, — I might say vanity, — and was very ready to display it.

"It would not be a bad idea to come to school here," I thought to myself. The amusing part was the disdain with which he treated amateur attempts. I modestly spoke of some of the things I had succeeded with.

"Yes, that's all well enough," he rejoined, "when you are not setting out to make money. That is the theory of fancy or pleasure gardening, but the real thing is very different."

IN A GARDEN

"You *do* consider it a profitable business?"

"Profitable!" There was a superb touch of scorn in his voice. "Why, I could mention a dozen men I know, who are making fortunes, and who, ten or twelve years ago, hardly had a thousand dollars. But they were not amateurs. They served a regular apprenticeship at the business."

I went up to dinner, and took a look at my own garden. I had some magnificent roses, young ones from last summer's cuttings, and others from divided roots. After all, was not the true meaning of practical knowledge, constant practice?

One thing Riker said that rather disheartened me, as applied to myself.

"I do not know any place that has the chances of this. From Northwood up to Truro, there is not a single greenhouse or nursery. I shall get the start of everybody with mine, you see."

At two there came a telegram from Eve, that simply said, — "Steamer in; all right."

Then I knew Lawrence Hildreth had reached New York alive. How strange we should all take such an interest in a person we had never seen.

At five Eve returned home. We went into the little office.

"Helen and Pryor are going to the theatre this evening," she announced. "Celia and her brother are at a hotel. I am so glad for her sake that he reached home alive! And, O Adam! are we to be in everybody's sorrows and joys?"

"We cannot help sympathizing with her."

That sounded almost indifferent. I did not dare say all that was in my soul. I was puzzled and confused with my own emotions.

Eve did not appear to remark this, or she was too intent upon her own thoughts, as she continued, —

"We all went to the hotel. Celia explained everybody and every thing beautifully; and the queer part was, that Mr. Hildreth proposed to be taken home where Celia was staying. She had written so much about us, that, you see, he feels quite as if we were old friends. Well, it put such an odd complexion on that matter! Of course he expects to get well, but it doesn't look so now. I never saw such a skeleton; but he has beautiful dark blue eyes, like, and yet unlike, Celia's; and there is something in his voice that goes to your heart. After a while it seemed to get settled. Helen was so good. She proposed she should go up-stairs, and give up her room: she is going to Asbury Park presently, and will make several little visits. And now, Adam, shall we open our house to the lame and the halt and the blind?" and Eve laughs, with tears in her eyes and in her voice. "I can see how pleasant it will be for Celia, and how dreadful it would be among strangers if he — if any thing happened to him." — How we always do pause and falter over that terrible word death! — "What shall we do?"

"Why, you have already decided the case in your mind," I replied, with a smile.

"But you" —

"We will consider Celia, and do as we would like some one to do to us," I said gravely.

"O Adam! you are so generous" —

"It is you who are always thinking of everybody."

"Well, we won't quarrel about our virtues," says Eve, with some of her olden gayety. "You know, after all, it is not quite as if the Hildreths were poor, and would depend upon us alone. We have only to be company, and encourage and keep Celia hopeful, and all that. We did not count on being as gay as we were last summer — and it is so lovely at Athens! It seems as if any one might get well here. Mr. Wilbur considers the air very fine and invigorating; and what with the hills in their changing beauty, and the soft-flowing river poetic enough for any one, and the drives winding about in veritable fairyland" —

"And the garden, and the chickens, and the porch" —

"And roses and hammocks and lazy-chairs and my good temper."

We both laugh there.

"Then, you do not so much mind if we have a hospital?"

"It may be a good training-school," I reply.

Merry as we made ourselves, I think we had some unconfessed misgivings of soul. What if the gray wing of grief and parting should be folded over our pretty home? For Celia's sake — that settled it.

Eve went down again the next day. Mr. Hildreth was extremely weak, — indeed, had not sat up five minutes since reaching the hotel. But he was so glad and thankful to be at home, as he called it. Eve detailed all the plan to Celia, who first made a faint protest.

"You are so good to render it possible! Mrs. Palmer said that day on the boat you were the 'dearest and sweetest girl in the whole world,' and I am sure it is true. But I am afraid we shall make you too much trouble. Still, you must believe nothing would be so delightful to me."

"It is all settled, then. As soon as your brother can stand the journey, you are to come. And you are not to think of the trouble."

Eve had taken a great bunch of fragrant roses that the sick man enjoyed wonderfully.

The day following we had no word, but early the next morning a note. There were no worse symptoms, only Lawrence was very restless, and did not seem to improve as they had hoped.

After that we heard every day. Pryor, Miss Gaylord, or Eve went down frequently. After a fortnight they decided to remove him. He would gain a little for a day or two, and then slip back. Celia was quite confident he would improve more rapidly at Athens.

I went down that day. A carriage brought him to the ferry, where Eve and I met them. Certainly Lawrence Hildreth did not look promising. Thinner he could not well be. His breath came in gasps, his eyes were sunken, his lips pinched and colorless; but there was a curious strength to his voice, a certain something that assured you he had not given up hope.

Joe drove him up from the station; and we both carried him up-stairs, he was so exhausted. Eve and Helen had arranged the room like a little bower, and brought up one of the reclining-chairs; but Hildreth begged to go straight to bed.

"You are all so kind, that I should be the most ungrateful fellow in the world if I did not get well now!" he exclaimed with a wan smile. "I never can repay you."

We were especially glad to have Celia back, as Miss Gaylord was going away for two weeks. Mrs. Wilbur and Miss Laverne were to spend some ten days or so at Saratoga with the Palmers. Mrs. Harwood had gone out to Detroit to visit the only sister she had living; and she would have taken Eve, if our dear housekeeper could have been spared. I *did* protest against her staying at home all summer; but she seemed so busy and cheerful, and kept so bright and rosy, that one could not banish her on the score of health.

We were both deeply engrossed in floriculture. We had been parting and slipping roses until we really had what might be called a rose-garden. From one well-known rose-grower I had purchased several beautiful varieties, and gleaned many useful hints from his catalogue, as well as from several of the rural papers we took. Every thing useful, Eve cut out, and pasted in her scrap-book. I sometimes felt as if, in spite of Mr. Riker, I should put up a real greenhouse. Joe and I enlarged ours, for I meant to put in a good many more plants. Pansies I knew I could raise successfully.

My vegetables did fairly well. Potatoes and corn yielded bountifully. Our cherries this season had not been so much of a success, on account of a storm; but prices had been higher, and the demand greater.

We had sold to the amount of five dollars' worth ; and Eve had disposed of some canned ones for the sum of two dollars and a half. My currants had been splendid. The worms had bothered me some ; but what with an infusion of quassia and dry ashes thrown up on the underside of the leaves, I had kept them in check. Mr. Riker rather smiled over my amateur efforts, but did say he had never seen such thrifty currants. From them we had received seven dollars and a half, besides all we wanted to use. To a hotel up above us, I had sent raspberries daily ; and though they were cheap, still my account of eleven dollars looked pretty fair. I had planted early tomatoes and cucumbers under cold-frames, and made a fair success of the first, and an excellent one of the second. Tomatoes I sold only while prices were high. Of course, mine were in small quantities, and I disposed of them to special customers. They brought me in five dollars and a half. We took our chance with them after prices came down. The first cucumbers I sold for seventy cents a dozen. For some reason, — care and study of soil, I think, — mine were exceptionally fine and growthy. They brought me in twelve dollars and ten cents. Our harvest apple was delightful : our peaches would do well, and the blackberries were still to hear from. So far we had taken in forty-three dollars and fifty cents, and seven dollars from chickens sold. I had planted hills of corn among some of my early vegetables, and by the time they were done with, the corn had a good start. Certainly, I improved my ground. I kept it rich and soft, working it frequently. I wanted to try my utmost in order to have a fair understanding of the possibilities of the ground. Mr. Riker's coming had spurred me to my best efforts. I think I made gardening more profitable than he did. His work was spread over too much surface. Two acres well cultivated would have given a better result. All his vegetables were too late for decent prices. Some he allowed to go to seed, but even in this he was not very successful. He progressed very well with his greenhouses: indeed, I thought this part of the business displayed more real capacity than any other.

After about a week, Mr. Hildreth began to show signs of improvement. Up to this period, one of the troubles had been utter lack of appetite. Eve and Celia concocted dainty dishes, and the fruit was especially grateful to him. Celia brightened up wonderfully, and the delicate tints came back to her soft cheeks. Mr. Estradura paid the invalid a visit nearly every evening, as Hildreth was a fluent talker in both French and Spanish.

"When I can come down-stairs," poor Hildreth would say longingly, as we talked of pleasures.

But we were not doleful. Indeed, Athens was becoming quite a lively place. There was a stir and life among the young people, a number of engagements, and several marriages. Pryor's lumber-yard was an undoubted success, and now he resolved to add a coal-shed.

"I shall take possession of Joe Crawford," he said to me. "He is going to make a splendid business-manager. Just look at the way he has worked up this parcel business, and carrying passengers and old ladies to and fro. Why, there has not been a young fellow, nor an old fellow, with vim enough to start the thing. But he is worth more than that brings him in, and he wants a special business training. I propose he shall sell out that scheme, and cast in his lot with me. After a little, I will take him in as a partner. I shall be married during the autumn or winter, and we have decided to live right along here. Helen likes it, and she loves Eve as a sister. Is she going to marry that Cuban, Thurston?"

"No," I returned. "She is not going to marry any one just yet."

"I should hate to have her. Oh, you needn't think I am going to keep watch and ward of her, like the desperate hero of a seaside novel! I love her dearly, and Helen knows it, but it is an honorable regard; and any man is the better for knowing and admiring your sister. I want her to stay here at Athens, where we can all see her; and I should hate any man who took her away. But if you want to glower at anybody, Ad, glower at Joe: he's utterly smashed on her, in spite of Miss Montgomery."

We both laughed at that.

Then he laid his business-plans before me. He could afford Joe a salary of fifteen dollars a week to begin with, — ten dollars to be taken up weekly, and the rest to remain. At the end of the first year Joe's money should begin to draw a certain percentage of the profits, that being turned over as well.

"I have figured it all out. At the end of three years, if all goes well with us, Joe shall be a partner. It is better than taking him in now, for he will see the value and the necessity of saving and getting ahead. And he is so honest, so trusty, so good-tempered. I wouldn't give him for half a dozen of the young fellows about here, though I have had two offers of partners already;" and he laughed.

"You are very good to him," I said, in some amazement, wondering if *I* would not have considered such an offer. But I could see Joe's fitness for the place, and I resolved not to envy him his good fortune. *Was* there any thing coming to me in the wide future?

Joe was astounded at first, and then wild with

delight. He rushed out presently, and went to hilling up some corn.

"That is just like him," said Eve, with a smile of merriment. "When Joe has any special good fortune, he has a sudden rush of gratitude, and always goes out in the garden to give thanks."

Joe was quite shrewd about his other business.

"I could get a young lad to do this, and to attend to office-chores, and work in the yard. But if any one wants to give me a fair price for it, he may have it."

The Wilburs returned, and Mr. and Mrs. Palmer were to spend the remainder of August with them. Bertha Brooke was to be married in October. Helen's marriage would leave Eve the only unmarried one of the gay company who had held carnival at our house hardly more than a year previous.

The 10th of August, Lawrence Hildreth ventured down-stairs. It was a very warm day; but our club-room, as Pryor called the pretty hall, was lovely and cool. Somehow we had taken the new-comer to our hearts, partly from pity and sympathy, partly from a certain admiration of his patient sweetness. He longed to get well with his whole soul. He was not tired of life, though, so far, it had given him some keen disappointments, and he had not reached his ambitious aims. Still, there was a good deal of the doing and daring left in him, and he made no useless moans: indeed, he had a most amusing strand of humor, of that quiet, irresistible sort. He and Eve kept up a curiously gay atmosphere. In some respects the similarity struck me as being quite remarkable.

We had a festival dinner to celebrate the event, asking in the Wilburs and the Palmers; and, Mr. Bradford happening up, we kept him to the feast. Helen had returned the day before, but was to leave us shortly, on another tour. We had a delightful time. Joe was so good that he ran down for the trains, and I had two hours of uninterrupted enjoyment. Hildreth had to return to his couch; but he joined in the feast of reason and flow of soul, — food and laughter. We had some fruits from our garden, flowers in abundance, and happy hearts that were not to be weighed or measured, but overflowed at every bright thought.

Hildreth was not so well the next day, and, for the first time, rather depressed. We had Dr. Rand, one of the Athenian physicians, but he had said very little about the case.

Celia asked me to call him in that morning. I stopped long enough to make several inquiries.

"It will be a long while before Mr. Hildreth recovers his strength, — if, indeed, he ever does, — but there is no imminent danger of his dying. He will find himself fluctuating a good deal when he begins to test his vitality, and his greatest aids will be patience and cheerfulness. Do not allow him to get discouraged. I shall have to talk to your sister about this;" and Dr. Rand smiled.

CHAPTER XVI

SOME IMPORTANT QUESTIONS

On the whole, we could see, by the end of August, that Hildreth had made a great improvement. He was out every day. If the girls could not go, Joe was always ready. He came down to his meals. He sat on the porch, or idled in the hammock, and sometimes picked out a few tunes on the piano. He evinced a wonderful interest in the flower-garden: indeed, we found we were all flower-mad together. Eve and Hildreth talked it over *pro* and *con*. He read her wise scraps of information, books and papers; and I do believe we all began to envy Mr. Riker his opportunity.

"You could have some nice greenhouses here," Hildreth said; "and since there is so much profit in cut-flowers, and they are generally sold at a distance, the rivalry would be no great matter. All the same, I should like to own Riker's plot of ground."

Just here an adventure happened to Eve. Mrs. Harwood sent her an excursion ticket to Niagara. She was to be put on the train in New York on the evening of the 2d of September, and would find her friend waiting for her at her journey's end, and they would have a little visit together.

"How can I go?" cried Eve in dismay.

"Celia and I can keep house," said Helen. "You have had no vacation, and you must not miss such a pleasure: besides, you could not well disappoint Mrs. Harwood."

"No," replied Eve thoughtfully.

An hour later, Sadie Palmer strolled over, and heard the news. Mrs. Wilbur declared that the day was lonely when nothing happened at our house to stir one up.

"I have half a mind to go myself," Sadie announced. "We were talking of a journey off somewhere. The sweets of Hymettus are occasionally cloying, and Mount Ida loses its charm. Let us away to fresh fields, — the Nile and the pyramids."

"So that is the complexion you put upon it?" said Hildreth. "But I give you fair warning, that, if you lose or otherwise make away with Miss Thurston, you had better plunge into the interior of Africa at once."

"Hear him, ye winds and waters," chanted Sadie in operatic style; and they had a rather brilliant war of words.

"I wish you would resolve to go," Eve said presently, coming out of a brown study.

That was the way the matter was settled. We bade Eve a reluctant good-by, still we were very glad for her to have the pleasure. Helen and Celia and Letty, and I might add Joe, who insisted on having a hand in every thing, kept house in a delightful and harmonious manner; and we had company every evening. But we missed Eve more than I would have thought possible. Celia, Lawrence, and I talked of her continually, or at least in snatches, and counted the days. But, alas! They came to New York, and then rushed off to Newport; and it was a full fortnight before we saw our darling. How could we ever part with her again!

Mrs. Harwood came over with her. Certainly, it would be necessary to enlarge our borders if we continued to keep a hotel. But somehow we distributed around, and were happy.

We paid our interest, but this time nothing on our principal. We had not quite an even hundred; and Mrs. Harwood insisted that we should not pinch ourselves, and that Eve must not wear herself with music-teaching in addition to her other cares. Lawrence Hildreth was wonderfully taken with our bright old lady.

I was amused with the sharpness with which she studied Estradura, as if she had some suspicions concerning Eve in the matter. There had been times when I had felt that only Eve's rare womanly wisdom had kept him on the safe side of friendship. However, an incident occurred which was to take him quite out of our lives for several years. The house he was with wished to send him abroad.

He had enjoyed his stay with us on account of the pleasant, homelike feeling, the ease and freedom, the reading, music, and merry chats. Then, he was extravagantly fond of the country and its various belongings, and at the last he left us with a very real sorrow.

Meanwhile the Hildreths were considering their future. A physician had advised Lawrence to go South for the winter, and he consulted Dr. Rand on the matter.

"I should like a breath of real invigorating air, such as comes in October. I am tired of a soft, warm atmosphere; and I have a great inclination to trust myself here for the present. But I do wish, above all things, to get strong enough to be of some use in the world."

"Then stay here," answered Dr. Rand. "I know of few healthier places. Should the winter prove exceptionally cold, it might be wiser to try a warmer clime; but I think we shall be able to brace you up successfully. However, at the first note of danger, I will promise to give you warning."

It was decided then that both of them would go on with us through the winter. Celia was to have one of the up-stairs' rooms for a studio, and paint at home part of the time, staying in New York on certain days. Her aunt was desirous of trying Florida, so she could have no compunctions about leaving her.

And now a new difficulty met us. Our admirable Letty had an excellent opportunity to go to work with a dressmaker at wages which were really tempting. It would have been unfair to keep her from what was evidently her best interests. But how could we supply her place?

"For," said Eve, "I do not feel like taking in an ordinary servant to waste and destroy my small patrimony. I think we will have to wait, and see what Providence sends us."

"A course of housework might be good for me," suggested Hildreth. "I hear such wonderful stories of Joe and Adam, that I am quite ashamed of my limited acquirements. And, you see, presently Celia and I might try your experiment — only she would earn the money while I kept the house."

The long, lank figure, sweeping, dusting, and cooking, was irresistibly funny to us all.

I found, when I made up my farm accounts, that I had done remarkably well. With the blackberries, pears, and peaches, my receipts had swelled to sixty-three dollars and seventy cents, leaving me the sixty clear profit. We had gone on selling some eggs, averaging enough every month to pay for our feed, and a little over; and now, to our surprise, we had eighty nice fowls, pullets and hens. Hildreth was much interested in them. The question at present seemed to be whether we should turn poultry-fanciers or florists.

This autumn the boarders who had by accident stumbled upon Athens, found so many charms that they lingered on; and a party of artists, well known to Miss Hildreth, took the spare rooms at Mrs. Ten Eyck's for the month of October, which proved exceptionally beautiful. Of course our house was invaded, and we did have some wonderfully enjoyable evenings, to say nothing of rambles and drives. Suddenly it seemed Hildreth made rapid strides in improvement. He took up gardening with a vim, and I found my occupation well-nigh gone. Our greenhouse assumed quite business-like proportions. We put in slips of roses, young and tender plants, and hardy flowers that we knew would bloom for a long while without fire, and live all winter. Then he began to cultivate young Riker.

Meanwhile, Joe's affairs progressed finely. He went to his new business; though nothing was said, outside of ourselves, about the partnership. The "boy" Joe found without any difficulty, and I was amused at the shrewdness with which Joe trained him. As Pryor said, there was the making of an excellent business manager in Joe.

He began to look mature and manly. The Montgomerys were very proud of him. Through the summer, another daughter had married; and Ruth wore a pretty, satisfied look, that was quite bewitching; while, it seemed to me, she adored Eve more fondly than ever. And presently they had a plan to lay before my sister. There was no further need of waiting for their marriage. They could keep house on ten dollars a week, they were quite sure; but the method they preferred from now until spring, was that Joe should remain, and Ruth come and keep house for us, making herself ready, meanwhile, for her own essay in the spring.

Such a novel idea took Eve quite by surprise at first.

"I should so like to live a while with you," Ruth explained. "You have such a pretty way of doing every thing, and Joe is used to it all. Mother would as lief have us home, but I'm afraid Joe wouldn't be satisfied; and father's ideas, about nearly every thing, are so different. And I know we should be real happy," she finished with a wistful cadence.

Eve debated within herself, and then with me.

"There would be some very nice points about such an arrangement," she admitted presently. "It is friendly, and I like them both. I hardly know how we can give up Joe. He seems just like a younger brother that we have cared for and felt anxious about, and whose prosperity is dear to us. I should enjoy their happiness. Our home-keeping is getting to be such an old, old story! Why, I am quite a veteran!" and she laughs with an infectious gayety.

"I do not think Joe would be comfortable under Mr. Montgomery's very depressing views of what you can do in this world," I said. "I should miss him very much. And then, if the Hildreths should go away presently"—

"Yes: I should find Ruth and Joe quite a delight then," Eve answered vivaciously; "and, though one ought not always consider economy, I do believe I should find it better, and at a less cost."

Out of my garden-money we paid the taxes, and the few repairs it had been necessary to make. We had our coal put in,—an abundance of it; and coal was thirty cents a ton lower than last year. Eve had some new attire; and we found that we were able, after all, to attack the next thousand dollars, so we paid one hundred. Miss Brooke was married, and we both went to the wedding. Sadie had gone to housekeeping up near the Park, and insisted Eve should spend two solid weeks with her when "fun" really commenced.

Pryor was to be married the day before Thanksgiving, in church, at two in the afternoon, and go to Washington. If our house had not been full, I know he would have proposed boarding with us: in fact, I think he felt annoyed because Hildreth was there.

"I certainly should be tired of having such a skeleton around!" he exclaimed rather disdainfully one day.

But I never enjoyed an autumn more. Now and then we drove out together — Hildreth was such a wonderfully companionable man. He had seen so much; and he had an admirable memory, vivid, compact; and his descriptive powers were fine; his eyes keen; his love of beauty deep, ingrained. What a wealth of asters and golden-rod! what gorgeous sumach! what shades in the fields of green to brown! what magnificent ripening of the leaves! Every beautiful tree impressed itself upon his memory.

There was another pleasure we shared, — boating. The banks of the river were a series of pictures. We used to float idly, drinking in the alluring sweetness of air, the golden-freighted ripeness of the summer, that still lingered as if loth to leave us.

Idle leaves fluttered from some overhanging trees, and drifted down; birds called from shore to shore; insects hummed and droned sleepily. I used to like to hear him talk of the marvels of Brazilian forests at such times; and yet he admitted that he always longed for his native clime.

I think I sympathized with Hildreth's disappointment in his life-plans. He had set out to make a fortune. During his first year, he had been ill a long while with a fever. Then part of their plans had miscarried at a loss; but prosperity seemed within his grasp, when the second illness attacked him; and he had stubbornly resolved not to give in until, during a dangerous relapse, his physician told him that his only hope for life was in leaving the country at once. His business was in the hands of his partner, to be wound up, or disposed of; and though he would realize considerable, it was far short of the limit he had set for himself.

"Still," he admitted, "I believe I shall be content. It seems to me I have had more real delight since my return, wretched as my health has been, than in the years of my desperate chase after fortune. If Celia and I can be as happy as you and your sister!"

So we talked and rambled about. He was so different from Pryor! Oddly enough, now that I had come to know Mr. Bradford better, there was a peculiar similarity in some of their views, while the men themselves were widely different. Had the clergyman grown broader, more to the needs and levels of every-day nature? He used to drop in frequently, and we had many a pleasant talk.

Then the leaves began to fall. There was a storm of days, a dreary, sodden kind of storm, with sullen gusts and thick skies. We started our heater, and, oh! the delight of our glowing grate. Hildreth used to lie in the reclining-chair just in the changeful radiance and warmth. One of the girls would read, the other occupy herself with some fancy-work. What a pretty, comforting picture they made when I came in after the trains were through with, and speeding on in the storm!

After that we had the late Indian summer. Hildreth suffered from touches of rheumatism, but on the whole his condition was encouraging. He did fret a little about not being able to take up some kind of business.

Joe decided to be married early in December, as soon as Pryor came back and was settled. I thought it altogether too soon, but did not oppose it very strenuously. Eve, woman-like, became more and more interested; and now I think she would have been deeply disappointed if any change had occurred in the plans. Ruth was to be our housekeeper. Joe was to "favor" me a little, as he termed it, to favor Ruth a good deal as I expected, and both were to have their home. Eve and I decided it would be worth that, but Joe insisted at first that it was quite too generous.

"Why, I shall not spend any thing," he declared. "I shall soon get together my share of the world's wealth. Thurston, if ever I do any thing to forfeit your esteem and friendship, I shall be a scoundrel of the deepest dye."

We went down to the city to see Pryor married. The wedding was a stylish one: the bride looked charming in a deep wine-colored satin with garniture of velvet. Pryor beamed with pride and happiness. The Gaylords were all pleased, and we saw many familiar faces in the church. They were to spend two or three weeks in New York after their return, Pryor coming up every day.

The Montgomery wedding was to be at home at first, Montgomery *père* being opposed to so much fuss and flummery as going to church. But Mr. Bradford said something to Ruth about the church being the proper place for such a solemn service; and somehow Joe evinced a decided desire for it, and presently it veered around that way. A cousin of Ruth's, who was to be married a few months later, was to stand, with her lover. So they decided to be married in church on Thursday evening at seven, have a wedding reception, and leave at ten, taking the train to Philadelphia, and returning Monday morning.

It seemed so strange to me. Indeed, I could hardly admit to myself that it was right for Joe to settle his future so young. One could not have wished him a more admirable helpmeet. Yet I must say Joe had done better than many of the young men at Athens, whose future eighteen months ago seemed much more promising. I concluded that mine could not be a sanguine nature. So far Joe had kept himself perfectly sober, and still reported every Saturday night. Indeed, I am not sure but that in our last tryst before his marriage, both were very near to tears.

"Thurston," he said, with a great, joyful tremble in his voice, "I'm the happiest fellow alive. I would not change places with any one."

The marriage was certainly a pretty one. Both looked their best, and Joe was handsome enough for any one to be proud of. Ruth was fair and sweet in her flowing white, and an abundance of white chrysanthemums. I must say here that Hildreth and I were trying some experiments with these in *our* greenhouse.

We all went to the reception; and it was quite

charming, thanks to Eve's planning. Then we kissed our young travellers, and they went out to test the sweet and the bitter of the world for themselves.

"I should like to cry!" exclaimed Eve, when we returned home. "Do you know, Adam, I feel as if it was our very own son who is speeding away to this unknown country. It *is* strange how Joe has come into our hearts."

"Put me in the lonely place," entreated Celia.

Eve went and twined her arms about the other's neck.

"See here, Thurston," said Hildreth, in an odd, whimsical manner, "suppose you adopt *me*, then? I shall want to belong to some one. I'm too utterly thin to be left out in the cold."

We all laughed at that. And yet, can anybody explain the inexpressible sadness that comes over one now and then, —

> "That resembles sorrow only
> As the mists resemble rain"?

We were all, I think, in the state of feeling where the soul reaches out blindly; where the new life is a formless thing; a spirit, moving upon the waters, dimly conscious that some truth will be evolved to change the old existence. Even the laugh seemed a cover merely for some deeper emotion.

We four were alone the few days that followed. No guests came: I think, indeed, Mr. Bradford was the only one who called. Pryor was busier than the mythical bee.

"To tell the truth, Thurston," he said Saturday evening, as he dropped in for the train, "I don't believe I could get along without Joe. I begin to have a wonderful respect for the manner in which he manages every thing. Joe will make a rich man if he should live, and a first-class man as well."

Dear Joe! My heart beat unwontedly at this praise.

Sunday was crisp, clear, and one of those uplifting days when the hours seem so full and long, and bound about with a heavenly satisfaction. We staid at home in the evening, and read and sang. I always remember how lovely Celia looked that evening.

But we came to a new phase of life. We always were, I think, having new phases. It grew colder, quite winter-like indeed; and Joe returned about noon, looking so serenely and joyfully happy, that I envied him.

The last of the week they moved. Joe told me privately, that while mother Montgomery was as good as an angel, the old gentleman was just too queer for any thing. "And he is continually saying *you* will never get back the money you have put in your house; and that Pryor, Corwin, and two or three others, will be the ruin of Athens. If his property is worth a good deal, so is yours: if all this business down by the river, and the new houses being built, depreciate values, he had better sell out now, before he goes any farther."

Joe was at home with us, of course; but it seemed a little odd about Ruth at first.

"It is just the same, in one way, as if we were boarding with you," Eve explained. "You are the mistress of a certain department. You must invite your friends to visit you; and when you and Joe want to go out for an evening, or a day, I will step in, and take the reins of government."

By Christmas we were working harmoniously, and it proved a very pleasant arrangement for Eve; while Ruth, who was quick and ambitious, learned many useful ways and bits of knowledge that somehow came natural to Eve. Joe was idiotically happy, we said; but he took our *badinage* in good part.

We four went down to the Palmers's for a Christmas dinner. All Sadie's family and the Wilburs had been invited. It was very bright and jolly; and once again Eve had to relate experiences of living over a railroad station, which she did in her most amusing manner.

Soon after this an incident happened that settled some matters definitely, although we did not understand all its bearings at the time. A friend of the Hildreths wrote for Lawrence to come out to Minnesota. There were fine business openings; and his town was the centre of health and length of life, according to his accounts. So Lawrence proposed he and Celia should make a visit, and if they found it of incalculable benefit, they might try it permanently.

"I am very well satisfied here : still, if it should be best for you" — and Celia made a curious pause.

"Then marry him to some nice girl, and come back to us," said Eve in a spirited manner.

They went about the middle of January. Every three days one or the other wrote, so we had two letters a week. But we missed them sorely. Was life becoming a graver matter? Mrs. Harwood came over and staid a week with us, and brought Eve what she termed a lot of old finery.

"What you don't want, you can give away," she declared with her short, bright laugh. "But you have such a genius for remodelling; and some of these garments are not the kind to give in charity, or bestow upon your washerwoman."

"I should think not, indeed," said Eve afterward, as she and Ruth inspected them. "Why, it is as much of a treasure as aunt Carry's trunk of goods; and that. I believe, dressed me for a year. My dear Adam, next to being rich yourself, is the possession of rich friends."

But we *did* miss the Hildreths. I think I made another discovery "about these times," in the parlance of an old-fashioned almanac. Was it Joe's and Pryor's infinite satisfaction that roused a longing in my soul that I had never experienced before? Or was it that the one who had gone out had taken something I had not understood before, — that one learned indeed, by missing it, how necessary it had become to the comfort and joy of one's life?

I knew by the want and hunger of soul, that could not be appeased by the sweetest and daintiest moods of Eve, — and it seemed to me she had grown strangely, awesomely sweet, — what it was that had befallen me. I had drifted into caring for another. I would not admit that it was really love. Fascinating as the glimpse vouchsafed me proved, I knew there were heights and depths that these vague imaginings barely shadowed. If a man allowed himself to love — if a woman loved — if he glanced into her eyes and saw the knowledge written there that nothing could ever entirely hide — the possibility was that delicious kind of torture that one returns to with a breaking heart, that one holds to his soul until the very forces of life are drained. And yet—what had I to offer that she would care to accept? She had a better position than I, she made twice the money I did — more than that perhaps. To take her, would be to mar her life. And I had tied myself here! I had shut out my own hopes of advancement. The delusive joy of having something of one's own in the shape of a home, cut me off from the greater joy. I must be manly enough to do my duty to Eve, and my whole duty to Celia Hildreth.

CHAPTER XVII

SWEET, FATAL KNOWLEDGE

I KEPT myself very busy. I was restless and unhappy, and did not wish Eve to have the faintest suspicion. Every moment I was at work somewhere. Our chickens — hens, rather — were doing finely, exceeding our last year's profits. We had many excellent layers: we fed for eggs, and had them too. It was cold weather, and prices ruled high. Then I had a plan for early strawberries and cucumbers. I had bought some old sashes, and put in the stray panes myself, and made others. My endeavors were to be in the nature of experiments, and I resolved somehow to make some money outside of my salary. I really *did* envy Joe his chance, and half wished I had cast in my lot with Pryor.

Helen came up and spent a week, and of course we had the happy husband. Pryor was so full of schemes, so hopeful. He had sold four of his houses, and was building two others, and working with all his energy to get another large factory to locate at Athens. I think their visit was quite a god-send to me: it broke up the mad, despairing, perpetual revery. Other men had seen possibilities, no doubt, and given them up as well; for give it up, I resolved I would. Some other woman might find it worth her while to marry me in the years to come, but my hand should make no blur in the delightful living of Celia Hildreth.

Pryor was wild on another idea. He wanted to build a summer hotel, and teased Eve to take charge of it. Eve and Helen discussed it with much seriousness.

"I'll do it before another year, I do believe," declared Pryor. "Why should we not make Athens a centre of attraction, when it has these pretty walks and drives, and the beautiful river for boating? Just give a place a push, and get some nice people to talk about it and visit it, and, if you have a delightful hotel, half the battle is won. Adam, here, can raise the vegetables and fruit, Joe can manage the transportation department, and the business will run as if by magic."

"It would be too late now," said Helen, "for you could not have it done and furnished in time; but I am quite sure it would be a success. See how many watering-places have started from the merest beginning!"

A few days after they had gone, I was rushing up home one bitter evening, when Mr. Bradford came striding down. "Horrible night," I said; but he did not seem to notice me. I hurried in, hung up my coat, and found no one in the dining-room, so walked through. Eve started up from somewhere with so strange a look in her sweet face that a sudden terror seized me; though a second after, I knew bad tidings must reach me first.

"What *is* the matter?" I asked.

She colored vividly, and turned away. There was such a peculiar droop to her shoulders, an air of something sorrowful pervading her.

"What brought Bradford up here this wild night? I met him flying along"—and then I halted suddenly. That curious consciousness, like a gleam of second sight, illumined me.

"My dear girl"—

"O Adam! I did not mean you to guess! I never was so surprised! I had not dreamed myself—if I had thought, I could have been more careful;" and her tender, deprecating voice broke with a long, sobbing breath.

There had been one wild bound of joy, then my heart dropped like lead. She did not care for him. If *she* were going to happiness—

"O Eve!" I cried vehemently, "you must not

let any thought or care for me interfere with a wish or hope" —

"No, Adam, it was not that. I love you well enough to make any needful sacrifice — oh, believe this! — and if you loved a woman tenderly, you ought not allow me to stand in the way of your happiness. But — I do not love Mr. Bradford in that manner. I am not fitted to be a clergyman's wife, and I am so sorry about it all. Forget it, Adam, and help me to forget it. He will see in time that it would not have been a wise step. O Adam! surely you are not tired of me?" and Eve clasped her arms about my neck, and laid her soft cheek against mine. "If I should never marry — that need not keep you single, you know. And when you *are* weary of seeing me around, you remember there is Mrs. Harwood" —

"My dear, dear girl!"

She gave a little, hysterical half sob, half laugh, and held me so strangely close. Had the flame of her soul gone out in that old time?

Joe and Ruth had come down, and were talking in the dining-room. We went out together, breaking up the tense strain.

"Wouldn't a cup of coffee go nicely?" said Ruth. "It is an awfully cold night. I do wish the Hildreths were back, don't you? or Mr. and Mrs. Pryor! The house hardly seems right unless it has some extra people in it."

She made the coffee. We had a little plain cake and some nuts. All of us possessed excellent digestions.

That was the last of February. March came in like a lion. For a week we had the worst winds I ever knew. The papers were filled with terrific accounts, and the damage to shipping was fearful. Western towns suffered tremendously. Then a lull, and, behold! spring seemed in our midst.

A telegram followed by our wanderers signalized the second beautiful day. They reached us by the early evening train, and quite a procession was at the station to meet them. Joe took Lawrence home in the wagon, for he seemed very much done up by the journey.

"I am afraid it has not been of much benefit," Celia remarked anxiously. "I am troubled about him. For the last three weeks I know he has been slipping back. And it has been such dreadful weather! I do believe there is no place like Athens!"

And when we entered the warm, bright house, with its lamps and cannel-coal fire, and its easy, well-used furniture, a sudden thrill seemed to sweep over us all. Celia glanced up at me with such an unspeakable radiance in her face, that I had much ado not to gather her in my arms; but in my soul I thanked her for the loving appreciation.

Lawrence stretched himself out before the bright blaze, and drew some satisfied breaths.

"Do you know, friends," he began, "that I *do* believe I have been homesick? You have all spoiled me. Celia wouldn't own it, but I know she is spoiled as well. And though we have seen much that is wonderful, it has tired me to death. As for cold, and storm, and blizzards, — well, I simply could not stand them. Of course, we should have taken it in the summer, but I wanted to know it at its worst; and I am not enchanted, though I must admire. Yet I am quite convinced it would not do for me."

We had a very thorough home welcome. Indeed, Eve was brimming over with delight; and there were sweet, half-bashful touches of cordiality in Ruth that were quite enchanting.

"Miss Eve," said Hildreth, when we had laughed and talked, and the clock had run on to midnight, "how is it that you know every art and ingredient that goes into home-making? The very atmosphere has caught the fragrance. The fires blaze as no other fires on the face of the earth; the chairs just fit you; the lamps burn with a soft, suggestive light; and — well, I have half a mind to say that you will never get rid of me again while I live."

A paleness flickered over Celia's face. Might there come a time when she would belong to us in a sad, sacred manner?

The next morning Hildreth showed plainly that he had dropped back a little. His cough was worse. He had lost flesh and strength. But the air proved really inspiriting. Even the frogs and turtles began piping; and martens flitted about with a short, jerky song, as if they were not sure whether it was best to scold or approve the weather.

I covered my strawberry-beds, after removing the mulch, and stirring the ground. They grew by the hour. In a sunny barn-window I had some potted tomatoes, that were looking splendid; and my young cucumbers were thriving. When Lawrence took his walk, he inspected them with a peculiar enthusiasm.

There was another cold snap and a snow. I covered some of my treasures, and watched them well; but in a few days it was pleasant again. We had some young chickens out, and I put those in the loft of the barn. By April it really was spring weather.

Suddenly Hildreth began to improve again. The deadly pallor vanished, the cough mended. He rode out, and took short walks several times during the day, and was getting a wholesome appetite. Celia was very busy filling urgent orders, and making up for lost time. She left on an early train, and did not return until dusk. She seemed unusually grave. Was she worried about Lawrence?

His South-American affairs were now settled, though at some sacrifice. He was master of seven thousand dollars, for which he had almost given his life.

We sat in the office one delightful afternoon, talking of the great subject of living,— how to make money, and not sacrifice every thing. "I started out to be a rich man," he said, with a little sigh. "I was willing to take it hard for the first ten years; and now I must take it comparatively easy all the rest of my life. A great many employments will henceforth be beyond my strength. But I have quite settled a part of my future."

I glanced up with questioning eagerness.

"You know, we have discussed floriculture so thoroughly, and found that we both have a genius for it. When a man has that, which must comprise love and patience to be of any real account, he can acquire the rest. It is coming to be one of the successful businesses of the future. Every year flowers are in greater demand. Let us join forces, Thurston, and do it in a profitable way."

"But"—I sat and stared. There was so much to say; and the old dream thrilled me.

"I spent all the morning at Riker's, and some new ideas entered my mind. I don't altogether like the man; and his methods seem too expensive for the result. With all his training and his opportunity, he is *not* going to succeed. He undertakes too many things, and stops too often in the middle. I have seen just such men in other walks of life. Last spring he borrowed one thousand dollars for a year. He has *not* made his living; is in debt now, and wants one thousand dollars more to enable him to go on at all. I have decided to advance him two thousand dollars, and take a mortgage on the place. I shall work with him part of the summer. I shall go elsewhere and study other methods. Next year he will want some more money. He is going to lose that place just as surely as that he once owned it; and there will be a chance. I shall not defraud him, nor make a hard bargain; but if *we* can agree upon it, Thurston, why not cast in our lives together? When I was in New York, talking over matters with a sensible physician, he recommended light farming — fancy farming; and I spoke of this, which he seemed to think would answer if I did not confine myself too closely to greenhouses during the winter. Two of us could manage admirably. What do you say to it?"

I was so surprised that at the first moment I could say nothing; then I gasped, —

"But you forget that I have no money."

"Well, some of the most successful florists have come up from one small greenhouse. I have money enough to buy the plot of ground, when it falls in, as it is sure to do. And, Thurston, I don't believe I could like or esteem a brother of blood any more highly than I do you. Well, let me go on, and tell the truth — nothing may ever come of it — but, if God should bless me with returning health, it will go hard indeed with me if I do not win your sister. Can you wish me God-speed from your heart?"

"Can I?" I cried joyfully as I grasped his hand. "My dear fellow!" then my courage failed. If others had sued to Eve, — only to know disappointment, — would Lawrence Hildreth be likely to win?

"From my *own* heart I can," I continued, recovering myself; "but Eve is — different from most girls. I mean that she seems to have no idea of marrying," I blurted out. "But she is the sweetest and dearest" —

"There need be no hurry. And if she should not smile upon your humble servant," — a curiously confident expression crossed his face, — "why, I should want *you* more than ever. I was not made for solitary life. I like people about me, a wide and diversifying interest. Your sister, I observe, is very similar in this respect. There are many points — well, she is the first girl that I have ever been drawn to in that coveting sense that I suppose always comes to a man when he thinks of marriage. Outside of this is the larger business question, for" — with a little smile — "I think no man has a right to ask a woman's love if he cannot take care of her; so business *must* be considered. Then, I have never believed it reprehensible to desire to better one's condition, to make money. I have almost given my life for it, which I don't mean to do again, for life has a new sacredness to me. I have an ardent love for flowers, and have studied the subject a good deal for the mere pleasure of it. Now I shall go into it from the profit point of view. You, I think, have a wonderful gift that way as well. I do not see why we cannot succeed as well as other people. Then, I *do* like Athens. I believe I feel better here than any place I have yet tried. So, if you are agreed, the minor points can be arranged, I am sure."

"I do not know how to express my" — and I paused for a word sufficiently comprehensive.

"Well, don't;" and a humorous smile lighted up his fine, tender eyes. "It will be business, you know; and you have done enough of it to realize that truth and straightforwardness make the best foundation. Now we will take up all manner of sharp study on the subject. Honestly, I do not like Riker's methods; he spends too much to reach a given result: and I think you have a wonderful economy of forces. That is one secret of success."

"Depend upon me for the very best that is in me," I made reply. Somehow, I was deeply touched. I could only think that my small efforts for Joe were being repaid fourfold.

Mrs. Wilbur and Mrs. Palmer were up a day or two after this. They had to inspect the young chickens. I had forty-five with three hens, though it had taken five hens to hatch them out. The ladies shrieked over my window of tomato-plants, with small green tomatoes the size of a cherry.

"Oh, you should see the strawberries!" cried Eve. And now the loveliness of the chickens paled.

The strawberries *were* doing well. I had kept them covered on the coldest days; the ground was rich; they had been aired and watered; and now some berries were nearly grown, and had a whitish look.

"You will sell them, of course," said Mrs. Palmer. "You never *could* be so extravagant as to eat strawberries at from one to two dollars a quart, and I shall engage some."

She laughed so mischievously, like the Sadie Brooke of old.

"Yes," I answered as gayly, "on the principle that farmers never can afford to use fresh eggs, or spring chickens, or any thing in season."

"But you certainly *will* have some to spare, so you can count me in. Why do you not have a great greenhouse full of them?"

"For the best reason of all,—I have not the greenhouse."

"You ought to have," said Mrs. Wilbur. Then she took a comprehensive survey of the place. "Mr. Thurston, I shall suggest to Mr. Wilbur that he build you a greenhouse, and we take the interest-money in flowers and early fruits—berries. Why, you might make money enough to pay for it all! You and Miss Thurston are the most wonderful people I ever met. And when you see Eve dancing around like a butterfly, you wouldn't suppose"—

"That I had an idea," interrupted Eve. "Why, *I* think I have ideas enough to furnish a whole colony. Why doesn't some association send me to the West, or to Florida?"

"Let such a plan be mentioned," declared Sadie, "and I shall straightway choke the mentioner. Besides, you are to have a hotel here in Athens, and a greenhouse. We shall fill the hotel with our most delightful friends, and we shall buy the contents of the greenhouses."

We went in for a lunch, and had a merry time. Afterward, Mrs. Palmer took me solemnly apart, to the great amusement of the others.

"See here," she began, in her eager, girlish way, "I just want to say to you, that, if you desire to start in any of these things, you shall have whatever money you want. Mr. Palmer will advance it, and I will be the security."

"Thank you a thousand times," I made answer from a full heart.

I may as well say here, that, of my strawberries raised under glass, I sold, during the first two weeks in May, twenty quarts at a dollar a quart, and fifteen at seventy-five cents. But we were like the farmers, — we did not eat any except the imperfect ones. They were large and fine flavored, for I kept them on until ripe; and I could have sold twice that amount. The plants had been forced beyond their strength, and most of them died through the summer; but I had plenty of others. My tomatoes did fairly well, and brought a high price; and my next lot was ready for sale before Mr. Riker managed to get any on the market. I had ten cucumbers which I sold for a quarter of a dollar apiece, but on the whole they were not a success: my next lot, raised under glass, proved profitable. Hildreth made note of all these experiments, putting down the mistakes for future avoidance.

There certainly *was* a boom in Athens. People looked about for houses to buy, and came to engage board.

"I should have gone at the hotel," Pryor declared ruefully. "I wish I *had* set myself about it last fall, but I was so full of getting married and other things. I could live here all the year round. I've locked up my money in some new ventures with Corwin, but I *could* hire some, I know. Let us hold a meeting, and hunt up an attractive site. There is a lovely chestnut-grove just above the Teall property, an elegant location. I am going to look after it."

Meanwhile our plans matured more rapidly than we imagined. Mrs. Riker had a child born, which died when a few weeks old. Eve had made a little acquaintance with her, and reported her as being quite discouraged about her husband's venture. She had been offered thirty-five hundred dollars for the land by her cousin; and she felt sure they could never realize fifty-five hundred, even after her husband had spent the two thousand dollars.

The latter part of May a business offer came to Mr. Riker. He had a cousin, a well-established nursery-man and fruit-grower in Western Pennsylvania, who had once asked him to come out. Now this man's two sons had gone out to New Mexico, where they had started extensive vineyards, and the elder Mr. Riker found he must have some competent help. He offered his nephew an excellent interest in the business, and it seemed too good an opportunity to miss. Mrs. Riker was very much in favor of his going.

If he *could* dispose of his business. He consulted Pryor, and threw out hints to Hildreth. Then he started off to visit his uncle, and returned more urgent than ever. Hildreth did not appear overanxious, and insisted upon an appraisement before he took any steps. A florist came down from Truro, who considered the finished greenhouse should not have cost more than seven hundred, and that the new one, when finished, would be worth one or two hundred more, being larger. But it still lacked a great deal, though there was a contract for completing it, and much of the material there. Then a man came up from Northwood, and offered four thousand for the whole thing. Riker asked six thousand. Hildreth came forward with an offer of forty-five hundred. The Northwood man reluctantly went a hundred higher, when Hildreth put in his last bid of five thousand, to hold good for the next fortnight.

No other offer came to hand. Mrs. Riker insisted that he should close with it. So Hildreth paid over to her the remaining three thousand dollars. There was not at this time much stock on hand, as Mr. Riker had been disposing of it in any quantity he could work off, and it was too late for vegetables to be of any great profit. So the first day of July Hildreth took possession.

"Now," he said, "I must make my two thousand dollars go a long ways. I can't afford to fly as high as Mr. Riker."

The partnership was next in consideration. That required some thought. At present I did not consider it advisable to throw up my position, though I could devote some time to the work. Then, too, I had not a little really valuable stock. Indeed, Hildreth admitted that my roses were extremely fine. We settled presently that the stock and labor should be a joint-partnership concern; Hildreth owning the place, and a fair rent being paid for it.

Everybody was wonderfully interested. Mr. Wilbur and Mr. Palmer offered to become my bankers, also our dear, lovely Mrs. Harwood, who came over and boarded a fortnight with us, and was greatly interested in the hotel project. Pryor had bought the ground, and plans were being considered. Eve,

Celia, and Helen were inseparables, and each drew plans until we could have built up the whole of Athens with them.

"Suppose *you* sell," Pryor said to me one day.

I stared at him, then I replied that I half wished I had the money for business purposes.

"Well, I struck something rather funny a few days ago. You remember the Mr. Benson that I took through your place,— the man who was so interested in poultry? He asked then if the place was for sale, and I said unhesitatingly, 'No.' I saw him on Tuesday in the insurance office of a friend when I was in New York, and we talked house and poultry. Maybe I put it in rather glowing terms," and Pryor gave a little chuckle. "He is a man of considerable means, has several children married; but his youngest son, a boy eighteen, I think he said, was badly injured a few years ago in a railroad accident, and is deformed somewhat. He has had a poultry craze for two years, and has a few thousand dollars of his own to invest. Mr. Benson has been thinking of buying a country-place, and wants to bring his son over to talk 'chicken' with you. Now is your time to sail in and sell your house. I may make an arrangement for him to come over, I suppose?"

For a moment I was astounded.

"I don't know about Eve," I replied.

"Eve is all right. She is going to take my hotel. She can keep a hotel splendidly. You may just count her out."

"What would you ask for the place?" was my hesitating inquiry.

"Five thousand dollars, and do not take a cent less. Let them come over. The place is in its glory, and your chicks beat any thing around here;" said he, nodding confidently.

"You couldn't get that for it."

"Give me leave. Well, I simply would not sell it for less than that. Why, every thing in Athens is worth more than it was two years ago. The Wilburs' building has enhanced this; and think of the new houses that have gone up! And the hotel will make things spin."

I drew a long breath, then hurried into the ticket-office, as it was train-time.

CHAPTER XVIII

TEMPTATION NO. II

My head spun as I walked up the hill to my dinner, which was still the evening-meal. I felt in a whirl of business. For two months events had rushed upon me, upon us all. But, oh! how more than beautiful it looked in the late sun-rays,— trees, flowers, velvety grass, the hammocks stretched on porch and lawn; Eve, Helen, and Lawrence disporting themselves! Celia was to remain until eight that evening, being very busy.

I have said little about her of late, not because desire had grown any less, but an intangible something seemed to stand between. How could I ask a woman to marry me when I could not do for her what she was doing for herself? I steeled myself to a curious patient waiting, and just now it was not hard to wait.

But, oh! how could I give up this delightful home? Dreams had chilled me to the marrow of being out of employment, of foreclosure of mortgage, of loss and trouble, of being compelled to go away; but *could* I leave of my own free will? Never had it seemed so dear to me. A crowd of happy remembrances flooded my mind. How Eve and I had worked and planned, and made all manner of ingenious adornments! How closely we had counted our money, she with a wonderful buoyant hope, I with clutch of desperation! Did she, would she ever, care for Lawrence? She had a curious — I was going to say motherly — way with her. She sent him in out of the damp; she made him go to bed when he was looking tired; when his voice grew weary, she would not allow him to read aloud. She even arranged his diet, and he gave in with a sweet sort of meekness. But what steps would he take to compel her to love him, when she liked him so much?

"What is the matter, Thurston?" he said presently, when we were about half through the meal. "You have not spoken a word. Are you repenting?"

"You will find that Adam possesses an immense capability of repentance, and a tremendous share of misgiving," said my sister, with a laugh. "But you must not allow him to infect you with his fears."

"So long as he grows magnificent roses, I shall forgive him and love him," was the reply. "And when the roses begin to fail, I hope I shall be strong enough to get up and thrash him. I am not sure but it is an event to be desired."

"Which?" I asked.

"I do not believe the roses will deteriorate," said Helen humorously.

I went down to the train, and found Celia looking tired enough with her day's work, and drove her up home in Joe's wagon.

"Isn't it time vacation begun?" I asked, with solicitude.

"I have just a few little things to finish up," she answered in a rather weary tone. "And this summer I mean to take a real vacation. I shall spend it nearly all in the garden. I do begin to envy you and Larry."

"We shall make you welcome in the garden," I returned, with a quick beat of the heart.

"Do you know," Celia said, turning her sweet face to me, "that I am so glad and thankful that Lawrence is going to be settled here? And he *is* growing stronger. Oh! do you remember the first time I walked up this hill with you? How strangely events get shaped, just by a chance word!"

Would they shape themselves to my desire, I wondered. She seemed so much nearer, so infinitely dear, in these worn and tired moods. I wanted to stretch out my arms and take her for all time. If my new plans worked well —

We could not do a great deal at this season of the year, but Lawrence and I spent our spare moments in "straightening up." We altered some things in our greenhouse, and began to hurry the other to completion. Many of the young trees and shrubs looked poorly. We decided not to buy much, but to bring all the cuttings we could from my house. We would make the ground profitable in this manner until we saw our way clear to do something else with it.

"One could easily build a house at the upper end," Hildreth said. "I do not suppose we shall even want two acres in greenhouses. But what a superb place for graperies! Really, one almost wishes for thousands to invest; but we must not rush on too fast, — rather take warning by our young friend's over-ambitious schemes."

It was a lovely plot of ground, and Mr. Teall's two houses were very handsome. He proposed to build two more on the avenue, and was much pleased with the hotel project.

It was a week after this, I think, that Mr. Benson and his son Walter came out. The lad was small and fragile-looking, with one high shoulder. There had been a wrench to the spine, but it was not a positive hump-back. He was fair, with a sweet, almost imploring face; and somehow my heart went out to him at once.

I took him through my chicken-yards. We had hatched out one hundred and twenty-three chickens this year, and had already used a good many. My Leghorns had been culled of every thing not quite true, and they were a handsome lot. They and some games were all that I kept separate. The young chicks were in a yard by themselves, and the hens in another, about thirty-seven extremely handsome fowls. I explained to him very freely my experiments and successes. I had not done it on a purely business basis, but I saw how it could be carried forward to a considerable profit.

"It would be good to have more land," said Mr. Benson. "I wonder if one could buy some of that lying above."

The remark startled me.

"If my son should make such a venture, I should want him to have a chance of success. It seems as if one ought to be able to do the work he is interested in, and there are things that would be much too wearing for Walter."

"I mean to try the experiment somewhere," said the lad. "And this is such a lovely place! I do not like real country; that is, large farms with houses ever so far apart. What a nice show of fruit!" and he glanced around. "Can you sell any of it?"

I told him I had sold both fruit and berries.

"Do you suppose, now, that a young fellow could make his living on a place like this — well, by branching out a little?" asked Mr. Benson.

"One young fellow certainly could. I have not given half my time to it, and it was very much run down when I came."

"You have matters in excellent shape. Now, Walter, do you imagine you have as much genius as Mr. Thurston?"

"This is my first attempt," I said. "I did not suppose I had any special genius for farming. I should not hesitate to undertake it on a larger scale."

"Is that your purpose?"

"Not exactly. I am to try raising flowers with a friend."

"You have a splendid showing here;" and he glanced about. "Will you take us through the house? Isn't five thousand pretty steep for a place like this?" and he turned rather sharply upon me.

"It is in excellent order, and there is a great deal that can be made profitable all the time," I said, with a show of being indifferent; "and I really had not thought of selling it until Mr. Pryor mentioned you."

Walter was really enchanted with the interior. I think Mr. Benson was very much pleased. He asked about the water and the drains, and inspected the cellar. Every thing was as neat as a pin.

Afterward I walked down to the station with them, and was a little amused by the backward looks they bestowed.

"We shall want a little time to think this over!" exclaimed Mr. Benson. "Walter may run up some day by himself, if you have no objection."

I said he would be welcome at any time.

Eve came down an hour later to walk up home with me.

"What did those people want?" she asked. "My mind misgave me. They had a sort of buying-look."

"Would you sell under any circumstances?" and I looked her square in the eyes.

"O Adam! it would be like selling your first-born." There was a touching quiver in her voice. "And yet—I wonder if I am mercenary?—if we *could* make something! And I'm half enchanted with the hotel project. I like stir and life and business. Oh! would you ever believe that *I* coaxed you to live in two rooms over a railroad-station?" and she gave a rather hysterical laugh.

"I wish you would tell me what a buying-look was like," I said with a sense of amusement.

"They had an air — I can't describe it" — looking perplexed. "And *I* had a presentiment. They *will* buy it, I know. And what have you asked?"

I told her Pryor's estimate and advice.

"Oh, my lovely, lovely house!" she cried, as we entered the gate. "There can never be any thing quite like you again! And I thought we were settled for life."

"But we need not go away."

"We need not? All the same, I think we will. And if it is best — well, we have been very, very happy. It is like a fairy story, and we can turn back to it with no regret. Every thing has been prosperous right along."

"Do you realize how steadily you have toiled to this end, my dear Eve? — how you have taught music and painting, and brought housekeeping to a fine art, and made economy a science?"

"Yes: I believe I have a genius for planning out all the housekeeping, and systematizing the work. I would rather do this on a large scale than teach music. I must confess that the hotel looks attractive to me; and, while I should not like to break up my own pretty, cosey home for that, if we could sell to an advantage, I should step right into that, and make another delightful centre. This, you see, is *my* genius."

"And are you never going to marry?"

I turned away to study something as I said this, for I experienced a qualm of insincerity.

"Suppose I should not? Well,—I shall soon be on the 'list,'" and she gave a gay little laugh. "But it is the fashion nowadays for women to be in business. If you are a successful business-woman, and make money, you do not lose caste. The romantic idea of a woman sitting in her back-kitchen window, in a faded calico dress, darning her husband's old socks, patching his shirts and trousers, has gone out of date. Confess, now, that I am ever so much prettier than she?"

Eve stands before me, straight, slim, and tall, with glowing eyes and cheeks, and the sauciest, most bewitching cherry-ripe lips. Alas for the poor household drudge! No, I should not like to see her in such a place.

"Then," she adds, a little more grave in tone, "Joe and Ruth will commence housekeeping some time this fall. There will be changes and changes. When we are too utterly homesick, we will come up here and roam around, and bedew the paths with our tears. Out of mine will spring a red, red rose, and out of yours a brier, ier, ier"—

I caught her in my arms and kissed her. She had managed Mr. Bradford in the most admirable manner. What it cost her, I knew long afterward. She would *not* allow any difference; if any thing, she went to church more regularly; she sang, she petted up the younger girls, she sent her choicest flowers to adorn the chancel, and took a hand in all good works, making herself so undeniably friendly that a man could not mistake. Eve certainly had the rare gift of transforming her lovers into friends. They could *not* resist her: they could not refuse to take what she offered them so frankly. I do not believe she had a better or truer friend in the world than Gordon Pryor, and I knew the time would come when Mr. Bradford would settle into a similar regard.

The last week in July was one of those curious summer anomalies, beginning with a thunder-shower one evening, then drizzling all night, and keeping up an east wind, moist atmosphere, and occasional rain for several successive days. Hildreth and I took advantage of this. We decided to turn at least two acres into fruit-growing for some years, quite certain it would be more profitable than regular nursery business. I had such hosts of splendid young currants, and others ready to slip, so we did quite an extensive business in transplanting. Indeed, like many others I had filled my place so full that I must have given or thrown them away. We decided also to take up a number of chrysanthemums. We cut squares large enough to enclose all the roots, and I don't believe they ever realized they had "moved." Then we drove down stakes; and when the sun shone again, we had awnings of cheap unbleached muslin that had been given a coat of oil, which we stretched over them, and the currants as well. I had used this to cover my chickens' coops in a storm, and found it admirable protection for young chicks.

We had on our place one very late peach. Half of it was dead the year we came; but I trimmed it, put wood-ashes about the root, and gave it two or three baths of hot soda-water. It bore about a peck of the most magnificent peaches I ever saw, ripening from the first until the middle of October. I planted all the pits, but only ten of them germinated. The second year I sold from it a basket of peaches for which I obtained two dollars and a half. I had learned that very early fruit and the very late commanded the best prices. I had budded several stray peach-trees, and also planted again. I had what might be called a swamp of young peach-trees; so Hildreth and I decided that we would devote one acre to a peach-farm, with rows of strawberries set between. There were fifty young grapevines Riker had planted out, but they had not been well cared for; and a few fruit-trees of various kinds. Two cherries were dying. Some of the dwarf-pears looked thrifty. We wanted to raise enough fruit to pay the tax on the whole place. Later on in the season we would transplant the peaches, raspberries, and blackberries.

We decided to devote one house exclusively to roses, and make those a specialty. We had received a catalogue from one famous rose-grower, and Hildreth had resolved to visit him in preference to sending an order by mail. I had numbers of roses, and some rarely beautiful, both in slips I had raised, and others from roots divided. We should take from our place all we could spare without impoverishing it, even if we sold.

The week Hildreth was away, young Benson came over. I let him see my poultry account, and imparted various bits of experience. To make hens lay in winter, to raise chicks of breeds that grew rapidly and could be put on the market early, and to keep some choice kinds, — pure, of course, — from which one could sell eggs for hatching, seemed about the greatest points. As for the rest, — good diet, cleanliness, and care in season, light and warmth, were about all the grand secrets. So far

I had kept mine free from vermin, had no contagious diseases, and very few cases of gapes. When my chickens were first hatched out, I put some kerosene under the mother's wings, and now and then a sprinkling of sulphur around them. While I had them in the loft, I took up a sod every day or two, and let them peck at the tender roots, and scratch off the dirt. I also fed them bits of meat and worms occasionally.

Walter had given the subject a good deal of study; but he said, —

"Why, how simple you make it all! It would be splendid to have an adviser like you. I wonder if you would be willing to counsel me occasionally, if I did get into a bad fix?"

"Certainly," I returned. "I do not pretend to be over-wise, but you are quite welcome to all that I have learned by experience."

Eve gave him the daintiest lunch, and then played an hour for him, making him sing a little. He had a sweet, but not very strong, voice.

"I should like to come here because you are not going away," he confessed, with a kind of wistful frankness. "People seem so nice and cordial at Athens. I like Mr. Pryor, and that Mr. Crawford is so bright and merry. It almost seems in the air."

"I think it is," replied Eve. "Athens always was a famous place, you know."

Pryor offered to take him up to see his friend Vanduyne, and drive him about a little, if he would come over again.

"You and Eve are bound to sell the place," I said.

They — we all, I think — settled upon a plan for the hotel. It was to be built so that a wing could be added any time; and would contain on the two floors above the first story thirty-two nice sleeping-chambers, with good closet-room, baths, and so arranged that rooms could be thrown into suites for family purposes. There was a handsome long drawing-room, two small reception-rooms, a reading and smoking room for gentlemen, besides the dining-rooms, which were arranged in three sections, with sliding doors, and could thus be converted into one large apartment. The kitchens were below; though the ground sloped somewhat toward the rear, which made them only a step or two below the ground at the back. Mr. Palmer and Mr. Wilbur were to advance the money for the building, leaving Pryor the more free with what he had, and in no immediate danger of foreclosure, since the mortgage was to run five years.

The first of August they broke ground, and began the foundation. There was to be a driven well and two large cisterns with force-pumps; as at present there were no water-pipes in Athens, although the matter had been discussed. Our greenhouses had been arranged with leaders to catch the rain-water, and lead it into tanks; and an old well had been cleared out and put in order, so we were tolerably well provided for.

Hildreth remained away five days, and came home glowing with knowledge and enthusiasm. He had invested twenty-five dollars in roses.

"And such a gorgeous place!" he declared. "It would fill you with envy! Of course we shall never have any thing like that, but I know I should have bankrupted myself if there had been any place ready to put so much stock. Yet we must not undertake more than we can attend to properly, and for the present we do not want to hire a regiment of help. But I have resolved to finish our other house. I have found a better method of heating, considerably cheaper than the contract Mr. Riker made."

This had been something of a bother to us. We had given the man notice on our taking possession; but he had come up immediately, and insisted upon doing the work at once. When we declined, he threatened to sue for breach of contract. This had not alarmed Hildreth, however; but the man had proved curiously persistent, and we as much in earnest to get rid of him.

Our cold-frames we went at ourselves. The foundation of one had been so poorly laid that the mortar was crumbling out. There was no end of stone and rubble; but I had succeeded so well with my own experiment, that I went at it with renewed courage. My lime, sand, and such materials, I could get at Pryor's for a trifle beyond cost. I did hire a stout Irish laborer for two days. We made two long rows of wall that would answer at any time for a greenhouse. The partitions were temporary, — put in more to support the frames than any thing else.

Miss Hildreth was much interested in our venture. She came down nearly every day: she and Eve took walks and drives in a leisurely way. There was no chance to take boarders this summer: we had our house full. Then both girls went to Asbury Park for a week, and Mrs. Wilbur persuaded them to take an excursion to Bar Harbor afterward.

Meanwhile the Bensons came over singly and *en famille*. Mrs. Benson was really captivated with the place. The abundance of flowers and fruit, the homelike aspect of every thing, won her completely. I left the matter in Pryor's hands; and the very day before the girls returned home, Mr. Benson came to hand with five hundred dollars to bind the bargain, and to learn when we would be willing to give possession.

I could do nothing until Eve's return. The very

first night we sat up until long past midnight, discussing it *pro* and *con*. That it was very dear to the whole four of us, we admitted. We even said there never could be such a charm about another place. But there were several points that made it appear desirable to let it go. The impending change which did seem for the best, the freedom of using the money in other ways, and having no divided interest, overbalanced the sentiment.

Yet the wrench was like parting with something out of one's very soul. We went about saying,—

"And must I leave thee, Paradise?"

in a mock-heroic way, but there were times when tears were not far from the surface.

Joe had settled upon a pretty cottage in Pryor's Row, as it had been christened by the Athenians. It had six nice rooms, with an excellent fireplace heater in the parlor that could be counted upon for keeping the second floor comfortable. They were to pay ten dollars a month rent, and had the option of buying it; but Joe thought he would rather wait and purchase more ground. They desired to get settled during the month of September. The Bensons did not want to wait later than the first of October, if they moved in the fall. Mr. Wilbur offered us his house for the winter, and we resolved to make that our headquarters; though Eve had suggested going back to the station. Mr. and Mrs. Pryor proposed to cast in their lot with us, and Eve decided upon a capable colored woman that Mrs. Banks recommended. So that was all settled without further difficulty. Our goods could be stored at the station; though some of them had been donated to Joe and Ruth, and a few we would take with us. It was curious how easily every thing seemed to get arranged.

CHAPTER XIX

WE ENTER THE GARDEN

On the 18th of September we met at Mr. Pryor's office, and bargained away our lovely home; sealed, signed, and transferred to Walter Benson, through his guardian, Edward Frye Benson, all right, title, etc., receiving therefor the sum of five thousand dollars; and we took up the mortgage, which our dear, bright-eyed Mrs. Harwood was ready to release, and she generously offered the money back to me if I needed it.

The Bensons would have preferred waiting until spring, but Walter was anxious to begin his venture. The money paid for the house he had received for damages from the railroad company — as if any thing could ever make amends to the poor lad for his maimed body! He would have lost some time by waiting, though he took his business at the most unprofitable season.

And now we — that is, Eve and I — came out of our business venture in this manner. We had owned our house two years and a half. The expenses against it had mounted up in this wise: —

Amount of interest paid	$300 00
Taxes for three years	119 56
Paper for walls	9 50
Finishing two rooms in attic	15 85
Spent for paint and labor	52 67
Miscellaneous repairs	22 60
Deed, recording, etc.	12 50
	$532 68
Add to this present amount of mortgage	1,700 00
	$2,232 68

We had now to deduct this sum from the five thousand dollars we received. We had paid one thousand three hundred dollars besides the current expenses. Out of the sum returned, four hundred and sixty-eight dollars was clear profit. This may not seem to the reader at all extravagant, but we felt quite well satisfied. Our home had been delightful, our living luxurious, I might say, for the fruit, poultry, and eggs had been abundant. My income from my position and the "farm" had been about six hundred and thirty dollars a year. Eve had averaged two hundred from her music and other matters, not counting the boarders.

So that in two years and a half we had increased our little hoard of seven hundred to two thousand seven hundred and sixty-eight dollars by dint of hard work, economy, and good fortune. Neither of us had experienced a day's absolute illness. We had won our share of the world's wealth, and done our duty by the bloated or plethoric millionaires.

I insisted upon dividing our fortune. I wanted Eve to take the odd hundreds, and let me keep an even thousand; but she would not, so we had thirteen hundred and eighty-four dollars apiece. Mrs. Harwood came up to the house, for Eve declared that we must have a party. The Pryors, the Wilburs, and our own six, were all the guests. Joe had just bargained away his express-business to a young man who meant to keep a hack for passengers, besides the parcel delivery, which was too much now for Joe to attend to.

The lad's prosperity amazed me more than my own. Most people would call it sheer good luck. There had been times when it seemed so to me; then I remembered Joe's industry, and the admirable quality of thinking no work beneath him. He had won Mr. Wilbur's regard by the cheerfulness with which he had done all kinds of chores at the time of the building: he had attracted Pryor by his persistency, shrewdness, and entire honesty. And he had won my love and that of Eve by the good, manful fight he had made on the side of temperance, and his cheerful, steady affection. Meanwhile, how many young lads had gone to ruin for want of a friendly hand stretched out at the crisis of their lives!

I think we were all the merrier this evening, because one would not allow the other to be sad. We said all manner of laughable things, and we *did* laugh over them: we ate our peaches, pears, grapes, and melons, with cake sandwiched between, and some most delightful coffee. Mrs. Wilbur declared it a feast of nectar and ambrosia. Then we adjourned to the parlor, and had some music, sang songs, and said good-night.

Was it that for the first time in my life I had allowed myself to dream that Celia might actually be mine? I went so far, she came so near, that at one point our lives interpenetrated. I had the divine glimpse of what was possible, I had a vision of what would be.

Our guests went away after midnight. The rest retired to their rooms. Eve went up to see that Mrs. Harwood was comfortable. I locked and barred, then sank down into an arm-chair in a most blissful reverie.

A light step startled me. Eve stood there with such a sweet, mysterious face. Then she stooped and kissed me.

"O Adam!" she murmured, under a long, tremulous breath, "I couldn't wait. I wanted to know. I have had it in my heart so long. I have loved her like a sister. Because I wanted to have it this way, I have felt almost afraid; and now"—

"But I have not asked her," I gasped. "I could not. I have always thought — what *did* I have to offer her? But to-night"—

"O you dear, delicious old goose!" Eve's face was hidden against mine, and its flush seemed to thrill through me. "Well, then, find out for yourself! This was why I thought it best to sell, to make a change, to leave you more free. I guessed when she was away last winter. Providence has interfered signally in your behalf; and if you haven't the pluck to go on, and 'ask for yourself, John!' why, then you must go mourning all your days."

She straightened herself suddenly, and kissed me once more, turned, but I caught both hands.

"Eve," I cried, "are you never going to have any confidence for me?"

"How can I, — if no one comes to woo?" she replied laughingly as she ran away.

I sat and dreamed a long while. After all, we had been very happy, though we had worked no miracles; and they are not possible on small incomes, in spite of romantic economists and imaginative statisticians. We had furnished, — simply enough; we had clothed ourselves; taken a daily paper, a weekly; and our library subscription had given us magazines as well as books. We had enjoyed an occasional theatre and concert, taken a few short journeys, and tried to keep in excellent physical and mental order; for there may be a good deal of existence that is no true living.

We awoke the next morning homeless. What a queer, lonely pang it gave one! I had a bit of breakfast with Eve; and, remembering a paper I needed, I went out to our pretty reception-room where we had enjoyed so much delight. A light step came down the stair. Eve tripped or flew, and had as many paces as a young colt; but Celia's movement was always the same, — elastic, but with a curious steadiness. I turned.

Did we both understand? I wonder how many hearts have been plighted without a word! I took her in my arms. The throbbing of her pulses thrilled me. I could feel the flush on her cheek, the tremulousness of the lips that met mine, and withheld not that first sacred troth, that exquisite surrender. It was martyrdom to tear one's self away, and yet I had to do it.

How impatiently I waited for my next glimpse! There was a crowd of people impatient for tickets, but I snatched one moment, and touched her hand before the train whirled her away; and it seemed as if a hundred things might happen, and we two never meet again! I resolved to follow her to the city: then I remembered how many important matters were waiting for my supervision.

Hildreth and I had formed our partnership. The remaining greenhouse was to be finished at his expense, and the rent was to be paid before any real division of profits. My own stock was a set-off to that he had taken from Mr. Riker, and now we were to put in our labor and money equally. I had stipulated with the Bensons for the removal of certain young trees, plants, etc., and was to devote all my spare time to it. We had promised possession the first of October.

Mrs. Harwood came down to inspect our new arrangements. I think she was wonderfully interested in our venture. I had brought over geraniums and various other plants. We had two strawberry-beds set out from runners I had struck in pots, and I had set out a number of annual roses and vines.

"If ever you should cover your five acres, you will have a fortune," she said. "Do not rush on too fast, but remember that you need never stint yourself of any thing necessary; and I am very glad that Eve can take a holiday."

It was not so merry that evening; but I know of one, who, if not caught up to the third heaven, still heard things that are too sacred to utter. I did not suppose we kept our secret from Eve or Lawrence; but they exhibited a wonderful wisdom, and left us quite to ourselves while they went over to settle some matters with our neighbors.

Somewhere in the talk I spoke of my present limited circumstances.

"The new order of greater equality between men and women has settled some points," Celia replied, with a lovely and convincing smile. "And while any true wife must always be dependent on her husband for many things, if she has a genius or a business that she can carry on without neglecting her home or his claims upon her, I do not see any pertinent reason for her giving it up. I am not a genius, perhaps, in the larger sense; but I have established a place for myself in the world, and have reached a point where I can make some money with ease. So for the present I prefer to go on; but I want you to feel, my dear love, that, if it was wisest and best, I should live cheerfully upon your income."

I called her an angel. I was supremely, idiotically happy.

Joe meanwhile made his nest ready, and transported his belongings thither. Mrs. Montgomery made some additions. Eve sent them our parlor-chairs and several ornamental articles she did not wish to store. The others, except some we intended to use, were boxed, and sent down to the station. Mrs. Wilbur declared that she hated to go away, and that we might count on her as a frequent visitor. Mrs. Pryor was to make the first essay in housekeeping. Eve and Celia had planned to spend some time in New York.

And at last the pretty house was dismantled. Still, we had no opportunity to mope over its dreariness; for the very next day some of the Bensons' belongings came up, with a woman to clean and to settle them. Our new handmaiden, a tidy colored woman of five and thirty, a relative of Mrs. Banks, had been with us for a fortnight, and we liked her very well. We decided to "even up" the cost of living, as there were three couples of us, and our rent comparatively low. Indeed, at first Mrs. Wilbur would not consent to any remuneration; but we placed it before her in a proper light, and our eloquence prevailed.

Mr. Wilbur had invested twelve hundred dollars for Eve in some stock that paid ten per cent. I placed mine at the bank, but I meant to make one or two small investments as I saw chances. I had another bit of luck. The attention of the company had been called to the lack of proper room for freight and express, and the superintendent had come up to inquire into the matter. I described the changes that had taken place since my coming to Athens, and gave Joe no small degree of credit in the part he had worked up so successfully. It was decided to tear out the small freight-house, and build a much larger place, putting in a broad, easy staircase, and connecting it with the room over the office. While we were discussing this matter, I asked for an increase of salary, and represented that I had done something toward working up extra business, and that the duties of the place were much more extensive than when I had first taken it, and that no doubt the hotel, as well as the natural increase of business, would add to the number of passengers. I also gently insinuated that I would not be at loss in obtaining a much better position.

When my month's pay reached me, I found my talking had been to some purpose. Five dollars a month was not very much, to be sure, but I took it with thankfulness.

By the last of October we made quite a show in our greenhouses. For our twenty-five dollars we had one hundred and thirty-five roses, some of them extremely beautiful; and we had made a very good friend of the Messrs. S. & Co. I had sixty of my own, besides a number of hardy plants in the ground. One of our cold-frames I had filled with some late chrysanthemums that I found were going to blossom finely. We had many choice geraniums, one very handsome white, that looked not unlike a small rose. Eve's passion had been bourvardias: we had them in all colors, and the dear old-time clove-pinks. Indeed, we had a very handsome show of carnations, and some splendid young heliotrope. We were to plant beds of mignonette and sweet alyssum, and also to do what we could in spring-violets. These things we thought would be as much as we ought to venture upon, for we had much still to learn.

We went in and took possession of our new home. The parlor was very large and on the north side. No provision had been made for heating this, but on the other side one Baltimore heater had been set. There was a sitting-room, dining-room, and commodious kitchen. Up-stairs on the south side were three spacious chambers, two on the north. Three were all we should want to use ordinarily. We might not be quite so cosey, but it would answer very well; and in case of need we could put up a stove or two. At present we could keep warm enough with a very moderate fire.

Walter Benson had spoken for my poultry. I had

thirty-five ordinary hens, mixed considerably with Brahma and a Houdan strain, eighteen elegant Leghorns with a really superb cock. I had kept these apart, and culled out every thing with the slightest off feathering or mark. Then I had about sixty pullets and cockerels, though we had been using up the latter sex. He took the hens of both kinds, and forty of the finest pullets, and paid me sixty-five dollars. I certainly had made on my poultry, though I had done it more to convince myself than for actual profit. Eve was quite jubilant, but we both decided that we did love the flowers rather more. In fact, Eve was a most enthusiastic greenhouse girl. I think the hotel project rather trembled in the balance, though the building itself was making rapid strides.

I insisted upon dividing my hen-fortune with Eve; and about this time she gave up her last music-scholar, although the fair ladies of Athens now formed a musical union, and expected to give several entertainments through the winter. They had a very delightful leader, — an enthusiastic, pleasant-tempered German.

My twenty remaining chickens I devoted to the family store. I was deeply interested in Walter's success, and promised to give him the benefit of my experience. Besides Mrs. Benson, there was Mrs. Gilman and her two children; and they did seem much pleased with their new home. The second week in October was cold, rainy, and unpleasant, but after that it was delightful weather. There was an abundance of grapes for them, some pears and a few apples. They bought a horse, and enjoyed the lovely drives, and we made them acquainted with several of the most agreeable of their neighbors.

I must not omit to state that our new business had already begun. Soon after Mrs. Harwood's return to the city, she had sent me an order for every chrysanthemum that I could cut. A young friend of hers desired to be surrounded by her favorite flower at her wedding. I had white, yellow, and four shades of pink, one very deep red, a beautiful feathery flower, very large and very delicate-looking. From an old root on the place I had raised eight elegant plants. I sent them without knowing their value, leaving it to her to arrange, and received in return a check for seven dollars, with word that some of mine were the finest in the display. I think we both felt wonderfully elated. We had hardly thought to sell them, or indeed any thing, so soon. And a few days later we had an order from Mrs. Palmer for our choice roses and all the bourvardia we had.

I was so near that I could spend a good deal of my

time at this new and fascinating employment; and, as soon as she had a little leisure, Eve must needs stray down, at which Mrs. Pryor complained loudly, until I suggested they might both come and live in a garden. Jane, our handmaiden, seemed left much to her own devices; but she was a good cook, and, the girls said, not extravagant.

Lawrence Hildreth certainly throve upon his new occupation. His angular frame began to fill out, and a healthy color came in the place of the pallor that I had concluded must be natural. He worked in a sensible fashion, leaving off as soon as he felt fatigued.

"I have too much at stake to overdo now," he would say with a smile. "My lessons have been sufficiently costly to make me heed them."

But we walked round about our plantation with high hearts. I had an enthusiasm here, that I had not experienced about our home: indeed, there had always been some presentiment of loss, some vague fear, that I could laugh at now. And I *was* very happy. I should have been an ingrate had it proved otherwise.

"But we shall never have this great place full," I said one day to Larry. "Every week it seems to grow larger to my eyes."

"I don't know as we shall turn it all into a garden," he replied. "On the avenue next to Mr. Teall's we may some day build a house, or houses, unless we get so used to living together that we shall never want to live alone;" and he gave a humorous smile.

There was a row of fine old maples along Rutherford Avenue; and we set out some trees on Linden Street, not enough to shade us in time to come. Mr. Riker had built his first greenhouse a little distance from the corner. We had a plan of some day adding to this by a pretty two-story structure, mostly of glass. We had seen one in Northwood that had captured our fancy. The greenhouse was eighty-seven feet long on Linden Street. The stone foundation was about two feet high, then glass for about thirty inches. The building was twenty feet wide: the peak of the roof was about eight feet, the path down the centre being sunk eighteen inches. On each side of the edge of the roof was fastened a leader that caught the rain from the roof, and at the end they both ran into a cistern. Here were situated the boiler-house and a coal-bin, a force-pump, and a closet for various useful articles; and from here ran the iron pipes used for heating in winter. Nearest the outside edge along both sides was a wide border for plants, while underneath various ferns and plants needing shade could be stowed. On iron braces was another wide row of shelving just high enough to clear one's head. In this we had placed our roses. The methods of ventilation were excellent, and on the Linden-street side the sashes were protected from an accidental stone by coarse wire netting that did not interfere with the light.

The other was far enough back of this to escape being shaded; the side toward the north being boarded, and the glass roof being pitched all one way, with shelves rising step-like for plants. This house was seventy-five feet long, and twenty feet wide, the heat and water arranged the same as in the other. We put our promiscuous plants in here, and the borders we prepared for our violets and seedlings. I had been gathering fine compost, and had brought from the woods several loads of rich soil, and piled up some good loam. We had altered this border, shoring it up with timber by the path. It was about forty inches wide. We made a foundation of rubble, sand, and earth, then mixed our soils for the top layer. We had now the whole thirty-five feet like a large garden-bed. We had ordered one thousand violets; and the day they came. Eve insisted upon helping us to plant them out. By this device we were spared any trouble of potting; though we left a space between, and kept each kind by itself. In this border we also set out fifty heliotrope plants, sowed our mignonette, alyssum, and at the end Eve began a bed of nasturtiums, one of her favorites. We had a number of boxes in which we placed three or four plants of heliotrope, and the rest of our hundred we kept potted.

Every spare moment through October we worked like beavers, doing some things in the evening. At the end of the month we were in tolerable order, and had bought most of our plants for the present. Twice we had gone to auction where private greenhouses were selling out. Our bills stood thus: —

135 roses	$25
15 roses	7
2 camellias	9
100 heliotrope	14
1,000 violets	95
30 azaleas	25
100 bourvardia	20
5 daphne	5
20 fuchsias	5
50 heaths	20
A job lot	7
	$232
Fertilizers	15
	$247
Flower-pots	·24
	$271

We had both greenhouses well stocked with these and the plants we had. We planted seeds of several other things, — choice petunias, snow-queen candytuft, and pansies, the last two in a cold-frame. Our two houses had looked large, but we began to understand that more would be needed another year, though we did not mean to have them so expensive. We saw now that Riker's ideas had not been quite so wild. Cold-frames I could manage tolerably well myself. I had become almost a mason as well as a carpenter.

The last week in October, Eve went to the city. Celia was to make her aunt a brief visit. I went down twice, and took them to see a play that was fascinating everybody, and to hear the "divine Patti." That we were enchanted, I hardly need state.

But, oh, how dreary the meals proved! We were not at home the alternate evenings, being so much engrossed; and Mrs. Pryor complained loudly.

"Really," said Lawrence in a dry tone, "everybody seems to have a claim upon Eve. What will there be left for a husband?"

"Take warning," I replied.

"But, you see, even a piece of cake might be better than none, on the half-loaf principle."

Lawrence had given me a most cordial and brotherly welcome when he knew of the bond between myself and Celia.

"Though I half suspected it when we were at the

West," he confessed. "She was always rehearsing the superior points of Athens, and thought it quite good enough to live in or die in."

But now that they had Eve in New York, they were not going to let her slip so easily. Mrs. Palmer and Mrs. Wilbur made so many engagements for her, that Mrs. Harwood could sympathize with Helen. There were theatre-parties, receptions, teas, and dances. She came home now and then quite as a visitor. Celia returned after a fortnight, so that I had her. Larry could take his turn going to the city, which he did quite often.

We had some cards and circulars printed, and we advertised in a paper at Northwood; for we were quite in earnest about making ourselves known. Orders from New York came to us, — through our good friends, I suppose. Now that outdoor flowers were gone, and hot-house blossoms rather scarce, new people might stand a chance. I found two places in the city where I could be sure of disposing of cut-flowers.

I had not expected a profit so soon, but by the last of November we had taken in thirty-five dollars. But now we were expending our ingenuity in heating and ventilation, which had to be narrowly watched. Our heater for the rose-house was too large, and we did have trouble in tempering it at first.

We found, too, that we had not planned judiciously. The heliotrope required more heat than the violets. We had "cut-offs" in the pipes, and thermometers at different places. On cloudy days we needed greater heat. The night temperature bothered us the most. Indeed, I slung a hammock, and spent two nights studying the alternations. There would be less trouble when the weather became colder: we really had to guard now against too high a range. The watering was more easily managed. An experienced florist told us not to water until a plant required it, — was, indeed, dry on the surface, and then fill the pots to the brim. Twice a week, plants were to be showered. Heliotrope and roses required extra fertilizing. We kept guano-water in a cask, and applied it to some of the plants twice a week, to the others but once.

Among the things I characterized as a job lot were numerous bulbs, — hyacinth, amaryllis, and lilies of various kinds. We resolved to bring our hyacinths into the market early, and covered them up in the mould a short distance from the pipes, potting them as soon as they budded.

CHAPTER XX

NABOBS IN A SMALL WAY

WE all kept the feast of Thanksgiving with Mrs. Wilbur. I petitioned for the "extra man;" and as I was in good repute with the company, he was sent without demur, though he did not come until noon. Lawrence and the Pryors had gone down in the morning. Jane must have thought her numerous mistresses sad gad-abouts; but she was given a day out as well. Joe promised to see that all went well with the greenhouses, which were like a first baby, — we hardly dared take our eyes off of them. But he was quite as much infatuated as we: indeed, I think only the aim of being a partner in a good business kept him from taking service with us.

The hotel was enclosed, and looked quite pretentious; though the prettiest part of the roof — a tower — was to be in the wing. Still, there were some ornamental peaks and windows. A wide piazza was to run across the front, and two bow-windows were to be set on the roof of this, with balconies for the windows above. We had decided that it must hold all of us the next year; for Lawrence and I could not be so far away, and Pryor was resolved to have Eve.

The day was splendid; rather crisp and cold, but with a magnificent sun. I took with me a box of beautiful roses, and had sent some to Ruth and Joe, who were to have the Montgomery household to dine.

How proud and exultant I felt as I stepped on the train! I believe I did not even envy our president, who considered himself one of the coming great railroad-men. I found them all assembled, waiting to welcome me. Mrs. Harwood was there, looking prettier than ever, and keeping Eve under her wing, like a hen with one chick; Mrs. Brooke; Mr. and Mrs. Palmer; Miss Laverne, the Southern cousin; Mr. and Mrs. Farnsworth, *née* Bertha Brooke; and our own six.

I am afraid we talked "shop." It was greenhouse and hotel, and yet we found time for no end of chaffing. They admired the roses enthusiastically: there were three of a new kind, that had made their first essay at blooming. We had some music, and I found we were all to go to the opera. Dinner was at four. It was a dinner of the season, of course, and we enjoyed it heartily. I took out Mrs. Harwood. Two friends of Mr. Wilbur's came in, a

Mr. Woolfe, and Mr. Bernard, who, by the way, was well acquainted with Celia. She looked so bright and winsome, that more than once I almost wondered how she had come to accept me, after all.

The evening was most delightful. We had a dainty supper afterward, then Lawrence and I wended our way homeward. Luckily for us, there was a midnight train. We cast a lingering look at the gleaming roofs that protected our heart's treasures, then trudged on up the hill.

"I declare," said Hildreth, "I feel as if I had taken a new lease of life, and might live to be a hundred. I grow stronger every day. Think of me last year at this time."

Somehow after that every thing went on with a rush. The freight-house was finished, and business seemed on the increase. Joe was here and there, his bright, manly face clear and smiling. Pryor almost flew about, as there was a prospect of considerable building. The "scratch-coat" was put on the hotel: the Musical Union gave a concert, which was splendidly attended at fifty cents a ticket, and passed off finely, leading to a talk of building a real hall, as the only one Athens could boast of was a rather poor affair over some stores. Then there were Christmas preparations. Celia was very busy; and I thought it too hard for her to come home every night, since Eve was away so much. She, radiant girl, was as gay as a butterfly, like the Eve I had known at aunt Carry's.

As for us, we made some mistakes, but, in the main, were successful. Our violets began to bloom, and the mignonette showed buds. Of course, there was a demand for every thing at Christmas-tide. I had brought down a tub of callas in the fall, intending to pot them, but had been too busy, until I found, with the warmth and watering, they were in bud. I had five out by Christmas. We had some calls from the little towns around, two large orders from New York, and numerous private orders. On making up our books the 1st of January, I found we had sold to the amount of sixty-five dollars, and could have done better if we had had the flowers desired. But we counted on quite a harvest during the month to come.

Our Christmas was not spent together, and I seemed to be the one counted out of most things. Eve went to Baltimore with Mrs. Harwood for a fortnight. Evidently she meant to hold my sister with a close hand; but she was so sweet and generous, no one could say her nay. The Hildreths had been hunted up by some Philadelphia cousins in a very cordial manner, and invited for holiday week. Christmas fell on Sunday. On Friday, Eve started.

At the last moment she had half a mind to decline.

"If Celia wasn't going! And you to be left alone!" she exclaimed pathetically.

"Some one *must* stay with the greenhouse, and the station refuses to carry on its business without a clerk. Besides, I am to take Christmas dinner with Joe."

Eve kissed me with a fond, lingering good-by. Then, on Saturday, Lawrence and Celia went. I think she, dear girl, would easily have declined the invitation; but Lawrence was very urgent, thinking to visit the Messrs. S—— again, and see their beautiful greenhouses in winter. The Pryors were to be in New York: indeed, we decided to shut up the house, and give Jane a holiday.

Sunday morning I went to church with Joe. I did miss Eve's voice in the singing. I must say I had never liked Mr. Bradford better. I certainly was coming to pay him a much higher regard, and he had quite won Joe's heart.

The week passed without any special incident. Letters came from all the travellers, who were enjoying themselves immensely: indeed, the Hildreths were to be kept captive until the second day of the New Year.

The first of January was simply magnificent. It

seemed like an April day. In the brightness of the morning sunshine was born Joe Crawford's baby, — a boy, — and both parents were wild with delight. I had brought up some lovely flowers for Ruth.

"And he is to be named for you, my best, my dearest friend," declared Joe, wringing my hand; "and if he will only be as good and noble and generous"—

"O Joe, hush!" I cried earnestly: "you must begin to see that you have used some strength of your own; that others have befriended you to more purpose than my few efforts" —

"But you were the first. You made it possible for me to accept the rest, for it to be offered to me. No, in my heart you will always be first, best; and though my boy will never understand it, he, too, will owe you a debt of gratitude."

"Not if he is saddled with such a queer old-time name. It was my father's fancy to call us after the first two, and Eve does very well; but Adam!" and I laughed with a little contempt. "Anyhow, wait until Eve returns home. She ought to have a voice in the name."

Mrs. Pryor came down, and insisted upon taking the first hug out of the baby. Indeed, Joe's baby created quite a sensation, in spite of there being so many babies in the world.

Celia and her brother returned delighted with their visit. These Philadelphia people were Hildreth relatives, and for a number of years had dropped out of sight, more by accident than design. They were loth to let Celia return, and wished both were to be settled in the Quaker City. Lawrence had enjoyed himself wonderfully, and came home full of plans and projects, and, if it had not been winter, would at once have plunged into building greenhouses.

"But we do look splendid," he commented enthusiastically. "I can't help thinking that I have struck just the right thing. Why, it fairly bewitches me; and I've caught up to you in love if I have not in knowledge. I've studied every spare moment, and asked enough questions to vex any one who was not a born florist. I told the Messrs. S—— about you too, and promised to send you next time. Ad, you must take a vacation. It is selfish for me to have all the good times."

I laughed at that. I was glad enough to see him looking so well and in such bright spirits.

We went back to our usual living. Celia staid home the remainder of the week. On Thursday it blew off very cold, and Friday morning it began to snow. All day the storm increased. Trains were delayed, roads blocked, and though about nightfall the snow ceased, it seemed more bitterly cold than before.

"I shall stay down all night," I said to Larry.

He insisted that he should, also, but I overruled him. I was a little afraid of some cold or trouble; and finally he gave in, for his greatest desire now was to be strong and well. About nine I took a blanket and hammock, and after looking at the fires and the dampers, and seeing the temperatures were right, I rolled myself in the blanket, and settled for a nap among my fragrant roses. It was a rather warm and sweet atmosphere, but I could sleep anywhere. I left my lamp burning. How the wind did roar and tear about in great gusts! I felt almost as if the houses might be moved off their foundation.

But presently I slept soundly, — three solid hours. It was two when I looked at my watch. I roused myself from my rather cramped position, sprang out, and glanced at the thermometer. It was fifty degrees, — hardly up to the mark for roses and heliotrope. I had brought all my largest plants in here, and they were showing bud. So I stirred up my fire. I wondered with a little shiver how the other house was doing, and dreaded to plough through the snow. However, there *was* a good deal at stake, and it was eternal vigilance here as well as elsewhere. So, wrapped in my blanket, lantern in hand, I sallied out, going up to my knees in snow. We had resolved, before another winter, to connect the houses. The biting wind shaved my face. I unlocked the door and entered.

I had not come a moment too soon. The highest temperature was forty-six degrees, the lowest forty degrees. I put on the draughts immediately. If I had waited until morning, my plants would have been ruined. For the next hour I watched and tramped around until it came up to fifty-two degrees. I knew it would rise a little higher, and that outside it could not well be colder; so I returned, and, finding matters right here, again settled myself to my hammock. Hard work, do you say? Well, as a lad in a Western station, I used to go out at one o'clock, and switch off one cattle-train that a freight and express might pass, there being but one track. If I had overslept, or been taken suddenly ill, a smash-up would have been the result. I have sometimes run up and down the track fifteen minutes on the coldest of nights, lest drowsiness should overcome me. Ah! this was heaven itself compared to that dreariness.

I slept until morning in my Eden. All things were right, when a far-off whistle roused me. I ran up to the station. The few who took this train had commutation tickets; but I always preferred being on hand, though it was now behind time. Then I began to shovel snow: I do not think there had ever been such a storm at Athens. The roads were impassable until the snow-plough came out. The trains wheezed and groaned along; but, oh, how lovely the world looked! The gray sky turned to blue: there were bars of faint yellow in the east, and presently a pale sun struggled through. We had been to zero in the night, and now were slowly crawling up, but the wind had ceased blowing.

Lawrence came down with my breakfast and some coffee, which we heated anew on the stove, and I toasted my piece of steak. We impressed one of the indolent Athenians into shovelling snow, — had our station-platform cleared, and some paths made about our greenhouses. Every thing was all right. Larry insisted upon being very grateful, but I would have it that the business risk was fully as much mine as his.

"And when we come to real living, it must be nearer by," said he. "I feel rather sorry that we are up there on the hill, but for Pryor's sake I wouldn't make any change. He is such a capital good fellow. But, Ad, I am thankful you *did* sell your house to so good an advantage."

Certainly, it was a piece of rare good fortune.

Pryor grumbled a little as well. He had never

lived so far away. He brought Mrs. Pryor and Celia down in his sleigh. They could not spend a long, dreary day alone in the house.

"If Eve does not come home, we will have to move down in town. What did possess us to take a house so far from the station!"

I laughed at this. "Why, it has never seemed any great distance to you all," I said.

"Well, we are lonesome without Eve,—that is the truth; and we have come to spend the day in the greenhouses," was the reply.

Down we went. We had the hammock and some stools. We envied no one Florida or Bermuda. The girls strolled around in the warm, fragrant atmosphere, did a little work, then rested, reading novels. It was a kind of fairy-land. They had brought some lunch, and Pryor came up from Joe's with some steaming coffee and cups. We had a regular picnic.

"What a silly thing to leave this space between the houses!" said Lawrence; "and how delightful it will be to glass it all over, and wander about at one's will!"

Celia considered this quite a brilliant scheme. They were about twenty feet apart now. We could put two rows in between, with a width of ten feet apiece, which would give us a fine lot of room.

We wandered about: we made love, — let me be honest; how could one help it amid roses and violets, and all sweet things? The sun sparkled over the snow outside, but the keen air nipped your cheeks the instant you stirred out. Well, we were in Arcadie.

The roads were quite broken and cleared up that day, and the weather some ten degrees warmer. I ventured to go home and go to bed, like a reasonable human being; and the next day the world was jolly with sleigh-riding. Lawrence went to New York with boxes of flowers, and brought home orders for the first heliotrope we could rush into market. It seemed to me that people were crazy about flowers. How could they be willing to spend so much money for such fragile, perishable things? Had I really touched the secret spring of a successful business?

There followed upon this three weeks of the most magnificent winter weather that could be imagined. The roads were kept white by a few lighter snowfalls. The sun shone nearly every day, and there were no violent alterations in the temperature: it was just steady cold. Two nights I spent in the greenhouse, but I need not have done so. It is the sudden changes that are so difficult to provide for. Celia took a holiday most of the time. We went sleigh-riding, and Lawrence was transformed into ticket-agent. He was quite a fair operator, as well; and no brother could have been kinder.

Eve went to Washington,—the gay little witch,—and had the best of times; stumbled over aunt Carry, who was visiting her daughter. Uncle Lennard was quite successful in some land speculations in Colorado; and aunt Carry was in the best of spirits, but much amazed that a pretty girl like Eve should be single still, and bewailed the misfortune of her being buried alive in a little country village. This time her sympathy included me; for some months after, uncle Lennard wrote to offer me a promising business opening, and thought it a sin that a capable young man should be wasting his time in a wretched little railroad station.

Ah, uncle Lennard! I would not have changed my Eden for all the money you were making!

During January we sold one hundred and fifty dollars' worth of flowers. That looked enormous to me. I went over the account several times to see if it was true. But we had such splendid luck with heliotrope and bourvardia, and there was always a demand for roses. I felt now that we might reasonably expect to succeed.

Now there came a thaw with a "muggy" week. This was worse than the cold. How to get the right proportion of ventilation and not chill, the right amount of watering, and how to provide for a sun that obstinately refused to shine, were important questions. But we came through it pretty well for new beginners. Some of our largest heliotropes blighted, and we cut them back. Some of our roses hung listlessly; but we had hosts of carnations, and no end of violets.

We planted now a hundred three-inch pots with cucumber-seeds, three to a pot. Where we could make room for them, we hardly knew; but some of the violets and other things would be done before long, and for a month, at least, we need not worry. Eve came home radiant. Joe and Ruth and the baby claimed her for a whole week: indeed, she was in danger of being divided around piecemeal. Where Lawrence was to come in, rather puzzled me. But distance all the rest, he surely did.

"I suppose you think it queer enough that I have not hunted up some one with a fortune," she said to me in a curiously defiant manner, as if that had been my plan for her. "Aunt Carry will consider that I have gone out of my senses, for she *did* pick out a rich old fellow in Washington who has worn himself almost to a shadow amassing a fortune. And there have been others. But I like *him*," — blushing warmly, — "for his manliness, his truth, and his sense of honor about little matters that so many people pass over;" and her eyes are lustrous as she utters this. "I could trust him to the uttermost, I could trust him anywhere, under any stress; and the world is full of evil deeds nowadays. O Ad, my darling!" and her soft arms are about my neck, her flushed cheek throbs against mine, "have we not both found the best, the sweetest thing in the whole wide world? Is it not Eden come over again? Who cares for the great Babylon with its strifes and envyings and hatreds? We shall be rich enough for our needs, and, what is immeasurably better, we shall be happy, gladly, joyfully happy. We shall not envy any nabob of them all."

I held her in my arms many minutes. Who dares to say other loves pale beside the one great soul-giving?

I think Pryor rather resented Eve's engagement in a queer, irritable sort of way; but everybody else took it fairly well. Sadie Palmer insisted that she had thrown herself away, and that, if she had shown good sense, she would have chosen a plumber, so she could have made sure of a trip to Europe. But we four were satisfied.

The baby's name, too, did get settled at last. It was simply Thurston. Eve and I stood for it. I endowed it with a silver cup and five dollars that opened the little lad's banking-account.

We exhort our young people a great deal on the subject of saving money, and there are tremendous economical essays in many of the more intellectual journals. I sometimes wonder how the writers thereof would live and save on fifty dollars a month. Here was my essay for four months. I seldom smoked. I rarely drank beer or any other liquor. Our housekeeping, as I have said, was a joint affair, we three men paying the bills; and we *did* buy at a considerable advantage. My cost of the living, including Eve's share, was as follows, under the head of board: —

October.	— Board	$26
	Clothing	6
	Incidentals	7
		$39
November.	— Board	$22
	Overcoat	20
	Incidentals	5
		$47
December.	— Board	$22
	Clothing	6
	Incidentals	3
	Gifts	7
		$38
January.	— Board	$18
	Shoes	5
	Incidentals	4
	Gifts	10
		$37

The reader will see that during four months, at fifty dollars a month, I had earned two hundred dollars. I had spent one hundred dollars and sixty-one cents. Consequently I had saved just thirty-nine. Incidentals with me meant my paper, car-fares, charities, and a very few personal wants. I was not severe on clothes. I seldom bought high-priced ones. During these four months I had hardly spent five dollars for Eve: she would have it so. Granting that I could continue this scale, which was hardly possible, I should save one hundred and thirty-six dollars in a year. I could take no journeys, rarely go to a place of amusement, must never be ill, and have no extra demands. Is not the subject of saving largely theorized upon when one has a small income?

I had lent Pryor my thousand dollars at seven per cent, on condition it remained six months or longer with him. I knew out of the remainder I could carry on current expenses with the greenhouse, and I would not have that lying idle.

Before finishing this chapter, I must say a few words about Walter Benson. I found him a careful little business chap. When one has a great love and aptitude for any certain branch, carefulness does the rest. I think these three are the component parts of most of the so-called genius. There is no such thing as luck, generally speaking. If you know how to do a thing rightly, and do it in that manner, success may be looked for with certainty.

He had the love and the aptitude. A cross hen rarely pecked at him. His voice and motions were all gentle. He was very ingenious as well. He had ninety-six laying hens and pullets, and he made them attend to their duty straight along by warmth, water, and proper food. In December he purchased an incubator that held two hundred eggs, and put in half that number. Testing them on the fourth day, he found fifteen of the number not fertilized. Of his eighty-five eggs he hatched successfully seventy-eight chickens, paying thorough attention to it. He made some artificial brooders that would hold about twenty-five, and kept them in these in a warm room for two weeks, losing five chickens. He had fitted up the barn-loft with a stove and a hot-water pipe to run under the brooders, and now he took them out there. They had sunshine, freedom, gravel, bits of green things, and proper food, and grew famously, being all of large breeds. He had seventy-three beautiful chickens, which he sold, at seven weeks old, for a dollar apiece. The next time he put in two hundred eggs, and had from these one hundred and seventy-eight chickens, losing only three or four. Of eggs he had an abundance at their highest prices. Clearly, he had a "genius" for it.

After February came in, our winter was very much broken. And, oh, how busy we were, — Celia with her pictures, Eve and Helen with the hotel, Lawrence and I with our greenhouse which grew more captivating every day! We learned to economize space. When our plants showed signs of giving out, we cut them back, put them in a cooler place, — infirmary, we called it, — treated them to fresh soil, and let them recover. Our geranium-slips were coming on finely, and we would have quite a host of bedding-plants. After the snow went off, I enriched my strawberries, and covered them with the sashes; and in a short time bud-clusters stuck up their defiant green heads as if they were outwitting somebody.

CHAPTER XXI

COUNTING THE GAINS

The 1st of April we balanced our books, as we had resolved to do every six months. So far it had been an experiment, though we did not mean to be discouraged if we had not come out quite square. We had found many ways in which we could improve. Our nasturtiums coming in bloom during March were eagerly snapped up, and brought us considerable profit. I told Eve that this rightly belonged to her; but she declared that she had been so in luck all winter, she would not take a penny of it.

I found now that we stood on this wise, —

EXPENSES.

Plants	$247
Circulars and advertising and fares	24
Flower-pots	36
Fuel	73
	$380
Half-year's interest	175
	$555

We had decided the business must pay the interest on the cost of the place at seven per cent, so Lawrence would not lose on his investment.

Our profit ran in this order: —

October	$21
November	37
December	65
January	170
February	145
March	163
	$591

I suppose you will think thirty-six dollars was small pay for half a year's work. It would not have done had we nothing else to depend on. I am aware that people have made more money on a smaller place. Our advantage was our increase of stock, our experience, our business being in good shape to go to work at in real earnest. We had bedding-plants and tomatoes and lettuce in cold-frames. Indeed, we began to sell the lettuce now; our first fifty heads bringing us in seven dollars, and giving us our ground to use over again. The last of the month brought us thirty-eight dollars for strawberries. In fact, our April sales mounted up one hundred and ninety-five dollars, and our expense for coal was trifling.

By the middle of April the hotel was practically completed. There was to be no papering at present, until after the walls had settled. Part of the woodwork was finished in oil or varnish, a little of it stained; and most of the walls on the third floor were left in a soft light-gray tint, very pleasant to the eye. It was plain, but comfortable and homelike; no great pretence, or straining after effect. Everybody was interested in the furnishing and naming, especially Helen and Eve.

I think Lawrence had quite a desire to marry, but Eve had some plans of her own. Pryor would have been heart-broken had she declined the supervision of the hotel: in fact, I think he felt rather fretted until she did agree to it. Jane had offered to come as general housekeeper, — a position she had held in a charitable institution. She had a cousin who was an excellent cook, and who had a son sixteen, and a daughter fourteen. On condition she could have these two employed, she would come for lower wages. Mrs. Pryor thought these young people could be trained in ways of usefulness, and Jane answered for their being "nice children."

Furnishing a place like this did seem rather appalling, but this had been thought of in the finishing. The parlors had a wide border of hardwood, in very pretty design, and the carpets would be more in the fashion of a large rug. On the chambers, matting would be largely used: some of the smaller rooms had painted floors and rugs. Celia brought out many very pretty ideas. I began to learn that Eve had not a monopoly of them.

Lawrence and I chose a rather large chamber on the third floor. It had two closets, was to have two beds. On the second floor were to be the Pryors, with Celia and Eve, and a family sitting-room, with a little studio for Celia. Our own rooms we furnished, and the sitting-room received general contributions. This was in the southern end also, and a side-stairs led directly to our chamber. So, in effect, we would be a little family by ourselves.

Certainly it was an unfailing source of interest; but, as it needed to be advertised immediately, a name was an urgent necessity. No one wanted to stand direct sponsor, though we tried on each other's names, and they sounded very well, but did not quite captivate our fancy. Joe humorously proposed "The Adam and Eve," as we could not have it Paradise or Eden.

"See here," said Gordon Pryor, "some of you go down and call on Mrs. Harwood, and ask the favor of her name. Harwood House has a tone and style about it. And it just occurs to me, that — may I be slangy, ladies and gentlemen? — Mrs. Harwood gave Athens its fortunate 'boost' into prosperity. I was awfully discouraged when you came here, Thurston, and thought I should look out some more thriving settlement. But Truro and Glendale had built up from nothing greater than a railroad station; and this place possessed finer capabilities, was more picturesque. Perhaps I had a high ambition in wanting to bring up a town; but why not do it here as well as at the West? You know how I badgered you to buy the Cassel place. I think I was making it a sort of test. And but for your charming Mrs. Harwood, there mightn't have been any luck at all."

"Why, that *is* splendid!" declared Eve. "I will go to New York to-morrow."

Mrs. Harwood accepted it as a compliment. She came over, and we had a royal christening. We had just "moved in," as the girls thought they could get along faster by being on the spot; and the living was like a picnic, with oceans of fun to ease the work.

Lawrence and I were busy as badgers. We packed away violets and every thing we could spare, and had a cucumber garden. Of our three hundred seeds, we had two hundred and nineteen thrifty plants. In the warm, rich soil they had thriven finely; and, as luxuries out of season bring high prices, we sold our first hundred for fifteen dollars, the next three hundred for ten dollars a hundred, and the lowest brought us in three dollars. In all, we had nineteen hundred cucumbers.

We had to hire an extra man in our garden, and took an apprentice, a friendless lad Joe had taken in out of the boundless pity of his heart, and who had a passion for gardening. I felt I ought to throw up my position, but Lawrence insisted that I did my share in off-hours.

Cut-flowers were dropping down in price, but the demand for bedding-plants began. It seemed as if half the people in Athens were flower-crazy, and from the little stations around they came daily. Indeed, the prestige of raising strawberries and cucumbers early in the season gave us a great mount on the ladder of fame.

"Well," said Mr. Montgomery one day, as he was sauntering round, "you do beat the Dutch; and my grandmother used to say they were hard to beat. 'Most ready to buy another house, I suppose? Young men like Pryor and you are making all the money! And that queer-looking little Benson, with his incubator! I never would believe there were any such fools in the world as to give a dollar for a spring-chicken or a quart of strawberries, and ten or twenty cents for a cucumber. Why, it used to take solid work to make a fortune years ago, not any such nonsensical fandangoes!"

He looked very much aggrieved, and eyed the greenhouses as if they were a positive injury to him. It was rather hard, when he had so confidently predicted my unsuccess.

We decided that we must have a new fence around our garden. There was a very fair picket-fence down Linden Street; and we had this strengthened with some extra posts, about two feet higher, from which were stretched two rows of barbed wire. At the bottom of the lot, a tight board fence three feet high, and three rows of wire above this. On Rutherford Avenue, we had quite a pretty wire fence, and now we felt well protected from mischievous marauders. Then we arranged our ground between the houses, which gave us two more long arcades, both having pointed roofs, and taking the sunshine beautifully, while they were quite protected from the sharp winds. We put in one more heater, and arranged some new leaders, that our rain-water should not go to waste. The cost of this, and the extra that Hildreth had spent in the fall, added about another thousand in value to the place. In here, we began to raise some stock for the coming winter.

During May, our sales for bedding-plants, tomatoes, and cut-flowers amounted to three hundred and ninety-seven dollars. We had also sold lettuce and some cucumbers, and had our out-of-doors beds arranged. My young peach-trees looked thrifty, and blossomed very nicely: my currants made a good show. It was such a delight to watch them changing day by day.

By the last of May ten rooms were engaged at Harwood House. Our new cook rejoiced in the high-sounding name of Bathsheba, commonly called Sheba. She was not quite as refined and lady-like as Jane, but she evidently understood her business. Tilly made a deft little waiter, and Homer exhibited signs of "handiness" that spoke well for his future training. By the last of the month we had quite a household, and only five rooms vacant. Mrs. Harwood engaged two rooms for summer quarters. Mr. and Mrs. Palmer, infant daughter and nurse, and a cousin of Mrs. Brooke's, — a Mr. Danforth, — came in their party. Then we had no fear of the hotel *not* being a success. We were all very much interested in it.

Eve kept the books, made out the bills, looked after household stores, and entertained. The master of the house, its acknowledged head, was Gordon Pryor, quite an important citizen of Athens, with his real-estate office, lumber and coal business; but Joe took most of the charge of this department. There was, of course, a good deal of talk about his having too many irons in the fire; and some of the old fogies predicted his speedy downfall. But I think Pryor quite knew what he was about; and though in certain respects he seemed venturesome, he had what is called a long head, and a shrewd one as well. He had started out to make Athens a live place, and he was doing it.

He had the pretty chestnut-grove cleared up, rustic seats arranged, and hooks put up for hammocks. Then he arranged a lawn-tennis court, and a club was speedily formed. The Musical Union was to meet once in two weeks in the hotel-parlor, and regale us with songs. He purchased two fine rowboats, and kept one or two carriages on hire all the time.

Of course he was to pay Eve a salary. Mrs. Harwood demurred a little at the whole arrangement, so did Hildreth; but Eve carried her point in a most charming manner. There was something quite indescribable about her. I think the French word "*chic*" expresses it. She had an elegant kind of dignity,—light, airy, but not frivolous. People would not be likely to offer her a slight to her face. Then she had such a joyous, inspiriting nature: every thing she touched seemed to come into shape at once. Joe had this same quality. Perplexity appeared rather amusing when they attacked it. Trouble lost its sharp edge.

We had a great surprise early in July, in the return of Señor Estradura with a pretty Spanish wife, whose large, soft dark eyes conquered you at once. His amazement at all things — changes, improvements — was absolutely laughable; and he insisted at once on being enrolled on the books of Harwood House.

We certainly *did* have a delightful summer. There were *musicales*, amateur theatricals twice, dancing-parties, and no end of out-of-door amusements. I think everybody enjoyed it immensely. Other houses were filled. People began to visit Athens as a much talked-of place, and were enthusiastic about its beauty; while its proximity to New York rendered it so accessible. It still had the air of a two-hundred-years-old country-town. There were famous old oaks and elms, hillsides, chestnut-groves; and this summer we christened our highest peak Mount Ida.

As for ourselves, we prospered. We worked hard, early in the morning and late at night, taking turns at office-business for a rest. Lawrence certainly throve upon it. We saw our way to larger things, — to prosperity, perhaps to fortune. The consumption of flowers and choice early fruit or berries is enormous. True, an immense deal comes from the South, from all over. People's desire for it may pall a little; but you set before them a dish of strawberries, ripened by the sun, fragrant with dews, and fresh from the vine, with a lovely, perfect flavor, and it *is* more enjoyable to a critical taste than berries picked within three or four days of ripeness. So with tomatoes. We raised some early ones in the greenhouse: we had others that blossomed while yet in the cold-frames. The later ones, I thought, would hardly pay for marketing; but the first fortnight my demand was beyond my supply. I had, too, an excellent customer in the hotel; though we made special rates with Pryor, or rather Eve, who proved as excellent a purveyor on a large scale as she had been on a smaller one.

We kept our man ten weeks, and paid him one hundred dollars; and we made forty-one dollars on the gardening he did for outside parties. We paid Fred Harrison five dollars a week for the first year. He was a strong, stout lad of sixteen, with a great love for the business, and unusual tastes. He boarded with a woman near by, who took him at a low price in consideration of his doing some work for her, which agreement I am glad to say he kept faithfully.

There were times when my heart smote me with a pang as Joe Crawford walked through the grounds with me. His whole soul was with us, and it seemed cruel to have him crowded out. But we could not do as well by him as Pryor was doing, which was beyond what he had first promised. Then, I do not know how he could have spared so efficient and trustworthy a man as Joe. They pulled together so harmoniously. Pryor had no mean little jealousies. I think he was as anxious that Joe should prosper as if he had been his own brother.

"It will all come out right in the end," said Joe in his cheery fashion. "Pryor is thinking of getting control of this piece of the Teall property on Myrtle Avenue; and if he does, I'm to have the lot down there, joining you. We'll have a gate; and Ruth and I can walk through at our leisure, and take as much delight as if it was really ours. And maybe you will let me come in and amuse myself trying experiments. It is better to keep straight on in the road of prosperity, than to turn aside and spend one's time getting established over again. But I shall always look at you two fellows with just a bit of envy down deep in my heart."

Dear Joe. He was welcome to the best we had! There have been several happy years in our lives; but with all its labor, that one might truly be called a golden summer. It was not free from perplexities, and sometimes I grudged the busy hours that kept me from my darling. But every day brought us nearer the time when our two lives would be merged into one. I do not know that our hopes and plans could have been more united by any tie. Now, in our days of youth, we meant to make some provision for the time that overtakes all, if life is spared, when toil becomes a burden, and one loses that keen relish for the struggle, the true time of enjoyment, when one has fully earned it.

It was a bright, glad, lovely summer. Celia used to repeat a little poem from a writer of some note in years agone, beginning, —

> "Oh, time is sweet, when roses meet,
> With breath of spring around them!"

and two of the last lines used to float through my brain, —

> "And naught can be so sweet to see,
> As old friends met together."

And there was a great meeting of old friends. The hotel and the growing charm of Athens called back most of the gay group who had participated in the frolic of the first summer in our own house. Mrs. Wilbur gave a really elegant lawn-party, the Randalls another, and Walter Benson insisted that we should accept the hospitalities of our old home. Estradura took his wife about the grounds, explaining in his vivacious Spanish his remembrance of an olden delight. Is it truly only such a brief while ago? So much has happened since that summer!

This with him is merely a visit, since he is to return to Europe in the autumn. Why, it seems as if almost a lifetime lay between.

We planned to be married in October, the four of us. We were to go on living at Harwood House: it was convenient, and in some respects less care. Eve's engagement was made with Pryor for a year, but she was to have a month's vacation. She had certainly shown that she could keep a hotel. Several of the married couples proposed to stay on through the winter; and three of the young men, whom I rather suspected of being charmed with the native belles, engaged steady quarters. Mr. Kingdon of the wire-works, a widower with three daughters, gave up housekeeping to go away for the summer, and on returning they settled at Harwood House. So there would be a family for the winter as well.

Pryor had arranged his house with due regard to heating. The steam-boiler stood about in the middle of the basement story; and the heat could be entirely cut off of the northern end, as he had not supposed there would be any demand for the rooms in the winter. So with the water. One could live in the southern rooms with no fear of freezing pipes, or trouble of any kind.

In addition to the " help," there had been a young colored man as waiter, and a laundress. This had been a scheme of Eve's. There was a splendid large laundry fitted up conveniently. The laundress had twenty dollars a month and her board. She washed and ironed regularly. The clothing of the boarders was taken at ordinary prices, Homer spent an hour or two a day at the washing-machine, and Jane occasionally ironed. When they fell behind, an extra woman was hired. There proved to be considerable profit in this, and the boarders were well satisfied.

Pryor had been getting his money out of his cottages, and resolved to enlarge the hotel; for we found there was call for transient accommodations, and a demand for meals. Parties rowed up the river, and wanted a dinner, or were out driving, and required refreshments of some kind. All these accommodations had a bearing upon the future of Athens, and Pryor had resolved to use every effort for its advancement.

As for us, our ambition was not a whit behind his. We improved every moment, every opportunity. Some mornings we were in our garden by daylight, and it repaid our care generously. We had a splendid out-of-doors rose-bed. Having so much space, we made nice wide paths everywhere, and our place was quite a resort of the hotel people. We built two rustic summer-houses, which we found extremely pleasant for ourselves. We re-arranged our rose-house, putting in the most profitable winter-bloomers, and those in greatest demand. Bon Silene, Sofrano, Mrs. Charles Wood, a beautiful tea-rose called Sunset, and a number of other hybrid perpetuals, we had found excellent. We had also managed admirably with heliotrope, and had a large plot of cuttings. But we found one of the greatest points for profit was novelty. A new flower, or a great quantity of something out of season, took like wildfire. We meant the coming winter to make money.

We laid out some new cold-frames on quite a different plan, digging about two feet down, and filling up one foot with soil. The sides we braced with timber. They were about five feet wide, and slanted to a fall of ten inches in that. Our timbering was raised a little, and the ground thrown up for warmth. We had here two rows fifty feet long, which lay to the south, and would take the sun all winter. On bitter cold nights we could cover them over; and in here we set many hardy things for use in the ensuing spring, and so had our heated houses to use for other matters. Our timber had been odds and ends from Pryor's yard, and our glass was very cheap. The labor we did ourselves.

On the 1st of October, our second term, as we called it, we stood thus: —

SALES.

April.	Flowers	$195
	Bedding-plants	87
May.	Bedding-plants	395
	Cut-flowers	150
June.	Cut-flowers	130
	Plants	180
July.	Flowers	156
Aug.	Flowers	145
Sept.	Flowers	132
	Plants	54
	Cucumbers, early and late	240
	Strawberries	67
	Other fruits and vegetables	78
	Outside gardening	41
		$1,950

The expenses for the six months were as follows: —

Paid to gardener ten weeks	$100
Paid to boy five months	125
For new plants	15
Flower-pots	10
Interest	210
Coal	7
Improvements	45
	$512

Subtracting our expenses from the income, and dividing that sum by two, gave us each seven hundred and nineteen dollars for our summer's work. I had saved from my salary an average of twelve dollars a month; and all my savings, including the interest on my thousand dollars, counted up five hundred and twenty dollars. So that now my fortune amounted to $2,247. I began to feel quite like a nabob.

We advanced our lad's wages to six dollars a week. Our coal had been put in: our autumnal work was pretty well done. In such a business, there always remains plenty of work, but we had resolved not to let one season's duties lap over into another. And in view of what was to occupy a part of this month, we thought it would not be wisdom to fall behind.

We found that we had nearly quadrupled our stock. Our four houses were as full as they could be crowded with regard to the well-being of our favorites. Our roses were in a splendid condition. We had kept on raising new ones, and now and then developed an unexpected variety through some queer freak of nature.

I must say a word here about my young peach-trees. I had now two rows of twenty each that would come into fine bearing another year. We had from them all about five bushels of peaches this year, and we could count on considerable profit. My blackberries I had set along the Myrtle-avenue fence. Some few might be taken by officious hands, but there would be an abundance left. They had grown tremendously, and would fruit finely another summer. It seemed to me that we could count on a clear income of over a thousand dollars apiece next year. I could afford to throw up the station, and sent in my resignation to take effect the 1st of October. I received a very kindly note in reply, — the business at Athens, passenger, freight, and expressing, had increased so much, that they regretted losing so honest and efficient a man. They would therefore advance my salary to sixty dollars a month.

Who shall say after this that corporations have no souls?

I explained that I had entered a more profitable and agreeable business, and thanked them for their generous offer. I could afford to retire from railroading, unless at some future time I should be elected director or president. Yet I looked around the old station and the little office with a pang of curious regret. There had been many hours of happiness within its walls.

An old friend that I had known on a Western road came to hand, — a Frank Tracy who had passed through quite a career. He had been married and divorced. His wife was somewhere, taking care of two children; and he was a jolly, improvident fellow of two and thirty, without money enough to bury him when he died. Socially he was not likely to come much within our circle, for our pleasures would have bored him. He drank a little, not to excess, played billiards and pool, and did some betting on horses in the season. In three months' time there had been so many complaints that he was removed, and the thing tried over with a rather worn-out married man of forty, whose wife came to live over the station. But it was not such romantic living as ours had been.

"I suppose," said Joe, "if some one had told me three years ago that I might succeed you at the station, and earn fifty dollars a month, it would have lifted me clear off my feet. And here I am on the high road to a fair competence, with the sweetest wife in the world and the finest baby, all because you hammered enough common sense into my head to see that it was better and happier by far to have something of one's own, instead of handing it over to a saloon-keeper. If there was half the anxiety that the poor man should have a home of his own that is displayed in inducing him to drink beer and rum, how much better off the world would be! There certainly will be a good deal to answer for at the last. And I am not sure but it will one day become one of the big factors in political economy."

I think Joe is right. I am not a bigot. But when

we talk of raising our fellow-creatures by education and art and a love of beauty, let us not drag them down with the other hand into blighting temptations.

CHAPTER XXII

WEDDING BELLS

"AND they were married, and lived happily ever afterward." I suppose that is the orthodox ending or beginning. Little did I imagine that Eve and I would find our fate and fortune in a small, sleepy, old-time country-town. But we had startled it out of its hundred-year nap, which, perhaps, has been better than "painting it red."

I fancy that a man's idea of marriage is, oftenest, going off quietly, and, like Mr. Wemmick, stepping in to be married, finding every thing ready with no fuss. But — well, Lawrence and I were in a manner patriots, and were ready to be sacrificed for our country.

It would have been a great disappointment to the Athenians, and to our own little circle as well, if we had not taken them into account. First of all, Gordon Pryor announced that the bridal feast, in whatever shape it was given, was solely his affair. Then, a double wedding was rather out of the ordinary. And there were so many friends — consequently, there was no resource but to resign ourselves to fate.

It seemed to me that Harwood House overflowed with guests. Many of Eve's girl-friends came over, — married now, of course, — but one could not forbid them hotel privileges, even if one had felt ever so hermit-like. The Hildreth cousins came on from Philadelphia; at least, three of them did, — two bright girls, and a very delightful young man. There were three more who were heads of families.

We were married in church at seven in the evening. The church was almost a garden of flowers. Mr. Wilbur gave away both brides. Mr. Bradford performed the ceremony with the kind of tender solemnity that goes to one's heart. We were convoyed back to the hotel, which was fragrant with flowers also; and —

> "The feast was set,
> The guests were met."

For two hours we enjoyed it all. We were not bored, we were not surfeited with good wishes; and we *did* appreciate the love and kindness and the enduring friendship, for some of it had been tried. At nine o'clock, Celia and I said good-by to the circle, and went out to try the new life by ourselves.

Lawrence and Eve had so willed it, since we could not both go away.

Where we went, it matters not. It was strange and new and sweet to have Celia all to myself. I saw visions through her artistic eyes. We planned out our lives, as I suppose all newly wedded lovers do. But the crowning delight of all, was belonging to each other. We had been sensible lovers, we had license now to be as foolish as we listed. I do not even think we were troubled about the opinion of those we met, whether or not they considered us newly married. It was a delightful, leisurely holiday in the glorious old autumn.

We ended in Philadelphia one Friday evening, expecting to reach Athens the next night; but, lo! the hospitable Hildreths, aided and abetted by Eve and Lawrence, had planned otherwise. They two were to come on Saturday evening, and we were all to return on Monday.

There were many things to see that day; but I obeyed Lawrence's behest, and visited his favorite greenhouses. Seven acres under glass was flower-farming on a large scale. It appeared to me that we were viewing all the beauty and bloom of the whole world. Ours was a sort of child's playhouse compared to it; and the well-informed, courteous proprietors were delightful men to spend hours with.

Many new ideas and suggestions presented themselves to my mind; but I found that, in the main, we were making our time count profitably. It is reaching a result in the best possible manner that is the test: the amount of time spent upon it is not the basis of a correct estimate. If the day should ever come when each man can do the work for which he is best fitted, and for which he has a love, — for the two things *must* go together to make a success, — there will be a great improvement in the productions of the world, and, perhaps, the inhabitants thereof.

We had a most enjoyable day, and at nine in the evening Lawrence and Eve made their appearance. The greenhouses had been left to the care of Joe and our young lad, who was progressing finely, being born to the business. How curiously fascinating Eve looked! I could not help watching her. The Hildreths were quite bewitched, especially the young man; and I ought not omit uncle Jared, a fine specimen of the half-Quaker school, whose "thees" had the endearing German sound when he used them.

A heavenly Sunday it was, but all days were transcendent. I was so glad to have Eve and Lawrence once more, and Celia's happiness was as fervent. Eve would always be the more brilliant, of course; and the added grace and dignity of marriage imparted something quite indescribable. And just here I ought to say that a New-York paper gave us quite a grand "send-off" on the occasion of our marriage, calling Eve a "beautiful society-girl well known in the city," and Celia "one of our talented young artists," and bringing Harwood House, as well as Athens, into prominent notice.

Still, it was very pleasant to come back home. There were warm welcomes on every hand: even the very flowers seemed eloquent. Joe's greeting, I think, touched me the most of all.

"I'm glad you are fast here," he added, between smiles and tears; "for if you went to any new place, I should pack up and follow. I don't know why, Thurston, but it just seems as if I could not stay in any place that didn't hold you."

"We are likely, all of us, to be fixtures," I replied cheerfully; "and I haven't seen many places that I like better. If we are not quite in the heart of things, we can get there in a few moments; and our little town has many beauties of its own."

It seemed so odd at first not to have to run up to the station every hour or so! I did oblige Tracy now and then; but I soon found that the more you granted, the more he asked, and so began to decline. And now I could throw my whole soul into my new business. We would have much more to take care of this winter. There were experiments to try; there was propagating by almost every method; the continual watchfulness of light, heat, soils; nursing up drooping plants; weeding out sickly, worthless ones. I never tired of it. Each day my soul seemed more thoroughly imbued with it, more content with the delightful toil that was pleasure under another name, — a thin disguise, perhaps.

Of course, we went on at the hotel. I added another to the suite of rooms Lawrence and I had shared, — a studio for Celia, that was library and sitting-room when we chose. She kept up her art connection in New York, going two days in a week, but relinquished her classes, devoting herself wholly to the pictures she loved, as she always had some orders waiting for her.

But we four spent a great deal of time in the greenhouses. Eve was quite an expert, always had been. Her love for a home and a garden had led me to take the first fortunate step in my career. I felt that I really owed my good fortune to her; and, though she had refused to take more than her half, my wedding-gift to her had been a check for five hundred dollars: and, oddly enough, Mrs. Harwood's had been the same, as she charmingly insisted on not counting her additions to the trousseau. Indeed,

I thought the wedding-gifts of both brides quite munificent.

By the time we were really settled, business started up amazingly. I had been haunted by a secret fear that we might overdo, have more stock on hand than we could dispose of; but orders poured in. Prices varied a little, to be sure, but choice flowers were always in demand. I used to wonder how people could afford to purchase such quantities of flowers. Lawrence and I kept very busy; but there was one delightful side to the matter, — if we wanted to go away for a few hours, or down to the city to any entertainment, we were our own masters. Our young man was very reliable, and Joe always insisted upon an oversight of things when were both away. Dear Joe! If any deed of kindliness brought back fourfold, you returned a thousand-fold. I used to smile when I saw him threading his way around, touching some lovely blossom with the tenderness one bestows upon a baby. How he did love all beautiful things! And how we all respected him for his manliness, his courage, and his true, earnest soul!

Seven years and more have come and gone since I took my first look at Athens; for now it is spring instead of autumn. One would hardly call us a sleepy little town at present. We have spread out our borders in every direction. Streets have been cleared up, built with rows of pretty cottages or more pretentious villas. Two more factories have come in, but they are all in the part below us, and down by the river; and there is a new station at Park Street for the greater convenience of the inhabitants. We have a handsome hall, a flourishing musical union, an amateur dramatic club, and some very attractive social life, a young men's gymnasium and reading-room; and, as we keep some of our best men in the Board of Excise, saloons do not flourish vigorously. We may be bigoted and narrow-minded; but I think, as a community, we have proved that there are higher and better moral tonics for the poor man than beer or whiskey. We have also a building association, of which Mr. Corwin — who, by the way, is prospering wonderfully — is president, Mr. Joseph Crawford vice-president, and Gordon Pryor secretary. It builds houses on the instalment plan; the owner paying so much yearly, which includes interest at six per cent, and a small amount of the principal, or a larger sum, as one elects. If, through sickness or misfortune, the payments cannot be met, they are added back to the whole amount for one year. No house is disposed of to an habitual drinker unless his wife has means of meeting the claims. The cottages, I am happy to say, are well built, if not so fanciful.

Indirectly, it has another side of profit for Joe and Pryor, in the sale of materials. So far, the demands have exceeded the supply; though Mrs. Harwood, Mr. Wilbur, Mr. Randall, and several other Athenians, are stockholders.

Gordon Pryor is a very successful business-man. His hotel is excellently managed. The added wing is larger than the main building; and during the season, which begins early and ends late, it is always full. There are several pleasant boarding-houses besides, and the current of summer pilgrimages to Athens is unfailing. Our pretty woods have been cleared up, we are at work on our roads, and boating on the river is one of our delights during the late summer afternoons and moonlight evenings. We have also a fair brass band that plays two evenings in the week, when people stroll around, or sit on the benches disposed about our little nucleus of a park, or haunt the broad hotel piazzas.

Eve's connection with the business management ceased the spring after her marriage. A Gaylord cousin, a Mrs. MacPherson, who had begun life with brilliant prospects, but was now a widow with two children, and only a few hundreds a year, came for a visit, and begged to try her hand. She was an attractive and very agreeable person, and succeeded so well that she was given the post, and fills it admirably. Her little girl is with her, her boy at school. Mrs. Pryor has two pretty children, of whom their father is immensely proud.

Thus relieved, Eve turned her attention to flowers, and became Lawrence's shadow. They are a happy couple, delightful as well; and I sometimes think, of all Eve's manifold gifts, there is none in which she excels more than in the culture of flowers, unless it is in their arrangement. She and Lawrence are like two children, — perhaps more harmonious than immature childhood usually appears. His health is excellent, his gaunt frame has filled out to handsome proportions, and they are noticeably fine-looking. They have one little daughter.

We have two children, — a son and a daughter. Celia still finds time to paint, and has done some excellent work. We haunt art exhibitions and club receptions, and I sometimes feel enthusiastic enough to paint a picture myself: then I remember the fate of Jack-of-all-trades.

We are building our new houses just as Lawrence planned, on Rutherford Avenue. They are together, and give the effect of one very imposing residence. The halls connect with wide sliding-doors, and we expect that only *portières* will divide us. We were so well endowed with wedding-gifts, and have accumulated so many treasures since that period, that it needed two houses to hold them. By autumn we expect to be settled. Mrs. Banks's daughter, Letty, is well married to a waiter in one of the large New-York hotels; and she — the mother — has petitioned for the post of Eve's housekeeper.

Walter Benson has prospered as well as ourselves. His portrait, his success, and a brief biography, graced a recent issue of a poultry monthly. He has taken prizes at poultry exhibitions, and keeps some most beautiful stock. When eggs are high, he manages to have them in tolerable abundance, and, with the aid of hens and incubators, is early in the market with spring-chickens. He has added two acres of ground at the back of the place, and is, I think, about as happy a young fellow as one can well imagine, in spite of his great misfortune. He plays delightfully on the violin, and spends many a pleasant evening with us. He has a kind of adoring fondness for Eve, and sometimes Joe is almost jealous. Lawrence is rather amused by the plainly exhibited preferences.

We have still a few of the old croakers left, or we should fancy we were quite in a world of our own. They complain that Athens has been ruined, and insist that it is quite impossible to get a fair price for property, since it has not gone up to the fictitious value of the swell times. Mr. Montgomery is the head and front of this party. So far, he has not disposed of a single lot. Two or three times he has partly bargained away several acres, then he thought he ought to have a higher price, and raised his figures, losing thereby his opportunity of selling. However, as he is not in a really important part of the town, his property can lie idle without so much detriment. He grumbles about taxes and improvements; and conceited, feather-headed young fellows running every thing, and ruining it as well. However, his land will be of some benefit to his children.

Lawrence and I have branched out considerably. We have now one acre under glass, and numerous cold-frames. Our "boy" is an intelligent florist, to whom we pay twelve dollars a week; and we have two more lads who are learning. Through the spring and early summer we require extra help; but we both devote our time and our brains to the enlargement of our business and its prosperity. We make a specialty of roses, both as to plants and cut-flowers, and have, I think, some of the most magnificent roses on the market. We also do something in the way of choice fruit. Our late peaches have been an astonishing success, and we have currants that can almost compare with cherries; but, as our flower-space increases, we shall do less with them, though we find them an excellent return for the time spent upon them.

Joe has achieved something better than his first dream. Hildreth sold him a pretty plot at the north-east corner of our lot, when we decided to build on the north-west. He has erected a very pretty Queen Anne cottage, not too ornate in style; and, as his grounds are just defined with a wire fence to keep children from trespassing unduly, he has all our wealth of flowers for his enjoyment, and he loves them with an ardor that often touches my soul. He is prospering in every way. Ruth makes a sweet and tender wife, and an admirable mother to her little brood of four. She and Joe were confirmed at St. Mark's, and Joe is a very earnest vestryman. Mr. Bradford is still with us, and has married a very lovely young English girl, who came to New York to spend a winter with some relatives. We all like her exceedingly, and every year "our clergyman" grows dearer to us. We are proposing now to build a new and more convenient rectory on a lot next the church, as we have received a very advantageous offer for the old one.

Our houses will be quite delightful. We have planned them ourselves, with nooks and corners and fireplaces to suit, to say nothing of closets. We shall do a good deal of the interior finishing ourselves, and we do not propose to be unduly extravagant so early in our business career. Indeed, we have found out many methods of helping along, of reaching a desired result without a great outlay of money. We make some mistakes, to be sure; but we rectify them by that best of all light, — experience. We both work: even Celia and Eve often lend a hand. Celia makes some five or six hundred dollars a year of her own, and Eve has done some lovely flower-pieces. But our garden does engross us with a curious fascination.

What, indeed, is more lovely, more satisfying, more comforting, than flowers! They are always appropriate: they cheer the cottage as well as the palace. Every year the demand increases, and it is rarely that the true florist fails of success. It requires close attention; but then, what business does not? Work seems the inexorable law for the many, and a business that promises a greater success every year is not to be held in light esteem. My idea of prosperity used to be a steady position at one hundred dollars a month; and, having exceeded that, I ought to be content, especially as the prospect seems to be, that ten years hence, if our business increases as it has so far, we shall have all we desire, though to many our desires may seem moderate. What matter, so long as they bring leisure, ease, culture, happiness, and an enjoyable social life?

We might have gone West on a ranch, and lived the half-solitary existence that cannot be evaded. Work among flocks and herds winter and summer is not all holiday-time. You cannot depute every thing to hired help. And it seems to me that at first there must be many pinches and sacrifices when one starts on a little money, as poor young men must.

There are, of course, the fruit-farms and vineyards of which marvellous stories are told, and the orange-groves of Florida. But trees do not fruit in a single season, and grapes must have time to perfect their strength for steady and profitable bearing. Even in these glowing lands, there needs to be years of waiting and patient endeavor.

And the land is not all filled up at the eastward. The same courage, hard work, and waiting, would make many of our desolate little country-towns blossom like the rose. True, the land is often held high for speculative purposes; but there is many a time when some entering-wedge may be used to an advantage. To be near good markets, is a great object. Flowers, fruits, berries, eggs, poultry, are always in demand. The best commands the highest prices and a ready sale. There will always be rich people who can indulge in extravagances.

As for us, we are satisfied with our garden. We sigh neither for ranch, vineyard, nor orange-groves, though we expect to visit them all in time. We enjoy having our friends about us, and within our reach such pleasant adjuncts as libraries, art-galleries, museums, theatres, singers, and noted speakers and lecturers that float hitherward from time to time. Ours is a kind of idyllic life; and when some one of the four reads aloud a good novel or a stirring poem, we give thanks that we have achieved the "garden." To us it is a bit of the old Paradise.

IRENE E. JEROME'S ART BOOKS

THE "PERPETUAL PLEASURE" SERIES

"The sketches are such as the most famous men of the country might be proud to own. They are original, strong, and impressive, even the lightest of them; and their variety, like a procession of Nature, is a perpetual pleasure."

A BUNCH OF VIOLETS. Original illustrations, engraved on wood and printed under the direction of GEORGE T. ANDREW. 4to, cloth, $3.75; Turkey morocco, $9.00; tree calf, $9.00; English seal style, $7.00.

The new volume is akin to the former triumphs of this favorite artist, whose "Sketch Books" have achieved a popularity unequalled in the history of fine art publications. In the profusion of designs, originality, and delicacy of treatment, the charming sketches of mountain, meadow, lake, and forest scenery of New England here reproduced are unexcelled. After the wealth of illustration which this student of nature has poured into the lap of art, to produce a volume in which there is no deterioration of power or beauty, but, if possible, increased strength and enlargement of ideas, gives assurance that the foremost female artist in America will hold the hearts of her legion of admirers.

NATURE'S HALLELUJAH. Presented in a series of nearly fifty full-page original illustrations (9½ x 14 inches), engraved on wood by GEORGE T. ANDREW. Elegantly bound in gold cloth, full gilt, gilt edges, $6.00; Turkey morocco, $12.00; tree calf, $12.00; English seal style, $10.00.

This volume has won the most cordial praise on both sides of the water. Mr. Francis H. Underwood, U. S. Consul at Glasgow, writes concerning it: "I have never seen anything superior, if equal, to the delicacy and finish of the engravings, and the perfection of the press-work. The copy you sent me has been looked over with evident and unfeigned delight by many people of artistic taste. Every one frankly says, 'It is impossible to produce such effects here,' and, whether it is possible or not, I am sure it is *not done;* no such effects are produced on this side of the Atlantic. In this combination of art and workmanship, the United States leads the world; and you have a right to be proud of the honor of presenting such a specimen to the public."

ONE YEAR'S SKETCH BOOK. Containing forty-six full-page original illustrations, engraved on wood by ANDREW; in same bindings and at same prices as "Nature's Hallelujah."

"Every thick, creamy page is embellished by some gems of art. Sometimes it is but a dash and a few trembling strokes; at others an impressive landscape, but in all and through all runs the master touch. Miss Jerome has the genius of an Angelo, and the execution of a Guido. The beauty of the sketches will be apparent to all, having been taken from our unrivalled New England scenery." — *Washington Chronicle.*

THE MESSAGE OF THE BLUEBIRD, Told to Me to Tell to Others. Original illustrations engraved on wood by ANDREW. Cloth and gold, $2.00; palatine boards, ribbon ornaments, $1.00.

"In its new bindings is one of the daintiest combinations of song and illustration ever published, exhibiting in a marked degree the fine poetic taste and wonderfully artistic touch which render this author's works so popular. The pictures are exquisite, and the verses exceedingly graceful, appealing to the highest sensibilities. The little volume ranks among the choicest of holiday souvenirs, and is beautiful and pleasing." — *Boston Transcript.*

Sold by all booksellers, and sent by mail, postpaid, on receipt of price

LEE AND SHEPARD Publishers Boston

THE DOUGLAS NOVELS BY AMANDA M DOUGLAS

A WOMAN'S INHERITANCE.
"Miss Douglas's Novels are all worth reading, and this is one full of suggestions, interesting situations, and bright dialogue." — *Cottage Hearth.*

OUT OF THE WRECK; or, Was it a Victory?
"Bright and entertaining as Miss Douglas's stories always are, this, her new one, leads them all." — *New Bedford Standard.*

FLOYD GRANDON'S HONOR.
"Fascinating throughout, and worthy of the reputation of the author."

WHOM KATHIE MARRIED.
Kathie was the heroine of the popular series of Kathie Stories for young people, the readers of which were very anxious to know with whom Kathie settled down in life. Hence this story, charmingly written.

LOST IN A GREAT CITY.
"There are the power of delineation and robustness of expression that would credit a masculine hand in the present volume."

THE OLD WOMAN WHO LIVED IN A SHOE.
"The romances of Miss Douglas's creation are all thrillingly interesting." — *Cambridge Tribune.*

HOPE MILLS; or, Between Friend and Sweetheart.
"Amanda Douglas is one of the favorite authors of American novel-readers." — *Manchester Mirror.*

FROM HAND TO MOUTH.
"There is real satisfaction in reading this book, from the fact that we can so readily 'take it home' to ourselves." — *Portland Argus.*

NELLY KINNARD'S KINGDOM.
"The Hartford Religious Herald" says, "This story is so fascinating, that one can hardly lay it down after taking it up."

IN TRUST; or, Dr. Bertrand's Household.
"She writes in a free, fresh and natural way, and her characters are never overdrawn." — *Manchester Mirror.*

CLAUDIA.
"The plot is very dramatic, and the *denouement* startling. Claudia, the heroine, is one of those self-sacrificing characters which it is the glory of the female sex to produce." — *Boston Journal.*

STEPHEN DANE.
"This is one of this author's happiest and most successful attempts at novel-writing, for which a grateful public will applaud her." — *Herald.*

HOME NOOK; or, The Crown of Duty.
"An interesting story of home-life, not wanting in incident, and written in forcible and attractive style." — *New York Graphic.*

SYDNIE ADRIANCE; or, Trying the World.
"The works of Miss Douglas have stood the test of popular judgment, and become the fashion."

SEVEN DAUGHTERS.
The charm of the story is the perfectly natural and home-like air which pervades it.

THE FORTUNES OF THE FARADAYS
"Of unexceptionable literary merit, deeply interesting in the development of the plot." — *Fall River News.*

FOES OF HER HOUSEHOLD
"Full of interest from the first chapter to the end."

Sold by all booksellers, and sent by mail, post-paid, on receipt of price.

LEE AND SHEPARD, PUBLISHERS, BOSTON.

Miss Townsend's Books

Uniform Edition Cloth $1.50 each

A BOSTON GIRL'S AMBITIONS
"There is nothing of the 'sensational,' or so-called realistic school, in her writings. On the contrary, they are noted for their healthy moral tone and pure sentiment, and yet are not wanting in STRIKING SITUATIONS AND DRAMATIC INCIDENTS." — *Chicago Journal.*

BUT A PHILISTINE
"The moral lessons, the true life principles taught in this book, render it one which it is a pleasure to recommend for its stimulating influence upon the higher nature. Its literary quality is fine."

LENOX DARE
"Among the best of her productions we place the volume here under notice. In temper and tone the work is calculated to exert a healthful and elevating influence, and tends to bring the reader into more intimate sympathy with what is most pure and noble in our nature." — *New-England Methodist.*

DARYLL GAP; or, Whether it Paid
"A story of the petroleum days, and of a family who struck oil. Her plots are well arranged, and her characters are clearly and strongly drawn." — *Pittsburg Recorder.*

A WOMAN'S WORD, AND HOW SHE KEPT IT
"The celebrity of Virginia F. Townsend as an authoress, her brilliant descriptive powers, and pure, vigorous imagination, will insure a hearty welcome for the above-entitled volume in the writer's happiest vein." — *Fashion Quarterly.*

THAT QUEER GIRL
"A fresh, wholesome book about good men and good women, bright and cheery in style, and pure in morals. Just the book to take a young girl's fancy, and help her to grow up, like Madeline and Argia, into the sweetness of real girlhood." — *People's Monthly.*

ONLY GIRLS
"This volume shows how two persons, 'only girls,' saved two men from crime, even from ruin of body and soul. The story is ingenious and graphic, and kept the writer of this notice up far into the small hours of yesterday morning." — *Washington Chronicle.*

The Holland Series Cloth $1.00 each
THE HOLLANDS
   SIX IN ALL
      THE DEERINGS OF MEDBURY
         THE MILLS OF TUXBURY

"There is a fascination about the stories of Miss Townsend that gives them a firm hold upon the public, their chief charm being their simplicity and fidelity to nature." — *Commonwealth.*

Sold by all booksellers and newsdealers, and sent by mail, postpaid, on receipt of price

LEE AND SHEPARD Publishers Boston

BOOKS FOR GIRLHOOD BY POPULAR AUTHORS

AN AMERICAN GIRL ABROAD.

By ADELINE F. TRAFTON. 16mo, cloth, illustrated. $1.50.

One of the most bright, chatty, wide-awake books of travel ever written. It abounds in information, is as pleasant reading as a story book, and full of the wit and sparkle of "An American Girl" let loose from school and ready for a frolic.

ONLY GIRLS.

By VIRGINIA F. TOWNSEND, Author of "That Queer Girl," &c., &c. 12mo, cloth, illustrated. $1.50.

"It is a thrilling story, written in a fascinating style, and the plot is adroitly handled."

It might be placed in any Sabbath School library, so pure is it in tone, and yet it is so free from the mawkishness and silliness that mar the class of books usually found there, that the veteran novel reader is apt to finish it at a sitting.

THE DOCTOR'S DAUGHTER.

By SOPHIE MAY, Author of "Our Helen," "The Asbury Twins," &c. 12mo, cloth, illustrated. $1.50.

"A delightful book, original and enjoyable," says the *Brownville Echo*.

"A fascinating story, unfolding, with artistic touch, the young life of one of our impulsive, sharp-witted, transparent and pure-minded girls of the nineteenth century," says *The Contributor*, Boston.

SALLY WILLIAMS.

The Mountain Girl. By Mrs. EDNA D. CHENEY, Author of "Patience," "Social Games," "The Child of the Tide," &c. 12mo, cloth, illustrated. $1.50.

Pure, strong, healthy, just what might be expected from the pen of so gifted a writer as Mrs. Cheney. A very interesting picture of life among the New Hampshire hills, enlivened by the tangle of a story of the ups and downs of every-day life in this out-of-the-way locality. The characters introduced are quaintly original, and the adventures are narrated with remarkable skill.

LOTTIE EAMES.

Or, do your best and leave the rest. By a Popular Author. 16mo, illus. $1.50.

"A wholesome story of home life, full of lessons of self-sacrifice, but always bright and attractive in its varied incidents."

RHODA THORNTON'S GIRLHOOD.

By Mrs. MARY E. PRATT. 16mo, cloth, illustrated. $1.50.

A hearty and healthy story, dealing with young folks and home scenes, with sleighing, fishing and other frolics to make things lively.

The above six volumes are furnished in a handsome box, for $9.00, or sold separately by all booksellers, or sent by mail, postpaid, on receipt of price by

LEE AND SHEPARD, Publishers, ... Boston.

BOOKS FOR YOUNG LADIES BY POPULAR AUTHORS

SEVEN DAUGHTERS.

By Miss A. M. Douglas, Author of "In Trust," "Stephen Dane," "Claudia," "Sydnie Adriance," "Home Nook," "Nelly Kennard's Kingdom." 12mo, cloth, illustrated. $1.50.

"A charming romance of Girlhood," full of incident and humor. The "Seven Daughters" are characters which reappear in some of Miss Douglas' later books. In this book they form a delightful group, hovering on the verge of Womanhood, with all the little perplexities of home life and love dreams as incidentals, making a fresh and attractive story.

OUR HELEN.

By Sophie May. 12mo, cloth, illustrated. $1.50.

"The story is a very attractive one, as free from the sensational and impossible as could be desired, and at the same time full of interest, and pervaded by the same bright, cheery sunshine that we find in the author's earlier books. She is to be congratulated on the success of her essay in a new field of literature, to which she will be warmly welcomed by those who know and admire her 'Prudy Books.'" — *Graphic.*

THE ASBURY TWINS.

By Sophie May, Author of "The Doctor's Daughter," "Our Helen," &c. 12mo, cloth, illustrated. $1.50.

"Has the ring of genuine genius, and the sparkle of a gem of the first water. We read it one cloudy winter day, and it was as good as a Turkish bath, or a three hours' soak in the sunshine." — *Cooperstown Republican.*

THAT QUEER GIRL.

By Miss Virginia F. Townsend, Author of "Only Girls," &c. 12mo, cloth, illustrated. $1.50.

Queer only in being unconventional, brave and frank, an "old-fashioned girl," and very sweet and charming. As indicated in the title, is a little out of the common track, and the wooing and the winning are as queer as the heroine. The *New Haven Register* says: "Decidedly the best work which has appeared from the pen of Miss Townsend."

RUNNING TO WASTE.

The Story of a Tomboy. By George M. Baker. 16mo, cloth, illustrated. $1.50.

"This book is one of the most entertaining we have read for a long time. It is well written, full of humor, and good humor, and it has not a dull or uninteresting page. It is lively and natural, and overflowing with the best New England character and traits. There is also a touch of pathos, which always accompanies humor, in the life and death of the tomboy's mother." — *Newburyport Herald.*

DAISY TRAVERS;

Or the Girls of Hive Hall. By Adelaide F. Samuels, Author of "Dick and Daisy Stories," "Dick Travers Abroad," &c. 16mo, cloth, illustrated. $1.50.

The story of Hive Hall is full of life and action, and told in the same happy style which made the earlier life of its heroine so attractive, and caused the Dick and Daisy books to become great favorites with the young. What was said of the younger books can, with equal truth, be said of Daisy grown up.

The above six books are furnished in a handsome box for $9.00, or sold separate, by all booksellers, and sent by mail, postpaid, on receipt of price.

LEE AND SHEPARD Publishers Boston

Bright and Breezy Books of Travel
— — — BY SIX BRIGHT WOMEN — — —

A WINTER IN CENTRAL AMERICA AND MEXICO
By Helen J. Sanborn. Cloth, $1.50.
 "A bright, attractive narrative by a wide-awake Boston girl."

A SUMMER IN THE AZORES, with a Glimpse of Madeira
By Miss C. Alice Baker. Little Classic style. Cloth, gilt edges, $1.25.
 "Miss Baker gives us a breezy, entertaining description of these picturesque islands. She is an observing traveller, and makes a graphic picture of the quaint people and customs." — *Chicago Advance.*

LIFE AT PUGET SOUND
With sketches of travel in Washington Territory, British Columbia, Oregon, and California. By Caroline C. Leighton. 16mo, cloth, $1.50.
 "Your chapters on Puget Sound have charmed me. Full of life, deeply interesting, and with just that class of facts, and suggestions of truth, that cannot fail to help the Indian and the Chinese." — Wendell Phillips.

EUROPEAN BREEZES
By Margery Deane. Cloth, gilt top, $1.50. Being chapters of travel through Germany, Austria, Hungary, and Switzerland, covering places not usually visited by Americans in making "the Grand Tour of the Continent," by the accomplished writer of "Newport Breezes."
 "A very bright, fresh and amusing account, which tells us about a host of things we never heard of before, and is worth two ordinary books of European travel." — *Woman's Journal.*

BEATEN PATHS; or, A Woman's Vacation in Europe
By Ella W. Thompson. 16mo, cloth. $1.50.
 A lively and chatty book of travel, with pen-pictures humorous and graphic, that are decidedly out of the "beaten paths" of description.

AN AMERICAN GIRL ABROAD
By Miss Adeline Trafton, author of "His Inheritance," "Katherine Earle," etc. 16mo. Illustrated. $1.50.
 "A sparkling account of a European trip by a wide-awake, intelligent, and irrepressible American girl. Pictured with a freshness and vivacity that is delightful." — *Utica Observer.*

CURTIS GUILD'S TRAVELS

BRITONS AND MUSCOVITES; or, Traits of Two Empires
Cloth, $2.00.

OVER THE OCEAN; or, Sights and Scenes in Foreign Lands
By Curtis Guild, editor of "The Boston Commercial Bulletin." Crown 8vo. Cloth, $2.50.
 "The utmost that any European tourist can hope to do is to tell the old story in a somewhat fresh way, and Mr. Guild has succeeded in every part of his book in doing this." — *Philadelphia Bulletin.*

ABROAD AGAIN; or, Fresh Forays in Foreign Fields
Uniform with "Over the Ocean." By the same author. Crown 8vo. Cloth, $2.50.
 "He has given us a life-picture. Europe is done in a style that must serve as an invaluable guide to those who go 'over the ocean,' as well as an interesting companion." — *Halifax Citizen.*

Sold by all booksellers, and sent by mail, postpaid, on receipt of price
LEE AND SHEPARD Publishers Boston

www.ingramcontent.com/pod-product-compliance
Lightning Source LLC
Chambersburg PA
CBHW030551300426
44111CB00009B/933